IMPOSING ORDER WITHOUT LAW

IMPOSING ORDER WITHOUT LAW

American Expansion to the Eastern Sierra, 1850–1865

MICHAEL J. MAKLEY

UNIVERSITY OF NEVADA PRESS | *Reno & Las Vegas*

University of Nevada Press | Reno, Nevada 89557 USA
www.unpress.nevada.edu

LIBRARY OF CONGRESS CATALOGING-IN-PUBLICATION DATA

Names: Makley, Michael J., author.
Title: Imposing order without law : American expansion to the eastern Sierra, 1850–1865 / Michael J. Makley.
Description: First. | Reno ; Las Vegas : University of Nevada Press, [2022] | Includes bibliographical references and index. | Summary: *Imposing Order Without Law* examines the history surrounding nineteenth century American settlers in two remote regions—the slopes of the Eastern Sierra Nevada and the Honey Lake Valley—who used extralegal means to establish order in their communities. The book reveals the use and effects of group violence used to enforce community edicts which transformed the Native people's world into colonial outposts." —Provided by publisher.
Identifiers: LCCN 2022013845 | ISBN 9781647790738 (paperback) | ISBN 9781647790745 (ebook)
Subjects: LCSH: Social control—Sierra Nevada (Calif. And Nev.)—History—19th century. | Vigilantism—Sierra Nevada (Calif. And Nev.)—History—19th century. | Frontier and pioneer life—Sierra Nevada (Calif. and Nev.) | Violence—Sierra Nevada (Calif. And Nev.)—History—19th century. | Sierra Nevada (Calif. and Nev.)—Ethnic relations. | Sierra Nevada (Calif. and Nev.)—History—19th century.
Classification: LCC HM661 .M34 2022 | DDC 303.3/3097944—dc23/eng/20220425
LC record available at https://lccn.loc.gov/2022013845

Manufactured in the United States of America

FIRST PRINTING

The paper used in this book meets the requirements of American National Standard for Information Sciences—Permanence of Paper for Printed Library Materials, ANSI/NISO Z39.48-1992 (R2002).

To exceptional editor
Margaret Dalrymple
and to my good friend
and sage consultant
McAvoy Layne

Contents

Acknowledgments

I am indebted to a number of people who have assisted on this project. Matthew Makley suggested it, gave it direction, and advised me throughout. Dan Makley was the first reader and read a later draft as well, offering pertinent comments in both instances. Ron James, the dean of writers of early-Nevada history, devoted untold hours to reading and offering editing advice. His insights about the Comstock and Nevada greatly improved the manuscript, and his suggestions regarding cutting and rearranging material added clarity. An anonymous reader, provided by the University of Nevada Press, broadened the scope of the study by recommending current scholarship in the form of secondary literature.

Fifteen years ago, Mark Twain impersonator and scholar McAvoy Layne, "Nevada Traveler" David Toll, and I met for lunch in Carson City at the old St. Charles Hotel. We were joined by book editor Matthew "Becks" Becker and Nevada state archivist Guy Rocha. Recalling Eastern Sierra history, McAvoy dubbed the group the "Never Sweats." Over the years others joined the group, until today there are some thirty writers, researchers, historians, and former newswomen and newsmen who meet monthly, in varying numbers, to discuss current research or reminiscences. They form a resource of encyclopedic knowledge. Two Never Sweats, in particular, helped me with this endeavor. Larry Schmidt provided information on pioneer roads through the Great Basin and over the Sierra and referred me to sources of interactions between Native peoples and American newcomers. In discussions, Bob Ellison shared his unmatched expertise regarding the first American settlers in Nevada, and his influence is clearly illustrated in the endnotes by the large number of citations from his books, *First Impressions: The Trail Through Carson Valley, 1848–1852* and *Territorial Lawmen of Nevada.*

In 2005, the first time I worked with the University of Nevada Press, I was fortunate to have acquisitions editor Margaret Dalrymple counsel me and shepherd my book through the academic-press process of reader evaluations and edits. She worked with me on this study, once again demonstrating the value of an expert editor. Press director JoAnne Banducci has overseen and coordinated the project, lending her support right from the first time she and I discussed it. Along the way, Caddie Dufurrena and Curtis Vickers added insights and assistance. Sarah Patton, at the Nevada Historical Society, was expeditious and thorough in helping acquire the maps. As in several previous projects, beginning in 2011, Annette Wenda edited the copy. She, once again, corrected numerous punctuation and formatting mistakes in the text and innumerable mistakes in the endnotes. Virginia Fontana supervised the editing and design of the book, creating this final product. I am grateful to all.

Last, thank you to my brother Kevin and my wife, Randi, who each continually offered encouragement and enthusiasm for the project.

IMPOSING ORDER WITHOUT LAW

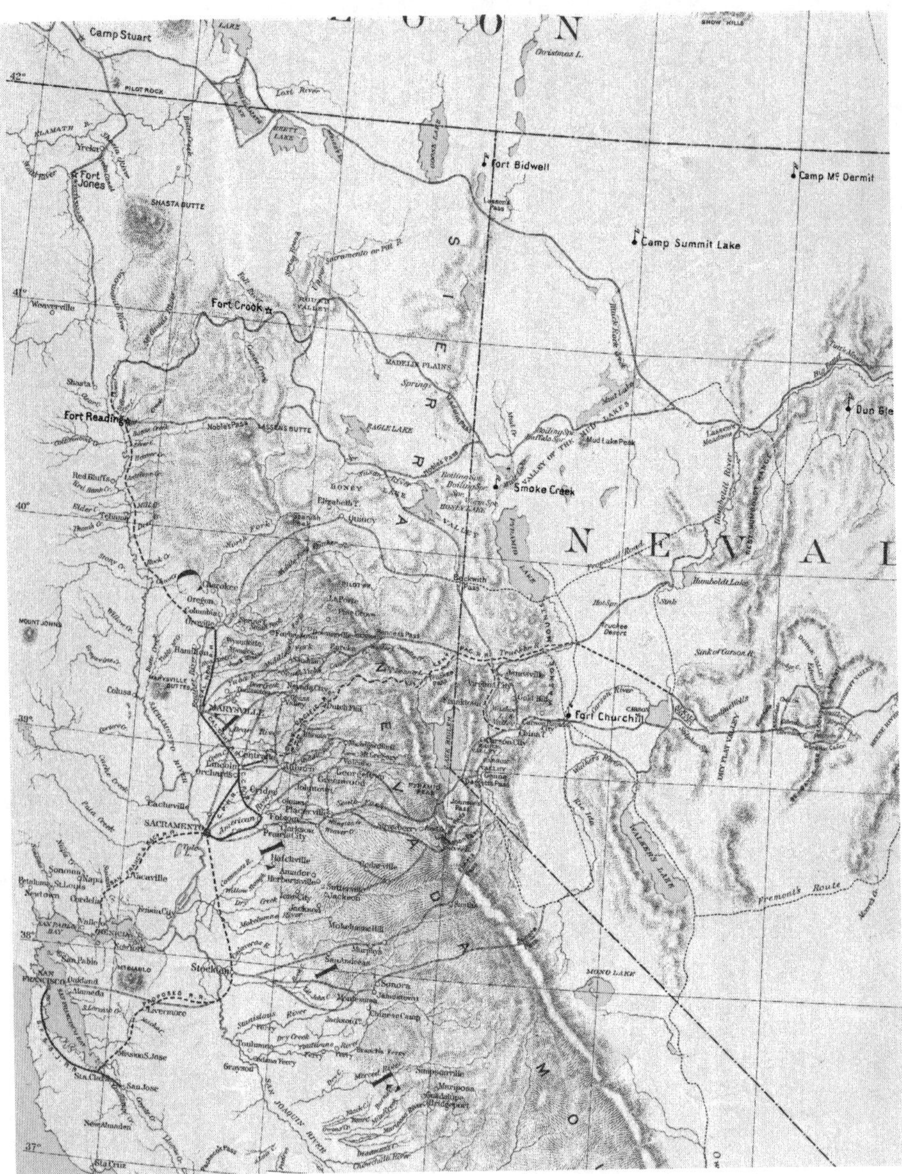

The US War Department's Territory of Utah (1867). The map shows the primary wagon roads coming from the Great Basin, leading into Honey Lake in the north and Carson Valley in the south. Following the Pyramid Lake War, the US military constructed and manned Fort Churchill and a half-dozen other forts or camps to protect white travelers and settlers. Note that Lake Tahoe is listed as "Lake Bigler." Courtesy of the Nevada Historical Society.

Introduction

In the 1850s, newcomers established two American settlements on the eastern slope of the Sierra: Carson Valley and, 120 miles north, Honey Lake Valley. Carson Valley was on the western edge of Utah Territory, in Washoe Indian land. It was more than 500 miles from the seat of government at Salt Lake City. Honey Lake Valley, in Northern Paiute Indian territory, was within California's boundaries but separated from the rest of the state by the imposing mountains. The two isolated communities refused to answer to the distant legal and administrative jurisdictions to which they were assigned. Plagued by problems in attempting to establish civil order and by conflicts with the indigenous people, factions addressed discord using various means, including group violence. How their efforts unfolded—the effects on the Native Americans and the Native Americans' effects on the burgeoning communities—is a story of upheaval, with far-reaching ramifications.

Nevada historian Sally Zanjani wrote the acclaimed *Devils Will Reign: How Nevada Began* (2006), which tracks the unfolding of the western Utah Territory as it transformed into Nevada Territory. Zanjani eloquently portrays what took place that led to Nevada gaining statehood. *Imposing Order Without Law* parallels part of the earlier work's time frame but focuses on the American settlement process in the region. It compares the Eastern Sierra's two earliest white communities, concentrating on the extralegal devices that each undertook. It proposes that western expansion to the region suffered from failures in leadership and the inability to maintain organized governance.

The white settlers saw the Eastern Sierra as beyond legal justice. Some wanted it to remain that way. Others sought to establish justice systems similar to those in the states, based in established American law. A third group wanted order, regardless of whether there were laws or not. Egalitarianism collided head-on with those claiming moral authority to

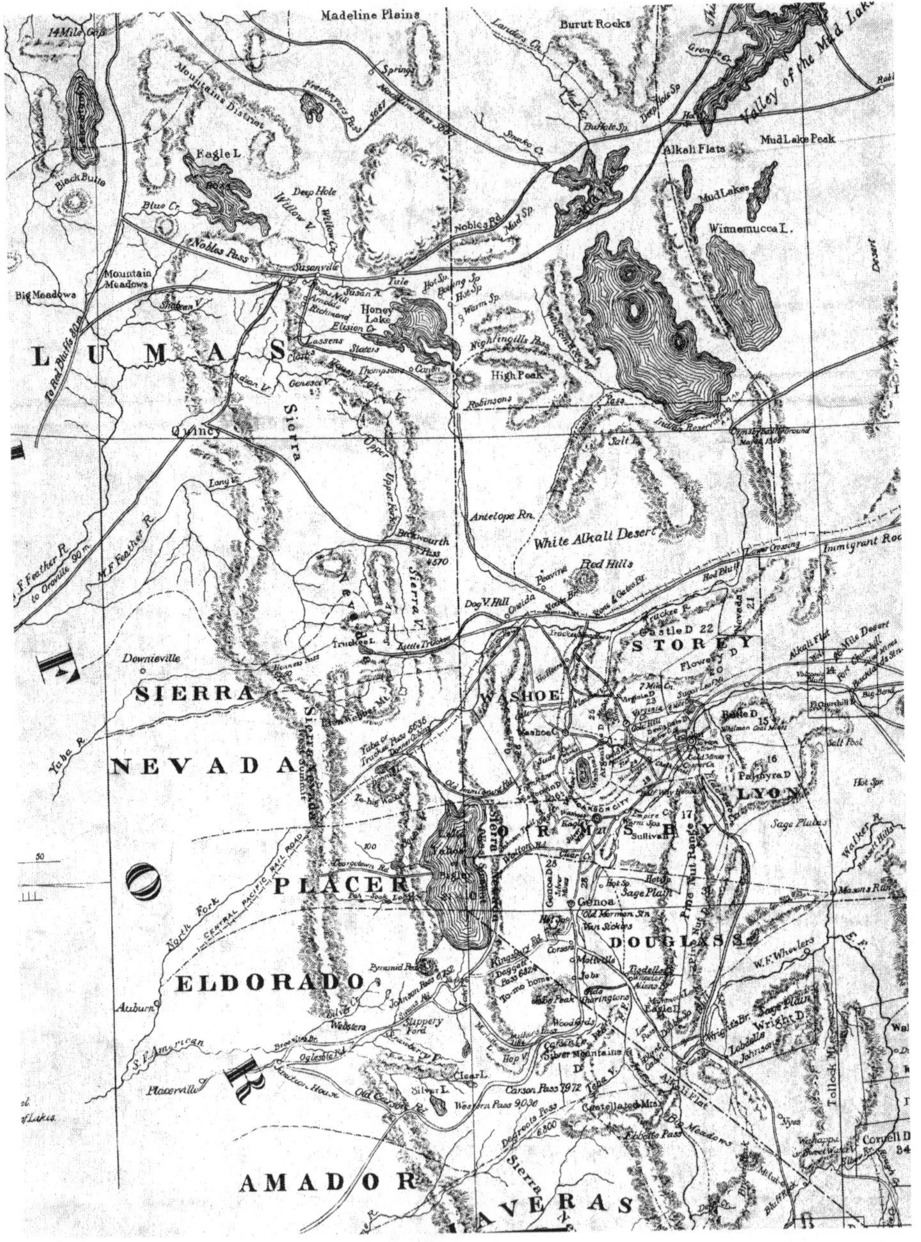

Degroot's map of Utah Territory (1863). In the east (*to the right on the map*) is the Forty-Mile Desert; to the west are the passes leading to California. Northwest of Honey Lake (*just above and to the left*), Susanville and the Susan River are listed, each named for Isaac Roop's daughter. Bordering Pyramid Lake on the south, the Paiute Reservation is identified simply as "Indian Reservation." In Carson Valley, the map identifies Genoa but adds the descriptive "Old Mormon Stn." The map labels the newly named "Ormsby County," as well as the properties of several key community figures, including Henry Van Sickle and Lute Olds. Interestingly, Thorington is listed, although he had been hanged five years earlier. Courtesy of the Nevada Historical Society.

establish law and order or to simply rule by edict.[1] The citizenry was a diverse mix: individualists rebelling against civil authority, progressives, reactionaries, boosters, and freebooters—all pursuing their own aims, removed from authoritative restraints. The extreme wing supporting those seeking order consisted of firebrands, always primed for a fight. The extremists among the individualists were outlaws.

The Native Americans found little justice dealing with the white settlers. Both Washoes and Paiutes tried diplomacy, and the Paiutes did service on behalf of the Honey Lake militia. For all of that, unreliable or dishonest American authorities allowed trespasses throughout the tribes' lands, including hunting and fishing areas, piñon-pine groves, forests, and fields.

The Anglo transgressions included violence that, employed by white people, differed radically from precontact Native people's aggressions. Because Native Americans lived across widely dispersed areas, their battles were not fought over land or conquest. Washoes would fight if intruders seemed hostile or if they sought to fish in their core area, Lake Tahoe, or hunt their deer. In general, Paiutes fought only over social issues: revenge over mistreatment of a comrade or a theft. The combatants were led by temporary military leaders who gathered others willing to fight for the cause. Once they met their immediate goal, the warring group disbanded. When the white settlers moved in, laying claim to the land, warfare changed, differing in scale. The white settlers' superior firepower disadvantaged the Indians, and the ever-growing numbers of settlers ensured the Native Americans' impoverishment.[2]

The white settlers who utilized force against the Indians were informed by the belief they were acting in the public interest, and so too were those attempting to institute security within the community. The chastising agents can be grouped into three principal categories: *militia,* standing armed forces called to meet emergencies; *vigilantes,* who came together to enforce systemic power and summarily punish criminals; and *mobs* caught up in *emotional contagion.*

In this context, emotional contagion refers to anger or fear rapidly spreading negative excitement in a crowd, creating an emotional atmosphere. Shielded by anonymity and security, a crowd will exhibit hostility and aggression directed at existing targets or scapegoats. In such circumstances, destructive mob behavior can follow. On the eastern slope, owing in large part to the absence of governing infrastructure, mob formation and aggression commonly went unchallenged.

This study describes how the inability to impartially adjust conflicting claims or assign appropriate punishments disrupted the communities and how the failure to consider Native Americans' humanity destroyed their way of life. Violence substituted for systems of justice, and, while at times achieving limited goals, more often it complicated and inflamed problems.

LYNCHING AND WAR

Two incidents, to be reviewed more fully in the body of the text, serve as microcosms for this study. The first was a lynching that raised passions from Salt Lake City to Sacramento. The second was the opening of the "Pyramid Lake War," in which Americans attacked the Paiute Indians, igniting a regional conflagration of historical consequence. The argument proposed here is that these events, along with others of a similar nature, demonstrate failures resulting from the communities pursuing retribution rather than justice. In the first instance, those claiming leadership fomented enmity toward an individual whose lifestyle they opposed, leading to his lynching. The second illustrated the hatred of Indians, as well as a cultural reductionism that engendered the belief that rather than individual Indians receiving due process, the tribe needed to be punished or exterminated. In each action, mobs formed, seeking revenge for unproved accusations.

The man lynched was William Thorington, known in the 1850s from Salt Lake City to San Francisco as "Lucky Bill." He was a gambler and an aggressive entrepreneur who seemingly never lost when betting or doing business. He lived in Carson Valley in the town of Genoa. Lucky Bill was the wealthiest man in the region, renowned for being a Robin Hood who helped emigrants in need.

In the spring of 1858, a large body of men from Honey Lake Valley rode into Genoa and joined with local vigilantes, arresting Thorington and several others. Thorington stood accused of being the leader of a band of robbers and of being involved in a murder. Without direct evidence, two of the arrestees were fined and threatened with banishment, but they and the others were then released. Not Thorington. He was put on trial in a people's court. Eighteen of those who had done the arresting formed the jury; twelve in agreement would decide the verdict. At Thorington's request, the testimony was recorded, and nothing in it implicated him in robberies or in the murder. Despite his apparent innocence, the mob hanged him.[3]

Major William Ormsby, the organizer of the vigilantes, was a community leader, a booster for the area's domestication. He died two years later at the head of a company fighting the Paiute Indians in the first battle of the Pyramid Lake War.

Numaga was the Paiutes' young leader. A newspaper at the time, using a white man's conceit, described him as "not only a superior Indian but a superior man, and one well calculated to prove a formidable enemy."[4] Numaga had previously assisted Ormsby in his efforts to establish public order, and Ormsby, up to the time of his death, professed to be a friend to the Paiutes.

The battle had been precipitated by the killing of several white people at a way station and by the burning of the bodies and buildings. Twenty years later, Eliot Lord wrote *Comstock Mining and Miners,* an authoritative history of Nevada's Comstock Lode sponsored by the US Department of the Interior. He commented on the "justice" that the Americans attempted to mete out in the Pyramid Lake War. The burning of the station had been represented to the citizenry as an "Indian outrage," and it prompted widespread calls for vengeance. Lord used a sarcastic voice in noting that many white settlers did not care that there was a distinct probability the station owners had been the original aggressors. He wrote: "It was enough for them to know that the Indians had assumed to act as judges and executioners, for pioneer lynch-law was very different from Pi-Ute lynch-law."[5]

BUILDING EMPIRE

The Thorington and Ormsby episodes exist at the confluence of a number of conflicts and acts of vengeance that illuminate American imperialism and the exploitation of the West. At the same time, never far from the nexus, was the belief that indigenous peoples needed to be removed. This idea hinged on a narrative of triumph and the belief in American exceptionalism. John Winthrop's "city on the hill" expanded

West, becoming John O'Sullivan's "Manifest Destiny," both of which had grown from European, specifically English, tropes of civilization versus savagery.[6]

Although violence filled the American political arena, the 1850s reinforced national incorporation. As the polarized interests of the North and South vied to control expansion across the continent, domestic tranquillity was disrupted by atrocities: Bleeding Kansas, Brooks's attack on Charles Sumner on the floor of the US Senate, Chief Justice Roger Taney's *Dred Scott* decision, John Brown's abolitionist raids at Pottawatomie Creek and Harper's Ferry, and Brown's hanging. In Salt Lake City, Mormons and emigrant confrontations eventually included the Mountain Meadows Massacre (1857), and the religionists' disputes with federal officials led to the Mormon War. On the Pacific Coast, vigilance committees summarily executed death warrants. In the fall of 1859, California's Supreme Court chief justice, David Terry, resigned his position to fight a duel and kill US senator David Broderick.

Neither conflicts over slavery nor the increasing threats of secession did anything to deter westward expansion. The influence of industrialization on the national economy was tethering increasingly global interests to the West. The telegraph and railroad would soon connect the Atlantic and Pacific Oceans. Quests for fertile soil, raw materials, and precious minerals gained new impetus, and it became imperative that the transportation corridor to the far West be secured. The process would include the establishment of way stations, settlements, towns, and forts.

After crossing Utah Territory's vast Great Basin, the central emigrant trail forked as it approached the Sierra Nevada. Each of the two trails led to an important gateway hamlet: Carson Valley, on the Carson River, and, on the less used Nobles Route, Honey Lake Valley. Within thirty miles of the Carson Valley settlement of Genoa were a number of farms and homesteads, as well as land being laid out as the Carson City town site and a haphazard placer mining camp whose prospectors were about to stumble onto the Comstock Lode. There were no American developments between the Carson communities and Honey Lake Valley. Atop the Sierra, between the two, was Lake Tahoe, the center of the Washoe Indians' homeland, which before the tribe's displacement had included Carson Valley and its environs. To the north, Pyramid Lake, on the edge of the Great Basin, was an important part of the Northern Paiutes' territory, as had been Honey Lake, previous to the white settlers' occupation.

Although driven by self-interests, many of the pioneers saw themselves as undertaking heroic action in expanding America's boundaries. The two new communities differed from many in the West in that the individuals claiming land there did not arrive from the eastern states. The first immigrants in Carson Valley were Mormons, or Latter-day Saints, who were seeking to establish hinterland for their religion's metropole, Salt Lake City. Subsequently, ranchers and tradesmen came from California. So too did the homesteaders, miners, and ranchers who settled in Honey Lake Valley. They came from California's towns and mining camps, moving west to east. Having already lived in the West, they understood its codes, values, and nuances.

ORGANIZED VIOLENCE

The Honey Lake Rangers were an irregular militia organized to fight against or punish Indians for alleged crimes against persons or property. The vigilantes in Carson Valley, calling themselves the Committee, formed when its members refused to submit to the Utah territorial government's administration of justice. There were antisocial ruffians who inhabited each of the groups, but upstanding citizens formed the nucleus of both the Rangers and the Committee. They embraced stand-your-ground chivalry, and, while intent on instituting their notions of law and order, they were liable to act barbarously or to follow disordered impulses of factionalism. Crimes, including murder, were excused when committed by members or supporters of their groups.

During the third expedition by explorer John Frémont, in January 1848, his troops engaged in a massacre of Native Americans at the Sacramento River. Estimates of the killed ranged from 150 to more than 700. One expedition member said the idea at the time was "that killing Indigenous Californians would teach survivors not to challenge whites." In April 1850 California passed two laws concerning the formation of companies that, between 1850 and 1861, funded "Ranger" militia units that recruited some 3,456 volunteers who would kill more than 1,342 Indians. The state of California provided "war bonds" that raised $1.1 million to pay for militia expeditions against the Indians in 1851 and 1852. Another $410,000 was appropriated in 1857. The federal government reimbursed more than $1 million to the state, even making a payment in 1863 when financially strapped by the Civil War.[7]

In his book *Murder State,* historian Brendan Lindsay points out that the killing of Native Americans was democratically imposed, as it was the result of local, state, and federal governments collaborating with the citizenry and abetted by the press. In fact, some newspaper publishers fueled the genocide, demanding that all levels of government work "to dispossess, displace, and destroy dangerous Indians." In 1853 one Northern California newspaper declared, "Let extermination be our motto." San Francisco's *Daily Alta California* reported: "Citizens are arming in all directions to march against the Indians and scatter them or exterminate them wherever they can be found." Furthermore, since prosecutors, lawmen, and courts refused to bring charges against the killers, Lindsay submits that essentially the killings were considered legal. In *An American Genocide,* Benjamin Madley agrees, calling attention to the fact that, as well as allowing unofficial amnesty, the state-endorsed slaughter justified the killers' actions and diminished cultural and moral strictures involving them.[8]

At Honey Lake, citizens contested paying taxes to California, and Rangers were not paid for fighting the Indians. Regardless, most male residents enlisted. Native people, who surrounded the white community on all but its mountainous west side, were perceived by many of the newcomers as inferior, making it easier for white settlers to mirror the actions of other California militias. At times unable to find the Indians who they felt were trespassing, the militiamen acted as terrorists, killing innocents they happened upon. In order to propagandize their actions, they utilized the fear-generating tactics of scalping victims and leaving them unburied.[9]

Scholars have noted that while reactionary terrorists despise "inferiors," they have a secondary conflict, or at least an ambiguous relationship, with constituted authority.[10] This was manifest on the eastern slope, as many denizens disregarded the governing jurisdictions in Utah Territory and California. In 1856 the US District Court judge for Utah Territory abandoned Carson Valley, condemning its "open rebellion to the laws of Utah."[11] It was three years before a successor appeared in the valley. At Honey Lake, the attitude led to the Sagebrush War in 1863, when a force of thirty Honey Lakers engaged in a shoot-out with a hundred-man posse from the ostensible California authority, Plumas County.

Romanticized, vigilance committees were seen as democratic, populist movements. Many were formed to assist functioning legal systems that were deemed too weak or corrupt or too respectful of suspects' rights. One historian coined the phrase "righteous hangmen" for Montana's vigilantes, several of whom went on to become successful politicians, lawmen, and judges.[12] Some vigilance committees were involved in class conflicts, and some had racist orientations; in the last quarter of the century, vigilante types were also recruited by wealthy cattlemen in efforts to concentrate landownership or industrial concerns in economic feuds.

In Carson Valley those who opposed Salt Lake City's governance petitioned Congress to create an entity separate from Utah Territory, and they formed a vigilance committee while awaiting recognition. Without jails to hold the accused or effective courts, summary punishment was the dominant feature of the judicatory regime.

During the California mining-camp era, 1849–58, there were more than fifteen lynchings a year as a result of vigilante tribunals. For the next forty-three years, between 1859 and 1902, the average fell to fewer than two lynch-court hangings a year. The second San Francisco Committee of Vigilance executed four individuals in 1856, and those actions almost certainly influenced Major Ormsby in the Thorington affair. The San Francisco organization was led by prominent businessmen. Their economic power enabled them to feed the public favorable news stories. A convincing case has been made that the leaders' motivations concerned the economics of disputed city land claims and political power. It is posited that their ultimate goal was control of the city's waterfront. The secret was kept from contemporary newspapers, and it went unremarked in nineteenth- and most twentieth-century histories. Instead, the Committee was acclaimed as having been a significant demonstration of civil righteousness. There was general acceptance that it had accomplished its ultimate purpose of establishing good government.[13]

The San Francisco vigilantes' constitution included an article stating: "No persons, accused before this body, shall be punished until after fair and impartial trial and conviction."[14] The Carson Valley trial fell far short of that intent. It featured hearsay and innuendo as evidence, and jurors afterward gave explanations for the conviction that were contradicted by the written record.

At the time Ormsby and other Carson Valley citizens formed the Committee, Honey Lake Valley was suffering unrest and unrestrained violence. In several incidents, in the spring of 1858, the militiamen pursued and killed Indians, guilty of crimes or not. In June the murder of a Honey Lake rancher by unidentified white men caused the formation of a mob, which included a large number of the Honey Lake militia members. They lynched a man while trying to get him to reveal information, mistakenly believing he had known about the killing. They then rode to Carson Valley, taking action with the vigilantes against Thorington.

In 1860 men from Carson Valley and the surrounding territory formed another mob to seek vengeance against Paiutes who, as mentioned earlier, had killed white settlers and burned down a way station. The Comstock Lode's massive gold and silver deposits had been discovered the year before, and newcomers to the area were especially susceptible to the rumors and emotional contagion that the Indians' action had generated. Rather than seek out those Indians involved or attempt to discern their motive, crowds cried for action against the entire tribe. In his history of Nevada, Michael S. Green notes that because of the attack, "old ties came unbound," and Green refers specifically to Ormsby, who disregarded his previous relationship with the Paiutes to help recruit the 105-man force that marched to fight the Paiutes at Pyramid Lake.[15]

Ormsby's contingent was met by Numaga and his warriors. The battle, the first of the Pyramid Lake War, ended with the deaths of 76 of the white participants and the panicked retreat of the survivors. Ormsby and another man, said to be an experienced Indian fighter, had led the company, but many of the participants had not known one another, and their allegiance was transitory. As might have been predicted, in the heat of battle, esprit de corps turned to panic. Undisciplined followers broke and ran, leaving their comrades, including Ormsby, to be killed.

OUTSIDE LEGAL BOUNDS

At the time of the white settlers' arrival in the western Great Basin, the Northern Paiutes and the Washoes shared generally permeable boundaries. Northern Paiute territory stretched west from what is today Boise, Idaho, to the Sierra Nevada and from the Blue Mountains of Oregon six hundred miles south to Owens Valley, California. The Washoes' homeland ran along the Sierra Nevada, from just below Susanville, California, south to Sonora Pass, California, and included Lake Tahoe.

The line between the two tribes sat east of Markleeville, California, and, in Nevada east of current-day Carson City and Reno but west of Pyramid Lake. In the 1850s, with American expansion appropriating their lands, all such boundaries became irrelevant.

Beginning in 1851, with the Indian Appropriations Act, the American polity promoted the reservation system, setting aside farmlands for the Indians. The intent was to separate Indians from the emigrants and to change their lives so they would not use the land the white settlers wanted. In 1860 lands around Pyramid Lake were apportioned as a Paiute reservation, but white homesteaders contested the area's classification. Without enforcement mechanisms, the tribe had to engage in disputes over Americans' encroachments, decade after decade.[16]

In the mid-1860s the agent for the Washoe Indians, a self-serving former politician, Hubbard G. Parker, attributed contraction of white diseases to Washoe "indulgences" and, due to their rapidly diminishing numbers, adjudged an earlier agent's request for land for the tribe "unadvisable and inexpedient." Incredibly, left to their own devices, the Washoes adjusted, living on the margins of white society without ever having a reservation. Both the Washoes and the Paiutes maintain their stature as federally recognized tribes to the present day, having adapted without being assimilated.[17]

The fate of some other Indians in the region was more immediate. Fighting against white people's encroachments, they were depicted as terrorizing without limits—instigating "savage war." Brutal attacks on either side were answered with retaliatory brutalization. The white populations on both sides of the Sierra had unmatched weapons. In 1854 the California Legislature made it illegal to sell or transfer arms to Indians, ensuring the newcomers' advantage in asymmetrical battles. These battles were part of the warfare and genocide that, along with the effects of migrant-carried diseases, reduced California's Native population from an estimated 150,000 in 1845 to fewer than 30,000 in 1870.[18]

Action by the US Congress, at the tail end of the Senate's "Golden Age" (1819–59),[19] greatly influenced settlement in the West. The Compromise of 1850 allowed some ten years of emigration by those who might ordinarily have signed up to fight for one side or the other in the Civil War. These young men, along with veterans of the war with Mexico and the Indian Wars, established a culture whereby militias and vigilante actions substituted for more developed systems of justice.

In 1857 the Carson Valley Mormons were recalled to Salt Lake as US troops moved to wrest Utah Territory governance from the religion's hierarchy. When the Mormons left, rather than lessening the political schism, it became more pronounced. Those who had been averse, and in some cases hostile, to the territorial government now demanded that the others, laissez-faire individualists and antiauthoritarians, comply with their mandates.

Carson Valley citizens, like those at Honey Lake, believed that might took precedence in personal honor; they subscribed to the idea that when threatened, an individual had "no duty to retreat." Western historian Richard Maxwell Brown has discussed at length the difference between England's common-law requirement to retreat because all homicides are public wrongs and the Americans' concept identified as "stand your ground." In 1856 a widely referenced American textbook on criminal law advanced the idea that rather than flight, the law commanded resistance. Supreme Court justice Oliver Wendell Holmes officially sanctioned the concept in *Brown v. United States* in 1921, stating that it was commonly accepted that if an individual believes himself in danger of death or grievous harm, "he may stand his ground and that if he kills [his assailant] he has not exceeded the bounds of lawful self-defense." He added, "Detached reflection cannot be demanded in the presence of an uplifted knife." On the eastern slope of the Sierra, attempts to impart justice were sustained by the notion that certain homicides were not outside legal bounds. Mob actions, the killings of innocents, shoot-outs, extrajudicial proceedings, lynchings, battles with the Washoe Indians, and war against the Paiute Indians followed.[20]

NOTE ON GEOGRAPHY, SPELLING, AND GRAMMAR

In discussing white settlements, use of the term *Eastern Sierra* refers to Carson Valley and Honey Lake Valley, the two earliest Eastern Sierra Nevada settlements. Established in the early 1850s, both are located in the northern part of the range. The town of Bishop, the first of the settlements farther south, was settled in 1861, outside the focus of this work.

Quotes in the text are written as they appear in the original sources, without an indication of spelling or grammatical errors. In some instances, [*sic*] markings would distract from what is being said, and in others the markings would dominate the extract.

CHAPTER ONE

ENCOUNTERS

It took little more than a decade for the Eastern Sierra to transition from the world of Native Americans to US incorporation. The first wave of American immigrants came west, following their dreams of landownership. In 1849 the number of homesteaders was eclipsed by tens of thousands of migrants inspired by the $300 million worth of gold that would be panned in California by 1855. On the eastern slope of the Sierra, the settlers engaged in entrepreneurial pursuits and fought the Native Americans and each other. In 1859, just east of the range, miners uncovered the exceedingly rich Comstock Lode, the first American discovery that required deep hard-rock mining. It led to the area's industrialization, and it ensured the abrupt end of the Native Americans' way of life.[1]

The pioneers who followed the emigrant trail to California in the 1850s suffered many hardships. The worst came on the journey's last leg. After months of travel, driving now-exhausted teams, they came to the Great Basin and the only river flowing west through it, the brackish, invaluable Humboldt River. They followed it for three hundred winding miles through sagebrush and saltbush valleys, across sand bluffs, and up ravines of low, rolling, treeless mountains, keeping wagons and animals well above alkaline riverbanks and swampy, deep sloughs. The geography was a constant threat. At the same time, Native Americans, losing food resources to each passing train, raided the pioneers' livestock.[2]

For the Native Americans, difficulties caused by Anglos had begun two decades earlier. At the end of 1828 and into 1829, Peter Skene Ogden had led a group from Canada's Hudson Bay Company into the Great Basin to carry out their "scorched-earth policy," exterminating the region's beavers to keep competing Americans from utilizing the resource. The actions, which gave the Humboldt its original name, "the Barren," destroyed a source of fur the Shoshone Indians used for winter clothing.

Celebrated trapper Joe Meek shot and killed a Shoshone at the headwaters of the Humboldt in 1832 because the Indian "looked as if he might" steal traps. The following year Joseph Walker, with Meek in his party, led an expedition that had occasion to confront a great number of curious Paiute Indians. The white men demonstrated gunfire, shooting at ducks, hoping the exhibition would be sufficient to allow them to camp for the night before leaving the area. The marksmanship impressed the Paiutes almost as much as the noise—which caused them to dive for the ground. The next morning, eighty or a hundred of the Native Americans approached. The white men were fearful of their intent. Walker instructed his men that in such a case, they needed a good start. Consequently, thirty-two of his men mounted their horses, surrounded the party, and opened fire. They killed thirty-nine and caused the rest to flee, "running into the high grass in every direction, howling in the most lamentable manner." Zenas Leonard, the company secretary, explained that the severity of their action was due to the fact that they were in country "swarming with hostile savages, sufficiently numerous to devour us."[3]

On the Walker party's return trip to the Humboldt Sink, a great number of Paiutes, perhaps twice as many as those who had sustained the earlier slaughter, seemed ready to fight. Walker ordered an attack. This time, Leonard reports, they "rode right over them," killing fourteen and wounding numerous others. The Indians, using bows and arrows, wounded three of Walker's men.[4]

Abuse of the Indians continued with the American western emigration. Bill Hickman, who gained notoriety as a Mormon Danite, or Destroying Angel, traveled along the Humboldt in 1851 with four others. At a place called Stony Point, the white men shot and killed several Shoshone men and a woman, scalping the men. Hickman bragged openly about the pleasure they derived in the murders, as ethnocentrism and chauvinism allowed the killing of Indians, regardless of circumstances.[5]

By the mid-1850s the Shoshone Tosa *wihi*, or White Knife band—named for the arrowheads and blades they made from a white-rock quarry—had declared open war against the white settlers. While other Indians killed the travelers' animals for food, still others worked in concert with white men, stealing stock to be traded or resold.[6]

The early-day explorers and mapmakers had been involved in less immediate forms of violence: their pathfinding and charting enabled the subsequent onslaught. Likewise, the migrating Americans were perpetrating passive violence by moving through Indian territory. In 1859, while the Interior Department was improving the northern route across the Great Basin, Captain J.H. Simpson led an expedition for the War Department to further develop the central route. That summer, at one of his campsites in the middle of Nevada, Simpson wrote, "Saw fine meadows for stock about the springs. Speckled trout weighing from 1½ to 2½ pounds caught in Reese's River. McCarthy brought in a large mess of ducks. Several Pi-Utes followed us yesterday and today—two armed with rifles." Armed Paiutes had reason for trailing the settlers. In a mostly barren landscape, every fish or duck taken by the Anglos was one less for the Native Americans.[7]

Improving the routes meant tens of thousands more white settlers would make the cross-country trek, stripping the few desert rivers of their grasses and grass seeds, game birds, and game. Knowingly or not, the travelers were clearing native species, thereby making areas of the Native people's homeland unlivable. In 1859 a federal Indian agent noted that the Indians who depended on the Humboldt knew from other tribes' experiences that roads heralded an onslaught leading to subjugation or destruction.[8]

When the emigrants finally reached the Humboldt Sink, on the western side of the Great Basin, they traded the danger of attacks for another perilous hardship: no water. In the Forty-Mile Desert, water and grass were replaced by silt and salt, remnants of an ancient inland ocean. The crossing became littered with parts of failed wagons, remains of animals, and shallow, simply marked graves.

As early as August 1849, the company surgeon of the Charlestown, Virginia, Mining Company, in a train with seventy-five travelers, described camping near a sulfur spring in a slough where thirst-crazed mules and cows had broken away from previous trains and become trapped, infusing the camp with the smell of the dead.[9]

Animals and emigrants were brutally tested in crossing forty miles of desert, lacking forage and water. It has been postulated that only a small fraction of the emigrants would have reached the western side of the desert had it been even ten miles wider. Another diary from 1849 demonstrates the point. After crossing the Forty-Mile Desert to within three miles of water, an emigrant's horse collapsed, unable to go any farther. The emigrant began to walk, periodically lying down in the sand.

> I thought I would never get through and laide down to kick the bucket; but I thought of home and it give me a little more grit and I would get up and stager along. I was so thirsty my tonge and lips cracked and bled but I was able to get to the water and after drinking a little—I dare not drink much—I felt better. Towards knight, I took some grass and water in my canteen back to the horse.... I poered water on the grass and he eat and then he went to the river first rate.[10]

After crossing the Great Basin, some two hundred thousand emigrants followed the Carson River Route. They took it rather than the previously favored Truckee River Route to the north or the highly touted, but less traveled, Lassen Route—even farther north. Those who followed the Carson left the nightmare of the desert to find what must have seemed the portal to the Promised Land: Carson Valley.

The valley is a fertile expanse fed by drainage from the Sierra Nevada and the eastern and western forks of the Carson River, snow water running out of the steep mountains. The valley, the river, a nearby pass, and, in the adjacent valley, the town that is the capital of Nevada are all named for Christopher "Kit" Carson. The mountain man, renowned as a guide, was believed to have explored and trapped in the area as early as 1839, and he crossed over the pass into California, serving as a guide on the first three of John Frémont's expeditions. The place-names were conferred some twenty years before Carson's notorious campaign of brutality against the Navaho people. The barbarity that he directed toward Indians did not affect his heroic stature. As part of the third Frémont expedition, he took part in the Sacramento River massacre, mentioned in the introduction. Shortly thereafter, he directed a similar action. After the Frémont party fought off a Modoc Indian attack, Carson led the slaughter of a village of peaceful Klamath Indians, and, during the week that followed, anytime the troop came upon one or more Indians, they killed them.[11]

Frémont's expeditions were intended to be scientific endeavors, and they included exploring, surveying, and mapping. His description of the Sierra Nevada was graphic: "Rising singly, like pyramids, from heavily timbered plateau, to the height of fourteen and seventeen thousand feet above the sea, these snowy peaks constitute the characterizing feature of the range, and distinguish it from the Rocky Mountains and all others on our part of the continent."

Although he miscalculated the maximum height of the peaks, the highest actually being Mount Whitney at 14,505 feet, it is generally recognized that its sharp-faced crests distinguish the Sierra Nevada from other American ranges. The mountains run 400 miles, north to south, parallel to the Pacific Coast, 150 miles away. Frémont described how winds from the Pacific Ocean sweep over the "great mountain wall" of the West, loosing rain and snow and leaving only dry winds to move across the eastern slope.[12]

Frémont's observation explains the limitations of the watershed on the comparatively barren east side of the range and why the Eastern Sierra's waters are coveted. The Carson River's west fork begins in the range above Hope Valley, named by the pioneers who paused there, resting their animals, before their last push over the Sierra to their California destinations. The Carson's east fork, a larger stream, originates at Ebbetts Pass, traditionally held as the crossing point, in 1827, of Jedediah Smith and two associates, the first white Americans to cross the Sierra Nevada. Meeting in the center of Carson Valley, the two forks of the river were lined with willow brakes, cottonwoods, and natural meadows. In 1850 Mormon entrepreneurs began setting up a station at the valley's most auspicious site, below the timber line but above the river's sloughs and adjoining meadows.[13]

Abner Blackburn is credited as the first of the Americans to pan for gold at Gold Canyon, just below the Comstock Lode. He was among a party led by Captain Joseph DeMont, who decided that selling supplies would pay better than mining. Blackburn wrote that in the valley there was cold water coming from the mountains, abundant pines lining it, and plentiful feed for stock. He said that it was ideal for business and that they built a station out of pine logs and a corral for their animals.[14]

The area had been equally bountiful for the Washoe Indians. Before the white settlers arrived, the Washoes controlled Carson Valley and a large swath of the Eastern Sierra. The range was a high mountain stronghold for the Washoes. The center of their world was Lake Tahoe, at 6,200 feet of elevation. The lake is 72 miles in circumference and more than 1,600 feet deep. It was formed by faulting, glaciation, and volcanic action that two million years earlier created a 500-square-mile basin guarded by eastern and western crests. In 1859 Captain Simpson, of the Army Corps of Engineers, described the lake valley as a beautiful park of green glades and stately pines, reaching a height of from 100 to 150 feet, 8 and sometimes 10 feet in diameter.[15]

The trees filled the mountainsides within the basin and its outlying slopes. Entrances and egresses into it were steep and narrow, 7,000 and 8,000 feet high. The Washoes traveled the passes in spring, living at the lake through the snowless months. It was the center of their world. They believed the water "breathed life" into all living things. Leaving the lake in the fall, they traveled to their sacred Pine Nut Mountains, east of present-day Gardnerville, Nevada, to gather the meaty pine nuts that were their winter staple.

Their winter settlements dotted the valleys abutting the Sierra, with bands living in permanent sites near streams or springs in distinct regional communities. The tribe had three main bands. The Welmelti lived in the northernmost area, bordering Honey Lake; the Hangalelti were the southernmost group, in and around Carson Valley; and the P'a-walu lived in the foothills and valleys in between. Protected by the Great Basin to the east and the Sierra to the west, the Washoes continued to pursue their traditional lives, undiscovered and undisturbed fifty years after the Lewis and Clark Expedition.[16]

The Washoe communities probably totaled no more than fifteen hundred members. On the bounds of snow country, they were nonequestrian. They engaged in cooperative hunting, fishing, and plant cultivation. Shamans, who were believed to gain knowledge from the spirits of antelope, rabbits, and deer, led some hunts. Hunt leaders regularly reconnoitered deer and antelope herds and organized other tribe members. Elders met and directed the maintenance of fisheries: which fish and how many could be taken each season. In the twentieth century, Washoe Manuel Bender recounted, "It was drilled into all providers of food that from one pool with 5 only 2 fish could be killed.... The practice was observed in game. So well established was this rule and so well observed that the white people merely took for granted that the fish and game were just prolific without any means to perpetuate the source."[17]

Countless generations had passed down the Washoes' knowledge of food sources, which included hundreds of edible plants and medicinal vegetation. The tribe's eco-management was developed to such an extent that the newcomers described the land as unexploited. The first pioneers to see Carson Valley lauded it in diaries. An Englishman declared: "[The valley] for soil, situation, and natural charms, eclipsed the most favoured localities in our journey. I got in an ecstatic mood on entering it, feeling as though I stood in fairy-land." A more pragmatic traveler said, "First rate grass. Beautiful springs coming from the snow mountains. The handsomest yellow pine timber I ever saw." Another said, "[It] presented a sea of the finest feed I had ever seen, untrod by domestic animals. By acclamation this was pronounced the most delightful spot we ever beheld." Unfortunately for the Indians, the last diarist concluded with words that others would soon act upon: "If there ever was a spot designed by nature for a stock ranch, it was this." Because the land was unfenced, the newcomers viewed the valleys, forests, and streams as sources of bounty free for the taking.[18]

Newcomers passing through and, more particularly, those who settled in Carson Valley and vicinity violated all the Washoes' precepts and standards of right. The homesteaders redirected the waterways and cut the riverbanks to spread water for cultivation, and they planted crops that replaced many of the Washoes' food plants and much of their pharmacopoeia. Within a few years, as immigration increased, the amount of land irrigated amounted to several thousand acres. Additionally, enterprising firms claimed large swaths of the outlying lands to clear-cut forests, harvest fish and game, and mine gold and silver.[19]

The tribes' history of isolation left them bereft of the language skills and knowledge regarding complex economic practices or nineteenth-century technologies that might have allowed them at least some defense against the American settlers and their industries.[20]

For a time, the Washoes' mobility allowed them to avoid most contact, hiding and observing the explorers and wagon trains. Once, in those early days, Washoes found an ox that had strayed, and they conducted tests to see its use. They packed it and led it around and experimented with riding it until, tired of its novelty, they killed, butchered, and ate it. Another time, in 1849, in the initial stages of the emigrant rush, several Washoes came into a camp and traded "glorious" trout, five pounds each, to a company for tattered flannel shirts and some hard bread and buns. After dinner, men from the company asked to borrow the Indians' bows to shoot at a tree. They all missed. The Washoes did not want to shoot but, when pressed, shot, and their arrows missed by as much as the white men's arrows. One of the white men, suspecting that the Indians were hesitant to show their skills, took a bun and stuck it to the bark, using signs to show that if someone could hit it, they could have it to eat. One of the Washoes raised his bow and released an arrow that pierced "the dimple of the crust."[21]

Although skilled with bows and spears, the Washoes were not numerous enough, nor their weaponry formidable enough, to raise a general resistance. The newcomers could therefore ignore how they were disrupting tribal life. In his book on the Washoes, anthropologist James Downs notes that many white settlers expected attacks and were contemptuous of people whom they believe lacked the national pride to do so. And what did the Washoes think of the newcomers? The Washoe term for *wild* was *mushege*. It was used to describe things like a bear driven from its den or a shaman evincing fearsome powers. In 1846 tribe members had surveilled the Donner Party. They had left food in places for the pioneers to find but saw the pioneers turn to cannibalism. In the next few years, they experienced the Americans' guns killing at a great distance, saw the way they plowed the earth and dug far underground, observed them clear-cutting the forests, and realized the unpredictability in their use of power. Into the twentieth century, the Washoe word for *whites* was *mushege.*[22]

In March 1851 Jacob H. Holeman, a nascent Indian agent assigned to Utah Territory, crossed the Great Basin and noticed the depredations by white settlers against Native Americans. He noted that the white settlers were not only taking possession of the country, killing the game, but in some instances were driving off the Indians themselves. There were two groups of white settlers in particular whom Holeman accused: the Mormons, who took possession of the Great Salt Lake Valley and the other rich valleys; and others living among the Indians, calling themselves "freemen," who induced Indians to drive off the stock of emigrants. The freemen then purchased the animals for trifles and resold them to the next train passing through.[23]

In his report the following year, Agent Holeman, who was stationed in Salt Lake City, wrote of the territory to the west. He reported that the previously plentiful game had been killed and driven off by the trains of immigrants passing through, "which has placed the Indians in such a condition that many of them are almost in a starving state." He went on to say that although the Indians had a savage nature and untamed habits, they had little intercourse with white settlers. The country's danger regarding plunder and murder was heightened because the lawless white people were more reckless than the Indians.[24]

Holeman also reported that the white traders, who set up along the trail to California, were committing more depredations than the Indians. The freemen traders offered the Indians guns, ammunition, and provisions if they would steal stock from the emigrants. When the agent confronted the traders, he recounted, "They laughed at me; they defied me and the laws; they told me there were so many of them that they could and would do as they pleased, law or no law."[25]

The nascent communities at the base of the Sierra did not have the same problems as those presented by the freemen on the trail. When Carson Valley was first populated by Anglos, they were merchants, busy with trade. In the summer of 1850, some twenty of them, from California, had set up tents using abandoned wagon beds tipped on their sides as business counters to sell to those coming in after the grueling desert crossing. Prices were high and business was brisk, as those travelers without money could trade their livestock.[26] When the traders' goods were gone, they returned across the Sierra. That same summer Captain DeMont's party of Mormons built a temporary log trading post near the confluence of the east and west forks of the Carson River. Years afterward a man who had immigrated to California wrote:

> They had quite a band of fat cattle and cows which they brought from Salt Lake; some of the fattest beef I ever saw hung suspended from the limbs of a big pine tree. Beneath the tree was a butchers' block, cleaver, and steak knife. They retailed the meat to hungry emigrants at six bits per pound; I have never since eaten beef that tasted so sweet as did that. In regard to improvements there was one store where they kept for sale flour, beans, tea, coffee, sugar, dried peaches, sardines, tobacco, miners' clothing, overalls, shirts, etc., etc. There was also a grocery where they sold whisky, bread, cigars and tobacco. They had a good-sized log-house completed

> all but the roof. I was informed that it was intended for a family dwelling and eating-house, you see the Mormon Station was well established and widely known in July, 1850, and the traders at that post were getting rich trading with the emigrants.[27]

After that first season, with the approach of winter, the traders sold the property to a Mr. Moore, who subsequently sold it to John Reese in 1851. It was Reese who led the first settlers, sixteen Mormons from Salt Lake, to the valley. Reese and his brother Enoch had established a general store in Salt Lake City in 1849. Hearing about Carson Valley from Captain DeMont's secretary, Hampden S. Beatie, who happened to be their cousin, they outfitted ten wagons with supplies. With nephew Stephen A. Kinsey and a small company, they crossed the Great Basin. They arrived at what was known as Mormon Station in early June. The station was replicating the Salt Lake City outfitting trade, and the Mormon Church's officers encouraged its establishment. Having families farming in Carson Valley would create a satellite, as was occurring closer to Salt Lake in Provo and Tooele. Wherever they could claim irrigable land, they believed they were blocking the evil influences of the increasingly industrial, urbanized world.[28]

The Mormons were developing a colony in San Bernardino, in Southern California, as well. In the 1850s, with Utah suffering droughts, grasshopper infestations, and Indian problems, there was some question whether San Bernardino might better serve as the center of the Mormon's Kingdom of God. The route into central California through Mormon Station, soon to be renamed Genoa, had been established by veterans, mustered out of the Mormon Battalion, traveling east in 1848. It soon became the most traveled of the emigrant trails. Although profitable, San Bernardino and Mormon Station were far removed from Salt Lake City, and the church would be unable to sustain authority over them. Urban historian Eugene Moehring explains that the Mormon incorporation plan's failure resulted from extending their network hundreds of miles beyond their power base with nothing in between to support them.[29]

Reese created a foundation for the Carson Valley colony that for a time succeeded as a Mormon outpost. He built a blacksmith shop, along with the trading post, and began to grow and sell crops.

After the 1848 Treaty of Guadalupe Hidalgo, Utah Territory was part of America's public domain. Congress provided for the establishment of land offices in various districts throughout the country, but, because of the contentious relationship between the Mormons and the federal government, the first Utah land office was not opened until 1869. Before that, Mormon officials asserted control over governing landownership. Brigham Young declared that as regarded farmers, every man could claim "what he could till."[30]

Reese took up large amounts of fertile land. His success brought a further migration of Mormons from Salt Lake and of non-Mormons crossing the mountains from California. Many of the non-Mormons, identified as "Gentiles" by the Mormons, and differentiated as such in newspaper articles, were gold seekers. Others joined the Mormons in starting businesses, developing the town, and claiming substantial lands on acreage in Carson Valley and in Eagle Valley to the north.

The rush to the West might have resulted in more chaos than it did if the miners and settlers had not brought ideas about law and order with them. In organizing land use, they concentrated first on drawing manageable property lines and then focused on ensuring that the lines were honored. They had no regard for the fact that they were dividing up Indian tribes' homeland. By November 1851 the settlers of Carson Valley had come in large-enough numbers that they needed to form a government. Over the course of three meetings, they organized committees and approved resolutions. The key determinations provided for the survey of land claims and the election of a magistrate and sheriff. There were ten men who served on committees.

Of the ten, four were soon involved in deadly incidents. The first to fall was Colonel A. Woodward, who had established a company for transporting mail between Salt Lake and California. He had been elected chair of those first meetings and was slain by Indians on the Humboldt River a few months later. Wash Loomis, a member of the Committee on Resolutions, was subsequently hanged for stealing in Los Angeles. Former Texas Ranger William Byrnes, elected the first sheriff, survived being shot, "perforated with ball holes," by a man named Haskill. The shooter had left Byrnes for dead. Said to have an iron constitution, Byrnes recovered and made periodic lengthy attempts to hunt down his assailant. He let it be known, after returning from his last such expedition, that he did not need to hunt for Haskill anymore. Byrnes lived a hard life after leaving Carson Valley, serving as a California Ranger involved in the killing of Juaquín Murrieta; he was a lawman in other jurisdictions and a prison guard; after fighting over mining claims and consistent hard drinking, he lived out his life as an inmate at the Stockton Insane Asylum.[31]

On October 3, 1853, the *Sacramento Daily Union* gave a succinct account of the other violent incident which involved a territory organizer named Jonas Barnard: "There was a fatal affray on Clear Creek, six miles below the Mormon Station in Carson Valley, on the 26th ult [meaning last month]. The parties were Jonas L. Barnard and a Mr. Dorsey—Mr. Barnard being killed, a pistol ball entering his right eye, and coming out the back of his bead." The short article concluded with the statement, "Mr. Dorsey was acquitted."

By December 1851 Barnard and his brother Frank and George Follensbee had joined W.L. and Frank Hall in establishing a ranch and a trading post in Eagle Valley. Early settler Henry Van Sickle, who at various times served as a county commissioner, county treasurer, and justice of the peace, recalled further details about Barnard's killing. Using frontier spelling, Van Sickle reported that the owner of a trading post on Clear Creek was assaulted by "a intoxicated man by name J.L. Barnard, who attempted to ride his horse into his place of business and upon being requested by owner John L. Dorn to refrain, and refusing got exasperated... borrowed a pistol and was coming toward Dorn's place of business, when within 15ft of the door, with cocked pistol, Dorn in self defense shot him dead." Van Sickle went on to confirm that Dorn was acquitted and added the remark, "Nearly every man either carried a gun or had one where he could readily get at it."[32]

The absence of a developed justice system was not the only difference between the two sides of the continent. The East's burgeoning factory system and industrial urban centers required workers' specialization and apprentice programs. The pioneer settlements needed the opposite. They required jacks-of-all-trades to sustain an agrarian, rural economy. The Mormons would send a nucleus of men to a new territory, men with essential skills, such as blacksmithing, masonry, and farming, so that inexperienced members had experts to rely on. Merchants, like John Reese, would serve as the territory's all-purpose businessmen:

importing, buying, trading, and selling all types of provisions and products. In Carson Valley, the Mormons and other settlers were soon joined by millwrights who built and ran lumber and gristmills.

In May 1852 the valley's residents held their fourth government meeting. It authorized anyone who built a sawmill to take up a section of timberland. Thomas Knott was able to claim a section. He was a Gentile who undertook the construction of a flouring and sawmill for another Gentile, John Cary, at the mouth of Woodfords Canyon, some twenty miles south of Mormon Station. Knott packed a 190-pound mill crank, an anvil, and other mill tools over the Sierra from California and used wrought iron that had been discarded by emigrants. "I gathered up 400 wagon tires and other wagon irons, and gathered together 40 or 50 log chains. In July [1853], I started the saw to sawing lumber before Migration came in from the states and Salt Lake."[33]

On December 1, 1852, after a year of the new government apparently sorting out surveying and recording issues, John Reese, the territory's leading citizen, now known as "Colonel," filed the first land claim under Salt Lake City's jurisdiction. Several other claimants followed that month; dozens made claims thereafter. Reese had seventeen acres under cultivation, some for small grains, but also ten for turnips that he sold to travelers for a dollar per each small bunch. In 1854 he had Knott build a grist- and sawmill for him. Within a few years that mill would become the object of a bitter court case between Knott and Reese that escalated into a conflict between Gentiles and Mormons.[34]

Reese sought to avoid conflict with the Washoe Indians. One account said that Reese sealed his claim to the land by paying Captain Jim of the Washoe Indians two sacks of flour.[35] If accurate, beyond its inequity, there would have been two problems with that transaction. First, without an understanding of the language, customs, or concept of American property rights, it would have been unclear to Captain Jim, whose Washoe name was Lenúka, what he was giving up for the flour. Second, although Captain Jim was by all accounts a Washoe "captain," or headman, the white settlers misconstrued what that meant. Headmen, shamans, healers, warriors, and animal bosses (hunting leaders) were important persons in their communities. However, each may have had only limited authority. Most served only within a kinship group or a band or for a limited amount of time, such as a hunting season or a particular battle. The tribe had no president or chief executive, no "chief." Individuals had great freedom of action. The headman gave advice but did not have judicial or enforcement powers. Even within a headman's group, each individual had the right to disregard his suggestions; adherence was voluntary. Years later, Charlie Rube, a nineteenth-century Washoe animal boss, said that he had "heard of no chiefs of [the] whole tribe before white man's time."[36]

Beginning with this interaction, Lenúka, who learned to speak some English, fell into disfavor with a number of tribe members. Although white settlers continued to seek him out, mistaking him for the chief, his actions eventually led him to be "witched and killed by a shaman named Wagotom."[37]

This initial agreement between Reese and Lenúka carried little weight with other Washoes. By 1852, being fenced out of their land and losing game and other traditional sources of food, they resorted to raids of retribution. Indian agent Holeman reported that the "Washaws" had been very troublesome. He said that the "many depredations which have been committed on whites in crossing the Sierra Nevada no doubt have been by this tribe." For all that, Holeman had difficulty finding the Washoes. He traveled to Carson Valley but was unable to make contact, meeting only stragglers he identified as "Pintahs" and "Washaws" (Paiutes and Washoes) engaged in hunting and fishing.[38]

That summer a report carried to Eagle Station, now the location of the Nevada state capital in Carson City, said that a band of Washoes had taken possession of several American horses. "A noted Indian fighter" named Pearson led Frank and W.L. Hall, owners of Eagle Station, and a man named Cady to confront the Indians. They found Native women moving belongings into the hills and then met a band of sixty Washoes prepared for battle. Pearson and W.L. Hall decided the odds were too great and returned to the station. Frank Hall and Cady decided to "play the friendly dodge" and remained to deal with the Indians. The Washoes accepted small gifts of tobacco from the white men and then let it be known that Hall and Cady should move on, which they did without recovering or even seeing the horses. Indian agent Major G.W. Ingalls reported that a few days later, Cady was riding along a trail and overtook an Indian and, "like a brave man," deliberately shot him.[39]

With other horses and livestock disappearing in 1852, the white settlers captured two Washoes: "a powerful man, dressed in a full buckskin suit," and a sixteen-year-old boy. They held them prisoner at Mormon Station for several days, until the man attempted to escape and a guard shot him in the back. The boy was so terrorized that those who held him let him go.[40]

There were other problems with cattle rustling in 1852. Jacks Valley is a small green oasis northwest of Carson Valley. It was named for Return Jackson (Jack) Redden, sometimes written as Redding or Reading, who lived there in 1851 and 1852. He and his Mormon kin—his father, three brothers, and a brother-in-law, along with men they consorted with—frequented the wrong side of the law. They were known for passing counterfeit money, stealing, and robbing. Back in Illinois, before they came west, Jack narrowly escaped when his father and oldest brother were arrested as accomplices in a murder during a robbery that ended badly. While Redden was in Jacks Valley, Indian agent Holeman wrote to the commissioner of Indian affairs, telling him that a Mormon cattleman, taking cattle to California, had been advised to paint the horns of his cattle. The report explained it needed to be done so that a Mormon named Reading, who was leading Indians in plundering immigrants near Carson Valley, would leave his cattle alone. Jack spent three months in jail at Salt Lake for horse stealing the year after leaving Jacks Valley. A year after that, his youngest brother and his brother-in-law were killed by tribesmen of an Indian whom the brother-in-law had murdered. Jack Redden had no trouble with the area's other settlers; his later life illustrates again the vagaries of the American West, as he served multiple terms as a Utah justice of the peace.[41]

Twenty-five miles northeast of Jacks Valley is Gold Canyon. Beginning in 1851, just above the Carson River, between one hundred and two hundred miners worked the gravel with rockers, collecting gold. Their average take was between five and ten dollars a day per man when they had water to work their claims. In the winter of 1852–53, a group of the miners decided to rob two supply trains traveling from Salt Lake Valley to Mormon Station. The teamsters fought back. A nephew of Daniel Boone led one of the trains. On January 1, 1853, the *San Francisco Herald,* which collected news from papers in outlying towns, reported: "Mr. B. dared them to combat; but like all other mobites and cowards, they left the road open for the train to pass on."[42]

On February 15 the *Herald,* using the ethnic slur "depredating greasers," reported that Mexican outlaws were rumored to be in the vicinity. This, along with the miners' attack, caused the people of Carson Valley to turn to vigilantism. The report read: "A vigilance committee was formed on Monday last for the purpose of ferreting out any evil doers; at least we are going to watch for them." No further mention of this group is ever made, indicating that they took no action or that actions taken were unsuccessful.[43]

With the precariousness of the initial attempts at local governance, another question arose: Were the people of the valley under the jurisdiction of Salt Lake City or California? Utah Territory, established in September 1850, included the valley when it created seven new counties that would later become the state of Nevada. The Mormon settlers were divided in their allegiance to Salt Lake City. In June 1852, after stopping in Carson Valley, a Mormon merchant, who had driven cattle to California, informed Brigham Young that the citizens there were intent on breaking away from Mormon authority. He accused Colonel Reese and his nephew Stephen Kinsey of being "the ringleaders" in opposing Utah's organization. Despite the fact that Reese would maintain close ties with Salt Lake and would move back there some years later to live out his life, the merchant claimed, "[Reese and the others] declare they will pay no taxes that are levied on them from that source and advise others to hold out in like manner until they get this valley annexed to California."[44]

That same year, William M. Eddy, California's surveyor general, was directed to map the state. A bill passed the state senate unanimously, allocating $8,000 for the task. The assembly reduced the amount to $3,000, a sum that was seen by friends of the bill as totally inadequate, but Eddy determined to do what he could. After a slow, difficult journey from Sacramento to Placerville, California—which necessitated that delicate instruments be carried by hand whenever the road got rough—Eddy used chronometer readings to determine that the town was approximately forty-six miles from the state boundary. He reported that it was common knowledge that it was at least sixty miles to Mormon Station in Carson Valley. Feeling certain the valley was outside the state limit, Eddy said he did not feel justified in traveling across the Sierra at the expense of the state. He wrote in his report that he was reluctantly forced to conclude that the valley was twelve to fifteen miles out of the state.[45]

The actual distance from the angles of the boundary to Genoa, formerly Mormon Station, is perhaps four or five air miles, although the closest distance by road from the state line is south of the angles and is some eleven miles. For purposes of jurisdiction, the entire area was ceded to Utah's governance. The finding caused resentment in the non-Mormon segment of the population. They accused the Mormon government of acting unjustly toward "patriotic citizens of the Union," as they saw themselves, and they threatened that they would protect their rights under the Constitution.[46]

Because of prejudice, persecution, and the collective memory of the murder of their founder, Joseph Smith, in 1844, the Mormons, calling themselves the Latter-day Saints, had followed their new leader, Brigham Young, to the West. They were claiming the prerogative of *expatriation.* In the eighteenth century, expatriation referred to the right of a country to banish its citizens. In the 1770s Americans refashioned the term to mean the right to withdraw from residence in one's native country. The new definition, although controversial and at times contested in the Supreme Court, was buttressed by the American Revolution. It was best manifested in Texas, beginning in 1820 and until the Texas Declaration of Independence in 1836, where thousands of early settlers crossed Mexico's northern border and claimed land by converting to Mexican citizenship.[47]

Mormonism was a communitarian experiment, a theocracy espousing egalitarian principles. Historian William Deverell notes that in the nineteenth century, its adherents were typecast as "ideal types of 'un-American characteristics.'" The Mormon elders maintained a rancorous attitude toward their American persecutors. Juanita Brooks, American West and Mormon historian, tells of an emigrant who kept a journal and wrote that while resting in Salt Lake City in July 1849, "He heard Brigham Young preach a sermon in which he declared that he would not hurt the murderers of the Prophet if they came here. No, indeed! He would not hurt them! He would only kill them so quick they wouldn't know what had hit them!"[48]

As pioneers traveled through Utah Territory in the early 1850s, newspapers in the West printed some testimonials about assistance given to the emigrants in Salt Lake City, but they could be drowned out by lurid stories or hateful allegations. An article that appeared in July 1852, in

San Francisco's *Daily Alta California,* accused the Salt Lake Mormons of treasonable language against the United States and of injustice, cruelty, and murderous threats against US citizens. US mail in Salt Lake City, the paper charged, was being opened and destroyed. The article described at length a book that contended Joseph Smith had been a "charlatan and cheat," that "he had gathered around him a gang of fools: the fools attracted rogues as the carrion attracts the vulture; and thus arose the Mormon community."[49]

Anti-Mormons contended that four aspects of the religion were repellant: the domination of the Latter-day Saints' lives by its hierarchy; the political subordination of its members, who thereby voted as a bloc in political elections; their exclusivism in business dealings; and, particularly damning, polygamy. Although it was long rumored, the church did not publicly announce the revelation regarding multiple wives until the Mormons were established in Salt Lake Valley.[50]

On August 24, 1852, at the direction of Brigham Young, Mormon elder Orson Pratt delivered a sermon in the Tabernacle at Salt Lake City. He said publicly what had been commonly acknowledged inside the religion and universally rumored outside it: the doctrine of plurality of wives was part of the Latter-day Saints faith. Pratt, a mathematician by training and a member of the Quorum of the Twelve Apostles of the church, justified the belief in large part by referring to the Old Testament, in particular to words saying that God's faithful should "take unto yourselves more wives, like unto the Patriarchs, Abraham, Isaac, and Jacob of old—like those who lived in ancient times, who walked in my footsteps, and kept my commands." Pratt asked his listeners: "Have you learned that the sons and daughters of God before me this day, are His offspring—made after His own image; that they are to multiply their species until they become innumerable?... How did Abraham manage to get a foundation laid for this mighty kingdom? Was he to accomplish it all through one wife? No."[51]

After Pratt's announcement, the outcry against the tenet was virulent and persistent. A Northern California newspaper, the *Nevada Journal,* described the "deleterious" effect of polygamy and called on every member of the Mormon hierarchy to be "punished for his beastly offences against virtue and decency." The remark echoed those of 1930s in the states, when, for example, Governor Lilburn Boggs of Missouri said that Mormon outrages "are beyond all description" and called for the religionists to be exterminated or driven from the state. By the mid-1850s both sides of the political spectrum were condemning Mormons. A California abolitionist introduced what became a conventional phrase, referring to slavery and polygamy as "twin relics of barbarism." A proslavery Missouri senator, speaking of abolitionists, turned the noun *Mormon* into a verb. In a letter to Jefferson Davis, he said: "We will be compelled to shoot, burn and hang.... [W]e intend to Mormonize the Abolitionists." As regarded Mormons, there were men soon to move into Carson Valley who would be in accord with those sentiments.[52]

CHAPTER TWO

Lucky Bill and Other Problems

It was entirely predictable that Lucky Bill Thorington would be a problem for those wishing to establish order. He was an agent of commotion, a fabled gambler throughout Utah Territory and Northern California. Thorington had earned a fortune inside camp tents at desert outstations like Ragtown, now Fallon, Nevada, and in the barrooms of Placerville and Sacramento. Historical geographer Archer Butler Hulbert wrote a perhaps apocryphal account, mentioning Thorington's wagering with the forty-niners at Ragtown: "But the most expensive thing here was experience in the thimble game operated by Lucky Bill, one of California's noted gamblers. Jerry Gullion staked his last ox and lost it; emboldened with whiskey, he lost his last dollar and five of G. W. Thissel's."[1]

Thorington came to Carson Valley in 1853. He was a native of Chenango County, New York, having moved with his parents to Michigan in 1848 before crossing the plains in 1850. Shortly after arriving in Carson Valley, he bought the recently constructed Woodfords Canyon sawmill from Thomas Knott and John Cary, and he acquired a ranch several miles from the mill, on the road toward Mormon Station. In town he built a home. He also continued his gambling, and he proved to be industrious.

Although he was not a Mormon, Thorington joined forces with Colonel Reese to build a toll road in a canyon that was difficult to pass through. The canyon, southwest of Carson Valley, had several names: Rocky Canyon, Big Canyon, Carson Canyon, Emigrant Canyon, and, ultimately, Woodfords Canyon. It was a vital link of the emigrant trail leading to the crossing point of the Sierra and beyond to Placerville, the mining town that had a population of fifty-six hundred in 1850, and then to Sacramento, with its twelve thousand citizens. The rocky bed of the West Carson River had to be forded twice in the canyon, and owing to the canyon's sheer towering walls and to an obstacle course of boulders to be twisted around, it was as difficult a stretch of road as any that the emigrants faced. Wagons, many with belongings inside, were deserted at the canyon mouth, and "piles of bacon and other valuable property" were abandoned in the canyon. In 1849 a traveler wrote about it in his diary, saying they had to cross the river several times. Some rocks in the road and the stream were as big as a nail keg, others the size of a whiskey barrel. "Finally," he wrote, "we encountered one as large as a sugar hogshead and proved too much for one of our wagons. The hind axle of the wagon broke. We cut the bed and put the hind wheels on the forward axle and made a cart, loaded the goods onto that and proceeded."[2]

Thorington and Reese straightened the road in some places, built around obstructions in others, and constructed two bridges. In 1855 the California surveyor general's chief field assistant traveled the road and approved the renovations. Thorington superintended the improved thoroughfare as a toll road.[3]

Reese was busy with his affairs. That spring it was reported he was doing quite well, as were individuals throughout the territory. In 1853 a newspaper in central California wrote that Reese had about a hundred acres of land under cultivation. It said fifteen or twenty other settlers were farming on a smaller scale and that some seventy miners were working in Gold Canyon, earning steady wages. The news report cautioned readers, though, that Indians were hostile and that visitors should travel in well-armed groups.[4]

The alliance of Reese and Thorington was uncharacteristic. Mormons generally sought to remain at a distance from the world that involved alcohol and gambling. Like many of the other early settlers, Reese related well to his partner. Thorington's neighbor Van Sickle, who served several terms as a county official and owned the largest landholdings in Carson Valley, vouched for the gambler: "Many stories might be told of his good acts that would put to blush those who make great professions of charity and love etc. but if a man gambled with him he was quite sure to lose his money. The narrator of this has often heard him advise people not to gamble." Another neighbor, A.H. Hawley, developer of the Hawley Grade Trail at Lake Tahoe, said that Lucky Bill was "a fine manly looking fellow...an open free hearted man; tis true he was a gambler but he was a very true hearted generous man."[5]

In his seminal *History of Nevada,* written in 1881, Myron Angel, an evident admirer, commented: "The country had no handsomer or merrier citizen in it than Lucky Bill, a name given to him because of the fortunate result that seemed to attend his every action." Angel excused Thorington's lack of education, saying it was modest because his "excessive animal spirits and vitality would not permit a close application to study." Hawley went on to give a physical description: "In form he was large weighing 200 pounds, and with broad ample shoulders, stood six feet and one inch in height; his head covered with glossy curling hair colored like the raven's wing, was massive, with a high classic forehead, and large gray mirthful eyes, looking out from beneath projecting eyebrows, that indicated strong perceptive faculties."[6]

The description is echoed in less Olympian but equally flattering terms by Van Sickle. Noting that Thorington was about six-foot-one, in his midforties, Van Sickle went on to describe him as "a fine looking man as one could find in a day walk, a gambler by profession and a man having many good qualities, a good worker at anything he ever undertook a better neighbor never lived near any man or a better friend to the weary traveler never lived."[7]

Thorington engaged in all forms of gambling, but his specialty was thimblerig. Also known as the shell game, it involves placing a small wax or buckskin ball beneath one of three cups and swiftly maneuvering the cups until giving a spectator the chance to bet under which it is located. The game is most often played to swindle bettors—the ball being hidden behind the player's fingernail and released beneath one of the cups that is not chosen. The second definition for thimblerig in *Webster's Dictionary* is "to cheat by trickery."

Rollin Daggett, a newsman who later became a congressman from Nevada, added to recollections about Thorington. While serving as editor of the *San Francisco Golden Era* in 1851, Daggett quoted Lucky Bill advertising his thimblerig game:

> Here gentlemen, is a nice, quiet little game conducted on the square, and especially recommended by the clergy for its honesty

> and wholesome moral tendencies. I win only from blind men; all that have two good eyes can win a fortune. You see, gentlemen, here are three little wooden cups, and here is a little ball, which, for the sake of starting the game, I shall place under this one, as you can plainly see—thus and thus—and thus; and now I will bet two, four or six ounces that no gentleman can, the first time trying, raise the cup that the ball is under; if he can, he can win all the money that Bill, by patient toil and industry, has scraped together.[8]

Thorington's wife, Maria, was described as striking and beautiful, with "coal black hair and huge brown eyes." Little is written of her, although it was said she became a favorite in town.[9] Their son, William Jerome, who went by Jerome, was twelve years old when he and his mother arrived in Mormon Station. Thorington seems to have been attempting to settle down by coming to Carson Valley. Besides his mill, he ran a trading post located for a time in a small brush tent. Once the toll road was completed, he supervised it and his ranch. He procured more land, brought the first fruit trees into the valley, and dug irrigation ditches.

Emanuel Penrod, a prospector who was later one of the original claimants of the Comstock Lode, had had a place in Eagle Valley, north of Mormon Station. He wrote that Thorington often said of himself that he "never worked nor never will." He went on to write in an inimitable style:

> But there is or was one redeamin quality in Luckey Bills favor, he was good to the poor and needy; he would always help a poor Emigrant and steal from all that would bite at his games; I say steal, for I think it nothing but stealing to play the thimble game; but the victim thinks he is only robbing player, and so I don't know which is the worst, the man who plays the game or the man who thinks he is robbing the man who manipulates the thimbles and wax balls. For fear all do not understand i will explain.[10]

As far as the "never worked" quote, it is belied by Thorington's enterprises and by the testimony of his neighbors in Carson Valley. It seems likely that the gambler used the self-deprecating characterization as part of his barroom persona, promoting thimblerig to lure potential bettors.

In speaking of Thorington's character, Myron Angel noted: "He was both generous and brave and his sympathies were readily aroused in favor of the unfortunate: or which in frontier parlance would be termed 'the underdog in a fight,' regardless of the causes that had placed the dog in that position." In the mid-twentieth century, writer H. Hamlin, utilizing the reminiscences of an old pioneer, said, "[Thorington] didn't inquire whether they were horse thieves or Mormon tithing collectors. His station was a rendezvous where the weary found rest and the hungry never were turned from his door."[11]

Something of this characteristic might be gleaned from an incident at his toll road. In the 1850s in Carson Valley, as in many parts of the West, sheep maintained a notoriety, perceived as an all-devouring scourge by cattlemen. Millwright Thomas Knott reported that in 1853, Kit Carson, assisted by a crew of Mexican sheepherders, drove five thousand head from New Mexico, through Woodfords Canyon, on their way to the gold diggings. Thorington allowed the sheep to cross his toll bridge for free, to the disgust of valley ranchers who most likely paid full fare for their stock.[12]

One other of Thorington's characteristics that needs be mentioned was his moral relativism. Although not a Mormon, upon settling among them in Carson Valley, he had a second conjugal relationship while remaining married to Maria. As society in the valley changed, that would cause him trouble.

Two other events in 1853 disrupted order in Carson Valley. On August 19 the *San Francisco Herald* reported that an unnamed man traveling through the valley had killed one of his employees in a fit of rage. The murder was committed in cold blood and was witnessed by several onlookers. The man was taken to Placerville, but "he was set at liberty, because the laws and courts of California have no jurisdiction over offences, however flagrant, that may be committed east of the mountains." The paper concluded: "As a consequence, nothing prevents [Carson Valley] being the rendezvous and refuge of robbers and murderers." Despite the efforts of its settlers, Carson Valley was considered a refuge for outlaws throughout the 1850s.

The second incident involved Indians versus white settlers, heightening ill feelings and raising further the demand for stringent law and order. On New Year's Eve 1853, there was a dance held in the upstairs of a log store at the mouth of Gold Canyon, some twenty-seven miles northeast of Mormon Station. Nearly all the men in the territory, perhaps 125, were present, but there were only 9 women, which represented three-fourths of all the women in the area. Despite the odds, the dance was a success, so much so that during the revelry, Washoe Indians drove off the celebrants' horses. The Washoes did not ride horses. Angel reported that when the white settlers caught up with them, the stock was recovered, "except two that had been killed by the Indians for eating at a general barbecue at Chalk Hill."[13]

The Indians would not have shared Angel's lighthearted tone. Such a blatant and daring foray may have been an attempt to answer miners who had begun prospecting in the nearby Pine Nut Mountains, encroaching on groves that provided the nuts that were the Indians' irreplaceable winter staple. That the Washoes did not expect pursuit after stealing the horses reveals their artlessness. Their action prefigured other failures in trying to replace lost resources.[14]

Gold Canyon, which is actually more sagebrush-covered gulch or ravine than canyon, had been producing incomes for miners since the first year of the decade, and in 1855 miners took out more than $100,000 in gold dust and small nuggets. They had previously lived in shanties made of sagebrush and juniper trees, many taking winters off when little water was available for washing the gold from the soil, wandering to warmer climes. With increased profits, they created Johntown, a camp that may have moved to various places in lower Gold Canyon. They built slightly improved houses out of stone and mud or canvas. Some had small stoves, but most used fire pits to cook their usual fare, potatoes and salted bacon. Although Johntown would be abandoned two years later, the increased activity further impacted the Washoes' nearby pine-nut groves that served the new arrivals as sources of firewood.[15]

In 1856 Colonel Reese and several associates brought Chinese laborers from across the Sierra to dig the Rose Ditch, a channel from the Carson River to Gold Canyon. It was intended to facilitate the washing of gold-bearing gravel by supplementing dwindling water during winters. The engineering of the ditch was flawed: the outlet proved to be higher than its head at the river. When it failed, the Chinese stayed, becoming miners themselves, although they were allowed only on claims that white miners had abandoned. They settled in an area first used by white settlers, which for a short time was called China Town before being named Dayton. Viewed through the lens of commodification and "otherness" by Anglos, the Chinese relied on their own customs and language and did not assimilate. They worked the flats below the mouth of the canyon, until moving into the canyon when the white miners had left.[16]

In Gold Canyon, as in all placer mining camps, the cost of supplies was high: sugar or coffee, $3 a pound, almost double what it would cost in the states; bacon, 37.5 cents a pound when it cost 10 cents in St. Louis; potatoes, 8 cents a pound, while at St. Louis they were $1.20 a bushel; and heavy boots, which may have cost $3 or $3.50 in the states, were between $6 and $10. Because of the prices, the Anglo miners tended to skim the richest locations of the auriferous ground and then move on. The industrious Chinese were more frugal and made do reworking the claims.[17]

The Chinese had their own store at China Town. After visiting the business in 1859, Captain Simpson, of the Corps of Engineers, described two attached rooms. In one, the Chinese American miners smoked opium: "It stupefies, rather than enlivens, and, when indulged in excessively, perfectly paralyzes the energies." In another room they gambled, and Simpson commented, "They have a large number of pieces, like dominos, and counters, and take a great deal of interest in the game; run through it with the greatest dexterity and rapidity." He went on to note, "They are represented as being very fond of gambling when they have nothing else to do, and not unfrequently lose all their earnings in this way."[18]

When the Comstock Mining District's regulations were written in 1859, as was often the case with such rules in the West, Chinese Americans—as well as Native Americans, African Americans, and Mexican Americans—were not allowed to own claims. When the hard-rock mining was conducted on the Comstock Lode, the miners' union demanded that the Chinese Americans be kept from working underground. Nonetheless, Chinese, and limited numbers of other minorities, found other employment. By 1870, of the 58,711 non-Indian residents of Nevada, 3,152 were Chinese Americans and 82 were African Americans—including a doctor, a restaurant owner, and 2 women milliners, as well as janitors, servants, and porters.[19]

A notable exception to the discrimination was the Mexican American mine, owned by Mexican Gabriel Maldonado. He made one of the first Comstock fortunes, buying Emanuel Penrod's original one-hundred-foot claim in 1859 and selling it in 1861. Maldonado showed others how the great silver mines of Mexico were developed, erecting two small smelting furnaces that enabled him to ship a large number of bullion cakes to San Francisco. Two other Mexicans quietly earned $6,000 in one season, using the Mexican patio process to rework tailings, the pulverized ore, taken from the Carson River below the mines. Eventually, the big companies caught on and began reworking the tailings themselves, collecting a high percentage of the pay ore previously lost. In the 1860s and 1870s, other Mexican miners developed profitable claims in the Candelaria Mountains, a district that was not as attractive as other areas to white miners because of the danger of Indian confrontations.[20]

William Wright, the leading Comstock reporter in the era, used the nom de plume Dan DeQuille (dandy quill). He estimated that after 1856, when forty or fifty Chinese settlers were able to mine certain parts of Gold Canyon, others followed until, between 1856 and 1858, there were no fewer than 180 Chinese miners working there. Their numbers and the distinctness of their culture stoked Anglos' nativism.

Once the Chinese were blocked from mining, they adapted by diligently laboring in alternate trades: raising produce, working in laundries, or serving as cooks. Another example is those who became wood peddlers, traveling several miles into the Indians' pine-nut forests, chopping up stumps left by the white settlers who had clear-cut the hills.[21]

The Chinese immigrants were seen by many white settlers as industrious to a fault. As early as 1852 some emigrants in California had saved their earnings and returned to China. Throughout the West critics protested that the Chinese immigrants were exploiting America, patronizing Chinese merchants, and contributing nothing to the American economy. At the same time, American workers, needing to protect their free-labor status, saw the Chinese immigrants as a threat for being forced to sign cut-rate labor contracts. Over the course of many years, those attitudes generated anti-Chinese agitation, leading to mob violence against them.[22]

The Chinese settlers in Gold Canyon were not a concern for the residents of Carson Valley. Rather, in the 1850s, agitation was caused by outlaws, Indian relations, contentions over government jurisdiction, and polygamy. As more non-Mormon settlers arrived from California, newspapers called for the state to annex the valley. On August 19, 1853, the *San Francisco Herald* supported a petition sent by residents to the California Legislature. It editorialized that Carson Valley's peaceable and law-abiding citizens needed more prompt and immediate protection from the government than they could get from such a remote location as Salt Lake City. The petition was passed by the state senate but not by the assembly. Its narrow defeat stirred Utah into action. On January 17, 1854, Brigham Young signed an act that provided for the organization of Carson County in the western reaches of his territory. The act stated that the governor would appoint a probate judge to divide the county into precincts and would hold an election to fill the various offices. Such action was to be taken "when he shall deem it expedient," and that would be more than a year later.[23]

On January 23, 1854, the *Herald* declared a further reason for a California annexation: the possibility that gold existed in considerable quantities along the eastern slope.

In July 1854 Colonel William Rodgers, a prominent citizen of the area, began a weekly pack-train service from Mormon Station across the mountains to Placerville. Rodgers, known throughout the territory as "Uncle Billy," was a respected frontiersman: an old scout who had also served as sheriff of El Dorado County, which encompassed Placerville, Lake Tahoe, and myriad small mining communities and which had an aggregate population in 1852 of forty thousand. The pack-train service may have been financed at least in part by Lucky Bill Thorington, as he and Rodgers were friends and were said to be business partners.[24]

In the summer of '54, two young men, who held strong opinions and were quick to act with fists or guns, arrived in Carson Valley: Richard Sides and L.B. Abernathy. They met, and became partners with, John M. Baldwin, a carpenter who had come to the area to build a saw- and gristmill, probably working for Knott, the millwright. The three men purchased land and moved onto a ranch at Clear Creek, a few miles northeast of Mormon Station. The tributary ran from the Sierra Nevada to the Carson River and was described by Captain Simpson when he passed through as a beautiful stream, ample for mill purposes.[25]

By 1854 Colonel Reese had expanded his successful businesses. One of his partners was E.L. Barnard (evidently unrelated to Jonas Barnard, who had been shot to death in Eagle Valley the previous year).[26] E.L. Barnard was another of the original government organizers and the first justice of the peace in Carson Valley. Reese and Barnard had borrowed $23,000 from Lucky Bill Thorington, using the money to buy a herd of cattle.

In March 1853 Justice of the Peace Barnard had presided over the district's first case. Reese was the plaintiff. He had sued to recover $625 for supplies furnished to George Chorpening, who had taken over the Woodward Company's mail-transport business after Woodward was killed traveling on the Humboldt. Justice Barnard had found in favor of Reese, ordering the forced sale of the transport company's assets: four mules, one anvil, two pairs of tongs, one broken vise, two hammers, one cold chisel, one bellows, one sledge, one compass chain, other surveyor instruments, and one revolver. The sale had raised $499, which, less $25 court costs, had been awarded to Reese.

Throughout 1853, Barnard had assisted in Reese and Company business, while serving justice with Solomon-like purpose. Then, in the fall of 1854, he drove the company's cattle over the Sierra into California, collected the money for their sale, and kept going. Magistrate Barnard had decamped with some $60,000. His treachery bankrupted Reese.[27]

The bankruptcy record reveals Reese's losses. On September 9, 1854, he signed over to William B. Thorington all of the (Eagle Valley) ranch and furniture. The ranch properties included the grain and hay raised on the ranch that season, eight yoke of work cattle, one cow, ten head of horses, sixty head of hogs, seventy chickens, all farming and blacksmithing tools, the dry goods as well as groceries and hardware in the store, and all household furniture and cooking utensils. Reese also relinquished his half of the Woodfords Canyon toll bridge and the Old Emigrant Toll Road. The transaction did not cause a break in his friendship with Thorington, but the bankruptcy caused severe problems between Reese and builder Thomas Knott.[28]

Reese had not paid for the grist- and sawmill that Knott had built for him earlier that year. In the transfer of property to Thorington, the mill was specifically excluded. Reese offered other property to Knott in lieu of payment for the mill. Knott refused. In light of the valley's business boom, each of the men wanted the mill. The disagreement would result in threats, charges of trespass, and two court cases.[29]

Thorington had redoubled his wealth, and his reputation as a Robin Hood was growing. Historian Angel wrote that, in the summer of 1854, Thorington had come upon a crying woman, distraught as she and her husband were being abandoned. Their partner owned the wagon and cattle that had brought them across the plains; they had supplied provisions. The provisions were gone; their expenses had been more than expected. The couple was broke. The wagon owner refused to take them farther. That night the wagon owner was persuaded to take part in Thorington's thimblerig game.

Thorington would let gamblers win enough early in the game to create an incentive to bet more. By morning the wagon owner had nothing left. Lucky Bill gave the man back fifteen dollars, bought him a new pair of boots, and advised him to head out for California and to never bet against a man playing his own game. Thorington then hired a driver and gave the bankrupt couple the wagon, team, and supplies that would carry them to California.

Angel told another anecdote about a luckless old man whose horse had died at Thorington's Woodfords Canyon station. The white-haired emigrant was trying to get back to the states. "'Cheer up old man,' said Lucky Bill, in his happy, inspiring, whole-souled way," and within a few days Thorington had outfitted him with "a fine roan horse hitched to a two-wheeled vehicle loaded with provisions for the trip." The historian concluded: "Numerous incidents of generosity like these are remembered by the early settlers of Nevada of this strange frontiersman, many of whose impulses were such as ennoble men."[30]

In his 1904 *A History of the State of Nevada,* Thomas Wren enlarged upon Angel's statement, saying, "Hundreds of instances are given showing [Thorington's] generosity and bravery. Many emigrants who stopped at Mormon Station had occasion to bless him for his kindness."[31]

Thorington's saga had another aspect: a love triangle. As indicated, he was said to have had two wives, although, with haphazard record keeping and his eccentricity, it is impossible to know whether the second woman was a Mormon-style second wife or his mistress. Her name was Martha Lamb.

Sarah Winnemucca was a charismatic Paiute, an exceptional woman, who, as a young teen, lived for a time, probably less than a year, with William Ormsby and his family in Genoa. As an adult, she served as a US Army scout and interpreter and wrote the first autobiography by a Native woman. In the autobiography she described those who lived nearby in Carson Valley. After first describing two neighbors, Dr. Daggett and Van Sickle, she said, "The next one had more than one family;

he had two wives, and his name was Thornton. The man who lived in the next house had still more wives. There were two brothers; one had three wives, and the other five. Their name was Reuse."[32]

The Reuses were John Reese and his brother Enoch, Mormons sub-cribing to polygamy. Thornton, identified as having had two wives, was the non-Mormon Thorington.

The mythical females of the West were generally presented as either good or bad. As social historian Elizabeth Jameson describes them, "The stereotypical good women were asexual, the 'bad' ones hypersexual hell-raisers or whores."[33] In reality, women settlers pursued unique opportunities depending on a wide variety of circumstances. In 1851 and 1852 Mrs. Louisa Clappe, known by her pen name, Dame Shirley, wrote twenty-three letters to her sister about Rich Bar and Indian Bar, mining camps on California's Feather River, across the Sierra from Carson Valley. There were very few women living in the mining camps. Her descriptions allow some idea of the heartiness required.

One woman is described as a "gentle creature [who] wears the thickest kind of miners' boots, and has the dainty habit of wiping her dishes on her apron! Last spring she *walked* to this place, and packed fifty pounds of flour on her back down that awful hill—the snow being five feet deep at the time." Another woman, Mrs. R., a "little sixty-eight pounder," lived in a tent house. Mrs. Clappe tells of a man praising her: "'Magnificent woman that, sir.... Why, she earnt her *old man*,' (said individual twenty-one years of age, perhaps,) 'nine hundred dollars in nine weeks, clear of all expenses, by washing! Such women ain't common, I tell *you*.'" A decidedly different tone describes Mrs. B., about twenty-five years old, working as a cook. She had left three children, including an eight-month-old, to come west and search for gold. While Mrs. B. worked, her two-week-old "lay kicking furiously in his champagne basket cradle."

Decrying the absence of domesticating refinements in the camp, Mrs. Clappe presents a long list of things she would do without that winter, including newspapers, church, lectures, concerts, the theater, shopping, calling and gossiping at little tea drinkings, parties, balls, the latest fashions, daily mail (they had an express once a month), vegetables—except potatoes and onions—milk, and eggs. How would her sister like to pass the winter with "no *nothing*"? The indomitable Mrs. Clappe answers for herself: "Now I expect to be very happy here."[34]

On the eastern slope, experiences were influenced by the sparsity of women's numbers. In the fall of 1855, there were perhaps fifteen women in all of what would become the state of Nevada.[35] In 1853, when it was illegal for Black and white people to marry each other, Charlotte Palmer, a Black woman, married Ben Barber, a white man, and they built a ranch outside of Mormon Station. Charlotte was hospitable and popular. According to one settler, if you passed by anytime near noon, they would insist you stop and have dinner. The local newspaper reported that at her funeral, in 1887, "the procession was one of the largest ever witnessed in Douglas County."[36]

On ranches, women's domesticity had a much-expanded definition. Work, as elsewhere, was generally divided along gender lines, with women tending the garden as well as the poultry and dairy, cooking on a woodstove, making clothing, tending the sick, and doing the housework; in addition, they were likely to be hauling water, chopping firewood, tending stock, shooting at wolves or coyotes, killing chickens, branding calves, and skinning game. Historian Page Smith comments: "When Eastern ladies were fainting at a coarse word or vulgar sight, their Western sisters fought off Indians, ran cattle, made homes and raised children in the wilderness."[37]

There were exceptions. Thorington's first wife, Maria, who was said to always dress in white and to make lace, lived with their son, Jerome, in a house on Genoa's main street, one of thirty or forty frame houses built there by 1857.[38] His second partner, Martha Lamb, lived at different times on two of his ranches: first in Fredricksburg, south of town, and then on one in Eagle Valley—presumably acquired from Reese. Whether she did any branding or skinning is questionable, as Thorington had plenty of money to hire hands. She is mentioned as being one of the provocations in a fracas between anti-Mormons and Thorington's partner Colonel Billy Rodgers. Several years after Thorington's death, she was named in a divorce case as having had an affair with a man whom she subsequently married.

It is possible to speculate about what life was like for Martha Lamb on the ranch outside of Genoa, while Thorington was necessarily spending time on his businesses, gambling, and seeing after Maria and his son in town. Regarding loneliness, another woman in the West wrote, "George went to the mountains yesterday morning to be gon all week…

after he had gon gave vent to my feelings in a flood of tears. It may seem foolish to those that have neighbors and friends around them. I get along very well through the day but the long evening and nights are *horrible.*"[39]

A large number of rumors accompanied Martha, none of which were ever corroborated. It was said that when Thorington died, she inherited half his property and that she was Maria Thorington's niece. Another version, the one spread by Thorington's enemies in Genoa, said that her real name was Martha Baker and that she came from the saloons of Sacramento. In a local Lassen County, California, history, written in 1916, Honey Lake pioneer William Dow said that he and some of the other Honey Lakers knew Thorington, or knew of him, in Michigan. Dow said that in the spring of 1852, Thorington went to Michigan and induced three young girls to come with him back west and that the other two girls' parents overtook them in Peoria, Illinois, and took them home.[40]

Territorial records show that on October 30, 1854, a George Lambe claimed land in Carson Valley adjacent to Thorington's, a little more than a year after Thorington had arrived, and that Martha Lamb sold the same property on November 11, 1859. There is no record of George Lambe's life in the territory. Nor is there evidence regarding what relation Martha was to George. The various versions color the story in significantly different ways. Martha was with Thorington by choice, but did he steal her from her home in Michigan or rescue her from saloon life? The other fact known about Martha is that sometime in 1856 or in the following year, she had a son named William R. Thorington.[41]

The relationship between Lucky Bill and Martha is integral to his hanging. Mormons insisted that the plural marriages of their leadership were heavenly commanded and chaste. The anti-Mormons likened the practice to slavery and declared it licentious. To those who opposed Thorington, the fact that by all appearances he was irreligious underscored the immorality of his relationship with Martha Lamb. Arnold Trimmer, a pioneer Genoan, believed that the relationship was the central motive for Thorington's killing. Trimmer's family arrived in Carson Valley one week after the hanging. Trimmer said that the charges against Thorington at the vigilante trial were just an excuse. The real reason he was hanged was because of Martha Lamb. Trimmer contended that once the Mormons left, the vigilantes were attempting to stamp out any evidence of polygamy.[42]

Several years after Thorington's hanging, Martha Lamb remarried. She lived to the age of eighty-three, dying in Inyo County, California, in 1914. Her version of her relationship with Thorington was taken with her to the grave. Her obituary in the *Inyo Register* reported that she raised four children, the oldest William R. Thorington, and it said she "held the respect and esteem" of all who knew her in Inyo County.[43]

At Honey Lake, the first white settler was a widower, Isaac Roop. He crossed the mountains in June 1854 after his mercantile business in Shasta County had burned down. He built the first non-Native American structures in the valley. They were located along the Susan River—which he named in honor of his daughter. Roop was a civic leader, having served as the postmaster and a school commissioner in Shasta. He was good-natured and popular. He had lost some $15,000 worth of property and goods in the fire and sought to begin again, building a house and way station. When others moved into the valley, he served as land recorder, loaned money, functioned as arbiter, and was said to be indispensable to settlers and emigrants alike.[44]

Honey Lake was part of Northern Paiute territory, which extended over some seventy-eight thousand square miles. The Paiutes had no central government; they never gathered as an entire tribe. Connected by lifestyle and the Western Numic language, they lived in bands of some one hundred to two hundred members. During the mid-nineteenth century, there were approximately twenty-one bands. Each controlled a traditional area for resource use that was respected by all other bands. Owing to the variability of high-desert weather, a band lacking a resource in a particular season could not be easily refused if asking to harvest in another band's area.

To their east, the Shoshones spoke a slightly different Numic language, as did the Southern Paiutes who lived in parts of Utah and in what are now northern Arizona and extreme southern Nevada. The Northern Paiutes' land centered in the northwestern part of today's Nevada, extending slightly into Oregon. Their high-desert lands in the Sierra Nevada rain shadow were dry but included the Walker River, the Susan River, parts of the Carson and Truckee Rivers, and many small springs and seeps, marked by green desert vegetation. Their territory featured, as well, the alkaline lakes: Walker, Pyramid, and Honey Lakes.[45]

When the white settlers began moving into Honey Lake Valley, the Paiutes accepted them, giving up areas claimed by the newcomers while continuing to live in other parts of the valley. They traded furs and game for things like articles of clothing. The tribe subscribed to their traditional system of individualistic democracy, wherein every individual decided on their own behavior and was responsible for such. However, they had a particularly influential headman named Winnemucca. He was not a "chief," although the white settlers considered him to be one, and he took on the role of a conduit for communication. In 1855 Winnemucca and the settlers of Honey Lake established a modus vivendi whereby the white people would complain to him if any Indian committed a depredation.[46]

The year after Roop went to Honey Lake, Peter Lassen, for whom Lassen County and Lassen Peak are named, moved into the valley along with a partner, Isodore Meyerowitz, and four others. Lassen is credited with being the first Anglo to have seen Honey Lake and had named it when passing through years earlier. He named it for the "honey dew"—a sweet, viscous substance deposited by aphids—on the wild rye on its shore. The six men prospected and, in October 1855, brought in provisions and cows, horses, and oxen to pass the winter at the lake (while Roop still wintered in Shasta).[47]

Lassen was a longtime Californian, having arrived to work as a blacksmith at Sutter's ranch in 1842. He had come from Denmark by way of Boston, Missouri, and Oregon. In 1843 he had helped recover stolen animals being taken to Oregon. Claiming land in Northern California, his ranch became a well-known landmark, and, in 1846, Frémont stopped there when the lieutenant's bellicose actions led Californio officials to run his expedition out of California and up into Oregon. A few days later, Lassen guided a marine lieutenant, who was carrying confidential dispatches from President Polk, through the wilderness to find Frémont camped at Klamath Lake. Three weeks later Frémont, leading a mounted column and a contingent of Delaware Indians back into California, incited American settlers, beginning his role in the Mexican War.[48]

Lassen was less successful when he guided emigrants on a new route to California's goldfields in 1848. To avoid the Forty-Mile Desert, Lassen took families in twelve wagons far north through uncharted, rugged terrain. He had difficulty blazing a trail, known thereafter as Lassen's Cutoff or the Lassen Road, and, very late in the year and out of provisions, the group was rescued by wagons coming down from Oregon. Although heavily traveled for a time, the additional mileage required in taking the Lassen Road caused the cutoff to be dubbed Lassen's Horn, likening following it to a journey around Cape Horn.[49]

Word went out in 1855 that there was gold in the streams around Honey Lake, and by the spring of 1856 miners, many from the Feather River in California, were making the trek east across the Sierra. The Feather River had produced legendary amounts of gold, attracting more and more prospectors until a number were squeezed out. Generally, those who came to pan the streams running out of the Eastern Sierra were not untested newcomers but were individuals who had been in the West for several years and knew the hardships of the frontier. At the same time, some of the newcomers were identified as "Indian fighters." If they came from California, that almost certainly meant they had taken part in one or more of the massacres of Native people, now termed the California genocide, which had begun in 1846 and would continue into the 1870s.[50]

It was commonly, albeit mistakenly, thought that the California state line ran along the summit of the Sierra. Not wanting to be part of the distant Salt Lake territory, in April 1856 the Honey Lake settlers formed their own government. Lassen served as the chair and was elected surveyor; Roop acted as the secretary and was elected recorder. The settlers agreed to twenty sections of regulations. Section 2 stated that each adult male was entitled to 640 acres, and section 5 stated that all claims had to be surveyed. The year had begun with two log houses, a little rail fencing, and a ditch at Honey Lake. By the end of the year, 36,840 acres had been claimed.

Other areas of agreement in the new regulations included water distribution and the settling of difficulties and disputes by citizens forming an arbitration committee. In substantiation of their good relations with the Paiutes, section 10 said: "Any person or persons misusing, maltreating, robbing or stealing from the Indians shall be considered an offender" and referred for punishment to a board of citizen arbitrators called by the recorder. This regulation was especially notable for that place and time as, across the Sierra, newspapers were discussing, and some were advocating for, the extermination of the Indians. An indication of the intensity of feelings is seen in an earlier *Yreka Mountain Herald* editorial that urged killing every last Indian, "and let the first white man who says treaty or peace be regarded as a traitor and coward."[51]

The proposed name for Roop and Lassen's new territory was the Paiute word *Nataqua.* Wistfully or humorously, it translated as "female." At the time, setting up camp in the valley were some one hundred men "and perhaps a few women." A register was kept at Roop's station house, and residents or those passing through could write in it. The pages for the last half of 1856 recorded the number of emigrants and animals in the passing wagon trains. It also had comments: "Girls very scarce non coming of any amount." And, "Why in 'God's name' can't some of the women stop here?"[52]

Writing about mining camps, historian Susan Johnson points out that in the Northeast, industrialization had influenced domestic roles for men and women, engendering responsibilities: for men, self-restraint; for women, application of moral sensibilities. She comments: "In the diggings, then, battles raged over whether white men had either reason or ability to practice restraint when apart from their collective better half." In Honey Lake Valley, in its formative stage in the 1850s, the answer would have been a resounding no. The virtually all-male society was volatile, with violence at times directed inward toward neighbors and toward outsiders on a regular basis.[53]

One of the few women at Honey Lake lived with Lassen's partner, Isadore Meyerowitz. In the casual contempt of the era, and also in dismissive histories in the twentieth century, she was identified only as "a squaw." In the summer of 1856, she, Meyerowitz, and three of their friends went out into Honey Lake in a boat Meyerowitz had built. It capsized, and although the three others made it to shore, Meyerowitz and the woman drowned.[54]

Beginning in 1857 men began bringing their families to Honey Lake. The earth produced with minimal cultivation, and animals could browse year-round as clumps of bunchgrass rose above the snow. Water fowl used the lake, and deer, sage hens, and rabbits the hills and brush. Life being so easy, the residents were dubbed "Never Sweats."

The 1860 Census showed that by then there were 355 males and 121 females living in the valley. In one incident in the era, a woman, Mrs. W. T. C. Elliott, exhibiting the reframing of gender roles in the West, involved herself in what was generally considered strictly male business. Mrs. Susan Elliott had two brothers of note. One was Richard Sides, who was living in Carson Valley. He was a big man, six-foot-two, and an unprincipled brawler, known for his temper and, perhaps owing to his physical stature, for being a sometime leader in Carson Valley. The other, William, was the first man in Carson County indicted for murder. Susan's husband, Rough Elliott, settled in Honey Lake. He had traits similar to her brothers'. Elliott was involved in numerous fights with guns and was a key figure in the hanging of Lucky Bill Thorington that took place at Richard Sides's ranch. Sometime during that affair Elliott met Susan Sides, and they married five months later.

Rough Elliott was away from his ranch one day when Plumas County authorities came to collect livestock in payment for what the county asserted were delinquent taxes. Elliott was one of forty or fifty Honey Lakers who were adamant about forming their own territory. They claimed their area was part of Utah Territory when confronted by Plumas officials and part of Plumas when taxed by Utah. In this instance when the authorities arrived, Rough Elliot was absent. Mrs. Elliott came out of the house with a shotgun and stood them off. Lassen County historian Asa Fairfield wryly notes, "There was no danger of her getting hurt for at that time women were very scarce and more valuable than horses, cattle or taxes."[55]

Susan Elliott later had occasion to demonstrate a different behavior in a similar situation. Because Rough Elliott bragged that he would not pay taxes, a year or two after the first incident, when the Plumas sheriff came to the ranch to collect, he brought a posse with him. Hearing what was at hand, Elliott had recruited a crowd of armed men to back him up. Arriving at the ranch simultaneously, the parties confronted one another. The sheriff and Elliott were "careless of their language" in discussing their differences. Everyone else sat unmoving on their horses, knowing that a wrong move could result in a number of deaths. When the argument got hottest, Mrs. Elliott came out of the house and, after a time of talking to the principals, insisted that everyone come in for dinner. Inside, tempers cooled, and they settled on a compromise that Fairfield noted did not cost Elliott much.[56]

The majority of the men who moved into the valley in 1856 took up mining in the creeks and gulches around Honey Lake. Thus engaged, there were no large-scale incidents of violence that year. Thereafter, things changed.

CHAPTER THREE

Domesticating and Agitating

In Carson Valley, during 1855 and the following year, an infestation of grasshoppers damaged the wheat crop, and there were sporadic incidents involving Indians stealing livestock, but the process of domesticating continued apace. Reese's new gristmill was making flour. The two sawmills could not keep up with demand, and three other mills would soon be built. Meanwhile, Mormon and Gentile rancor, smoldering for some time, began to erupt. Gentiles complained that the Mormons were threatening the prosperity of the valley. Just as they had the year before, in January 1855, they sent a memorial, or memorandum, to the California Legislature asking that Carson Valley be placed within the limits of California. This time the Utah government acted. In June, Brigham Young sent one of the church's twelve apostles, Orson Hyde, to organize the valley and ensure that the Saints maintained their western outpost. Hyde was accompanied by an escort of thirty-five men, including the US marshal for Utah Territory.[1]

On July 6, 1855, the *Sacramento Daily Union* urged California officialdom to negate Utah's action, arguing that the state should appropriate Carson Valley. It announced that Young had sent one hundred Mormon settlers there, and he was ready to send five hundred more, if need be, so that the area would not be annexed to California. The article recounted how the year before, Mormons had repaired two or three bridges at a cost of $800. Nominal tolls were to be levied to pay the expenses. By July, the paper said, $20,000 had been taken in, and the Mormons would not stop collecting. The non-Mormons were outraged because the "excessive tax" was turning away the emigration, crippling the valley's general business. The report continued, saying a public meeting had been held and a resolution had passed to protect emigrants from the imposition of tolls. The man reporting the dispute, a Mr. Montgomery of Ranch Camp, buttressed by the resolution, drove his cattle across a toll bridge without paying. Mormons followed him, threatening to sue for trespass in the California courts.

The newspaper did not identify those collecting tolls, but non-Mormon Lucky Bill Thorington was one of the primary toll-road operators. As indicated, he had been a half-partner in the construction and operation of the Woodfords Canyon toll road and had received Colonel Reese's half-ownership of it, along with the Emigrant Toll Road, in partial payment of Reese's debt to him. Thorington was deterring potential customers, yet, owing to his capriciousness, he would allow Kit Carson and Mexican herders to pass, with five thousand sheep, for free.

On July 22 the *San Francisco Herald* reported that a violent animosity had arisen between the Mormons and the Gentiles in Carson Valley. Besides *Gentiles,* the other term the Mormons used to identify non-Mormons was *Americans.* The Mormons did so to distance themselves from the populace in the eastern states. Mormon interpreter Dimick Huntington "informed the natives, 'We [are] Mormons not Americans.'" Anti-Mormons were quick to accept the designation, identifying themselves as "Americans," emphasizing their contention that Mormons were un-American—owing allegiance only to the church.[2]

By now California newspapers periodically attacked Mormons with provocative editorials. The papers called Mormons "miserable dupes," "fanatical followers," and "Utah Mahometans." The *Placerville Mountain Democrat* later labeled Brigham Young "an arch-imposter" and "supreme dictator," calling his lectures "harangues of fanaticism." The paper called his followers "unnaturalized foreigners of the lowest class," "fanatical instruments," "thieves," and "harlots." The *San Francisco Herald,* like several other California newspapers, picked up the story of Mormon taxes on toll roads, sarcastically dubbing Young "the Great High Priest of the Saints," describing one Carson Valley settler as having a half-dozen wives and forty or fifty children.[3]

Polygamy, the main source of incitement, brought condemnation as "damnable in its influence and pernicious to society and the welfare of mankind," comparing it to "primitive and animal habits" and, anticipating Darwin's theory that was several years from being published, to "the first animal existences—the shell fish and crab." Brigham Young was identified as "that prince of bigamists" and was accused of "immense scoundrelism." In November 1855, the *Shasta Courier* raised the stakes, writing, "It is said Brigham is down on the Union . . . and that the United States might go to h_ _l."[4]

Juanita Brooks pointed out that Mormon judge Orson Hyde had little enthusiasm for his job of organizing Carson County. He was fifty years old and had spent much of the previous few years on missions for the church. Enoch Reese alerted church elders that Hyde might be more willing to become established if he had a wife with him. Showing the importance of the Carson Valley outpost, Brigham Young responded, sending a letter to Hyde the next day, October 9, 1855. "[We] purchased a team &c. to go out to Carson County and take your wife to you. . . . We have done pretty well as they are going to start tomorrow morning." In early November, Hyde's wife arrived. She was Mary Ann Price, mother of one child. From the first, she proved to be another source of agitation to the anti-Mormons. Knowing the judge had other wives, they saw her presence as a flagrant example of the Mormon leadership's disdain for monogamy. The handful of women in the surrounding valleys signed a petition "protesting a government that forced polygamy upon women and compelled them to associate with a 'Scarlet Lady.'"[5]

The *Deseret News,* the Latter-day Saints newspaper in Salt Lake City, found the idea of ladies in Carson Valley humorous, using an illiberal conceit of the era to emphasize its amusement. It said that according to "a gentleman of veracity," in attempting to hold a dance in the winter of 1855–56, "searching the valley from the Humboldt to the Sierra Nevada only *three* were found and one of those was a 'lady of color.'"[6]

Judge Hyde stilled some of the Gentiles' animosity through tact and strong leadership. He ignored the polygamy issue while writing letters to California newspapers explaining how the territory was being organized. He wrote another supporting road building through to California, and he worked with surveyors to determine the exact position of the state line. On September 7, when it was found that most of Carson Valley lay within Utah Territory, he called for an election. It was to be held on September 20, 1855, at the county seat, Mormon Station. Mormons won most races by large margins, although the non-Mormons Henry Van Sickle and J. C. Fain won election: Van Sickle as justice of the peace and Fain, who had been the county recorder, as sheriff. Hyde laid out the town plat, and, in yet another tactful move, he changed its name from Mormon Station to Genoa, in honor of the birthplace of Columbus.[7]

On October 27 a special term of the court was held at Colonel Reese's house. At this meeting, water rights were addressed for the first time since the squatters' government made its determinations. This time, a decree was issued stating that water must be shared and not diverted. It was further determined that once the river left the valley, eight individuals were to be granted exclusive rights to remove portions of the Carson River water for mining or other purposes in the vicinity of Gold Canyon. Among the eight were Colonel Reese; his nephew Stephen Kinsey; two brothers named McMarlin, James, who was a county selectman, and John, named by Hyde six weeks later to be justice of the peace for the Gold Canyon Precinct; Sheriff Fain; and Judge Orson Hyde. With this instrument in hand, Reese hired the first Chinese laborers to dig what would be the failed Rose Ditch. Although the canal was poorly engineered, the idea of locking up river rights was sound. Within a few years the hard-rock mining corporations, needing river flow to power their mills, and the settlers, requiring irrigation, would battle over the Carson's water. The decree became obsolete when the ditch failed, and Hyde and most of the other signatories moved away.[8]

As Mormons were called or volunteered for assignment to the western edge of the kingdom, women arrived in larger numbers. In May 1856 a company of sixteen wagons began moving west with eleven men and forty-four women and children (the exact number of women was not delineated). The group was, in fact, only five or six large families with teamsters and extra hired hands. More women, but all were spoken for. At least one was ready to return as soon as possible. Mary Jane Phippen wrote home of the hardships. On the trip she had been forced to lead a young cow through deep sand. In her next letter she told of the birth of her daughter. Genoa was a disappointment: "Imagin a City with only Three Houses in it, no Streets tall pine trees and a great high mountain to look strait up to." In more than one letter she counseled: do not encourage anyone to come out.[9]

That spring the conflict between Colonel Reese and Thomas Knott, over Reese's debt and his mill, severely raised the level of animosity between Mormons and Gentiles. Early in the year, Thomas Knott left for Ohio to raise needed capital. He left his son Elzy, a handsome man in his early twenties, to collect the debt. The Mormon Reese could not pay the Knotts but would not sign over ownership of the mill. Instead, he leased the mill to a newcomer to the valley, Russell Kelley, who was to take charge on May 1. Elzy Knott, supported by the Clear Creek Ranch owners—Richard Sides, L.B. Abernathy, and J.M. Baldwin—and unspecified others, occupied the mill. For unknown reasons, the sheriff, James C. Fain, resigned his position and left the territory. On May 12 Judge Hyde appointed Kelley sheriff. Was Hyde giving Kelley legal license to act against the Knott crowd? Regardless of his motivation, it added intensity to the valley's political turmoil.[10]

On May 22, 1856, Colonel Reese filed a complaint with Hyde, charging trespass against Knott and his allies. As the trial was set to begin, rancor erupted into hostility. With the defendants menacing the court, Judge Hyde called on citizens to act as special deputies to keep order. The clerk wrote in the book of records:

> In consequence of the threatening and hostile attitude assumed by the defence the court thought proper to issue an order to summon a trope of well disposed citizens, as a precautionary and prudent measure to repel any violence that might be offered: where upon the following named persons were summoned and responded to the same:
>
> J. Hollinhead — H. Mott
> C. Merkely — J. Mott
> John Castro — Mr. Coper
> Enoch Reese — S.A. Kinsey
> John Reese — C.S. Daggett
> W. Fredrich — A. Mead[11]

The Motts, for whom the hamlet of Mottsville was named, were among the first settlers and cattle grazers in the valley. Kinsey was Reese's nephew and was county recorder. Daggett was the prosecuting attorney for the court. It is informative that in the small town, the plaintiff and his brother also were among those charged with keeping order.

When jurors were being selected, the defense rejected Thorington. Knott and Thorington were friends, but Thorington was perhaps closer to Reese, who had repaid him while failing to honor the Knott debt. The defense also rejected Luther "Lute" Olds, who owned a ranch near

Thorington's Fredricksburg ranch who, along with Thorington, was later put on trial by the vigilantes. In addition, the defendants excluded Justice of the Peace Van Sickle and two others. Witnesses for the defense included John Cary, who had sold Thorington a sawmill two years earlier and later acted as judge at Thorington's vigilante trial; B.L. King, a businessman from Eagle Valley, also involved in the vigilante trial; and a Mr. Perrin, presumably Solomon Perrin, an attorney for the court.[12]

There was no violence during the contentious proceedings. Much of the questioning was aimed at Reese. At one point, Judge Hyde declared that questions that could not be answered were improper and should not be asked. Hyde also disallowed two documents, one a purported lien on the mill presented by Knott's attorneys, the other a conditional transfer that Reese said was returned to him after he paid it in full. Perhaps demonstrating the laxness in which legal documents were drawn up in Carson Valley, Hyde deemed neither to be a legal instrument. The finding was recorded the following day: for the plaintiff, Colonel Reese. The defendants were charged $454. If they had not been already, they now became the most adamant anti-Mormons in the valley.[13]

The trial delineates the distinct split of the citizenry into two factions. Thorington, Olds, and Van Sickle were relative old-timers who enjoyed favorable relations with the Mormons. Thorington's relationship came despite the fact that Orson Hyde disapproved of him because he had prompted church members to stop paying tithings.[14]

Sides, Abernathy, and Baldwin were Thorington's enemies. Two years later they and defense witnesses Cary and King would play key roles in his arrest and trial. By that time, Elzy Knott had aligned himself with Thorington and hid from the vigilantes after they came for the gambler. At the vigilante trial, hearsay evidence that originated with Solomon Perrin, by then living near Honey Lake, would be crucial to Thorington's conviction.

The resolution of Knott's case against Reese came a year and a half later. Knott won a $20,000 judgment, although as late as spring 1860, final settlement was pending. Because of the appeal, the whole town of Genoa was under attachment, and lots could not be transferred.[15]

In July 1856 a train of one hundred individuals from Salt Lake City arrived in Carson County. They came to farm and do missionary work, but, more important to Mormon leadership, they came to ensure the

Mormons would win elections and control the territory. The anti-Mormons, bitter over the Mormon political ascendancy, began to rebel more publicly against Utah authority.

Hyde continued reorganizing the county despite the Gentiles' opposition. He called for another election, knowing the influx of Mormons had created a solid majority. On August 4, 1856, nine positions were contested. Only reelected sheriff Russell Kelley, who converted to Mormonism two months later, and Dr. Charles Daggett, elected assessor and treasurer, were Gentiles. No Mormon wanted to be charged with standing up to, or collecting moneys from, the Sides faction and the other anti-Mormons.[16]

Sides, known for his temper, joined his partners in refusing to pay the fine that they owed the court, as well as a judgment of $1,010 that Sides owed Reese in relation to an unspecified suit. Shortly after the election, Sheriff Kelley advertised the sale of the Clear Creek Ranch to satisfy Sides's debt. On August 16 Kelley organized a posse and led them out to the ranch. Sides had gathered a large, well-armed resistance to confront the sheriff. A Mormon settler reported on the outcome: "There was a few Knock-downs a good deal of swairing don and whiskey drank and finely ended in the Sheriff postponing the Sail." Hyde attempted to talk Reese out of further pursuit of the collection because the recently arrived Mormons, who might have supported the effort, were engaged in building houses for the winter. In this case Reese did not listen to the elder; he insisted Sheriff Kelley pursue the issue. Kelly tried a second time, but, with Sides and some forty collaborators waiting behind fortifications of heavy planking, the equally large posse merely turned around, abandoning the field before a battle ensued.[17]

Hyde wrote to Brigham Young, describing a portion of the citizens as "mobocratic," saying they were threatening to lynch the tax collector unless he refunded all moneys collected, including court fines. He complained that the mob would allow no Mormon with more than one wife to live and that they wanted to regulate everything. He concluded alarmingly: "There is no chance for us but victory or death."[18]

It was not just the Mormons and the tax collector the Sides crowd opposed. Shortly after they first held off Kelley and his posse, they held a meeting and vowed to drive Lucky Bill Thorington from the valley. Sides had some fifty supporters, but, owing to Thorington's popularity among other residents, the effort fell apart. On August 25, 1856, a community member who kept a journal commented: "They could not raise sufficient force to drive this Lucky Bill of his ranch and in failing in this they have stoped their proceedings for the present an are tolerable friendly."[19]

William W. Drummond, US District Court judge for Utah Territory, was a Gentile who had served in Salt Lake City and accompanied the new settlers to Carson County. He later announced publicly what Hyde had confided to Young and what the election illustrated: the Gentiles resented having to pay taxes that benefited Utah.[20]

Drummond summoned a grand jury, using the loft of the Motts' barn as their meeting place. During afternoons when the temperature rose too high, the proceedings were moved down to the blacksmith shop. The grand jury was ineffective, and it has been suggested that skeletons in the closets of the jury members may have prompted merciful perspectives. Although a catalog of complaints ranging from robbery and horse stealing to "concubinage" and gambling had previously been compiled, only two indictments were brought, and it was said neither "stuck." Angel's *History of Nevada* reported that a couple of men were convicted of grand larceny, but both of them escaped.[21]

The territory resisted Judge Drummond's authority. At one time he threatened "to iron" (jail) the jurors themselves for willful contempt. After six weeks of futility, he gave up, riding across the Sierra. Out of the valley, he declared, "It is sufficient for me to say that open rebellion now exists in that region to the laws of Utah which the Gentiles deem unjust and oppressive."[22] He never returned, and his successor did not make his way into the territory for three years.

Leaving Carson Valley, Drummond did not go back to Salt Lake City. In California he began a campaign against Brigham Young, the "Holy Priesthood," and the institution of Mormonism. He announced in newspapers that it was useless to send judges to Utah Territory, complaining that Young overruled decisions by federal officials and dictated to grand juries when to indict or not.

Drummond indicated that he had unsuccessfully attempted to secure indictments of men having multiple wives or when two or more women were cohabitating with one man. His concerns were soon revealed to be hypocritical in that he had brought with him to the West a beautiful lady whom he introduced as his wife. The *Sacramento Daily*

Union discovered and announced that she was a public character of some notoriety about Washington City (Washington, DC). His legal wife and children had been left in Illinois.[23]

Tensions between the Mormons and Washington had always been high, but in the latter part of 1856 they intensified. In Carson Valley the Mormons were in control, but the opposition to federal appointee Drummond had mirrored that toward Hyde. The Mormon elder said that resistance to his jurisdiction had been unceasing in every form, trivial and important, open and secret. Action against him had been exacerbated by the vocal attacks in the California newspapers.[24]

In September, Young sent Mormon elder and probate-court judge Chester Loveland to the valley. The following month Young ordered Hyde back to the metropole. This transference was the first sign that power in the valley would shift. On January 14, 1857, the Utah Legislature enacted a law requiring that all records of Carson County be returned to Salt Lake County. The legislation stated that the county was to retain its present organization until further directed by Salt Lake. It did not take long for further action. On April 13, Loveland adjourned county court until the first Monday in June. Instead, the court would not meet again until September 1859.[25]

In setting up their "Kingdom of God," the Mormons had traveled across the Rockies to be outside federal reach. They had arrived in the eastern Great Basin in July 1847. However, with the Treaty of Guadalupe Hidalgo, in February 1848, the region officially became part of the United States. Having lost expatriation status, in 1849 the Mormons held a convention, organizing a territorial government that they called the "State of Deseret." The federal government was dealing with conflicts over the admission of states as free or slave and over the designation of territories, and Utah Territory was created as part of the Compromise of 1850.

Wanting to direct their own affairs, Brigham Young and the church elders did not approve of decisions being made by federal land surveyors, judges, marshals, or Indian agents sent to Utah. Brigham Young wrote, "I love the government and the Constitution of the United States, but I do not love the damned rascals that administer the government."[26]

The Mormon citizenry followed his lead. Finally, in March 1857, the Utah territorial legislature sent a memorial to Washington, DC. Because the federal officials sent to Salt Lake did not meet the church's moral standards, its citizens would decide which federal laws they would obey.

Table 3.1. The population and number of families in Utah Territory's far-western settlements in 1857

	Population	Number of families	Mormon families	Gentile families
Carson Valley	225	37	20	17
Eagle Valley	90	14	10	4
Jack's Valley	50	9	9	—
Washoe Valley	150	25	25	—

Source: Daily Alta California, July 9, 1857, in Juanita Brooks's, "The Mormons in Carson County, Utah Territory," 19–20.

The election of James Buchanan as president exacerbated the problem. His cabinet believed the Mormons' actions amounted to treason and urged the newly elected and indecisive chief executive to take action.

In 1857 the population and number of families in Utah Territory's far-western settlements were mostly Mormon. This, however, was about to change. In March Sierra legend John "Snowshoe" Thompson, who skied across the mountains carrying the mail in winter months, brought word to Placerville that all Mormons were to be recalled to Salt Lake. Orders seemed imminent. Brigham Young was preparing to reduce the boundaries of the Mormon kingdom to fortify Salt Lake City.[27]

And with that, the Gentile US officials in Salt Lake City were feeling themselves more and more imperiled. They had sustained numerous overt threats and incidents of harassment. In one, a judge was threatened in open court. When he informed Brigham Young, the governor said that if the judge could not enforce the law, he should resign his position. A week later a mob seized the judge's legal papers and books, threw them in an outhouse, and set the structure on fire. On April 15 every Gentile federal official but one left the territory. In September the last of these officials, an Indian agent, fled after he was warned by Indians that he was to be murdered. Federal authority in Utah no longer existed.[28]

On the eastern slope of the Sierra, a newcomer moved in and quickly became the leader of the movement to break away from Utah governance. He also gave direction to the anti-Mormons, organizing a vigilance committee. Like similar vigilante movements, the group insisted that their concept of justice be imposed as a tool of social order.[29]

CHAPTER FOUR

Major Ormsby, Mormons, and Indians

Early in 1857, William Ormsby arrived in Carson Valley. He had strong features, a high forehead, high cheekbones, and a Roman nose. His hair was wavy, and he wore his curly, black beard neatly cropped. He went by the title of "Major," having served in the Pennsylvania state militia. He seemed a man of destiny, personifying America's progress in "winning" the West.

In 1849 Ormsby, at age thirty-five, and male family members, including brothers and his wife's brother, had come overland with pack mules to Northern California. One of his brothers, John, was a doctor who would become involved with state Democratic politics. John and William's brother-in-law John Trumbo would join Major Ormsby in business partnerships.

It was the era preceding the managerial revolution. Rather than salaried managers administering enterprises, family-run companies or partnerships predominated. Major Ormsby would be involved in a half-dozen such enterprises in Sacramento and another half dozen when he moved across the Sierra a few years later. With his brothers, he opened a Sacramento assay office and private mint, melting American River gold. They cast it into bars, rolled it into strips, and stamped out dye-marked coins with a sledgehammer. The business, producing hand-struck five- and ten-dollar coins, said to be extensive, was apparently unprofitable, and by the end of 1850 they had shuttered it. In Sacramento, Major Ormsby was also associated with a livery stable, a hauling business, and, partnering with Trumbo, a horse auction.

Within a year, Ormsby formed a mail and passenger stage line from Sacramento to Hangtown, soon to be renamed Placerville. The line then extended north to Coloma, California, where James W. Marshall first discovered gold, and then to Marysville on the Feather River. Ormsby had a strong sense of right and wrong, and, in January 1851, he was appointed to the Sacramento grand jury. He had married Margaret Trumbo in 1844 when he was thirty and she was sixteen. In 1852 he traveled back to the East and brought her and his daughter to California.

There is no record of Ormsby's activities in 1855 and 1856. According to Carson Valley pioneers, he left his wife and daughter again to join William Walker and his army of irregulars as they engaged in a "filibuster," a term used in the era to describe a private military expedition. Walker was an attorney from Tennessee who in the 1850s lived in both Marysville and Sacramento. During that time, he organized military expeditions into Mexico and Central America in failed attempts to expand America's Manifest Destiny. Unsanctioned by the government, although wildly popular with elements of the population who cheered expansionism, he attempted to overthrow the government of Nicaragua to begin establishing a Central American federation of proslavery states. He twice led groups of mercenaries to the troubled country before being captured and executed there in 1860. Many years later, pioneer D.R. Hawkins wrote to Asa Merrill Fairfield, commenting offhandedly that Ormsby had been a buccaneer with Walker in Nicaragua.[1]

In 1881 Thomas Knott wrote a manuscript titled *Reminiscences* in which he called Ormsby a "Walker filibusterer." Knott's manuscript was reprinted in 1947 by H. Hamlin, who commented further regarding Ormsby: "Very little is known about him, especially in Nevada. Mr. Knott called him a Walker filibusterer: who was one of the numerous lot that joined Walker's unsuccessful filibuster in Nicaragua in 1856.... Knott had evidently run across Ormsby's trail in Nicaragua as he was there twice." The fact that Ormsby was not mentioned in newspapers during 1855 and 1856 is circumstantial evidence supporting Hawkins and Knott's belief, because in all other years, Ormsby's activities or his normative statements were deemed newsworthy and were consistently reported.[2]

Ormsby came to Genoa with his wife and daughter, partnering with Captain William H. Smith in running a pack service. They also acted as agents for Colonel J.B. Crandall's Pioneer Stage Line, a tri-weekly stage service between Placerville and Genoa. At the same time, Ormsby rented space from Lucky Bill Thorington for the sale of general merchandise. Within a few months he bought lots in Genoa with his brother-in-law Trumbo, bought a store at the mouth of Gold Canyon, and invested in land in Eagle Valley with his clerk, Samuel Swanger. From the time of his arrival, he claimed leadership in all the pressing issues of Carson County. His mandate apparently came from his experience and age since, being in his forties, he was older than most.

At the end of July 1857, Ormsby was reported to be organizing a company to prospect the headwaters of the Walker and Colorado Rivers. He may not have led that expedition because a week later he was involved in a meeting formed to discuss seceding from Utah. Three days after serving on a committee of arrangements, on August 6, he chaired a meeting of men from ten communities. They came from as far away as Honey Lake, Ragtown, and the Humboldt Sink. The gathering was called to press for the creation of a territory composed of the Sierra eastern slope and large parts of the Great Basin (anticipating the state of Nevada). Colonel Reese was elected president and Isaac Roop, of Honey Lake Valley, as one of the vice presidents.

Judge James M. Crane had come to Genoa from California a month earlier. He was a friend of Ormsby's, and he gave a speech at the meeting that lasted a full hour. After the speech, he was elected to carry the memorial to Washington, DC, in what would be an unsuccessful attempt to gain recognition by Congress.[3]

On his own motion, Ormsby was the first named of nine individuals, including rancher Richard Sides, to draw up resolutions of intent. Ormsby was not looking to create innovative policies. He was part of American incorporation and the consolidation of capitalistic forces. Like many other frontiersmen, he wanted to form a society similar to those in the states. Carson Valley was unlike southwestern settlements influenced by Mexican culture and unlike San Francisco, which—with a population of perhaps fifty thousand—was multicultural. Out from under Salt Lake City's influence, the eastern slope might establish a system akin to older Anglo-American communities. The memorial they produced contained luminous, inflated prose: "[We] do not wish to see anarchy, violence, bloodshed, and crime of every hue and grade waving their horrid scepter over this portion of our common country." Its objective, appealing for approval of a new territory, reflected Ormsby's perspective regarding the need for law and order. The residents of the eastern slope, it stated, had been "without any Territorial, State, or Federal protection from Indian depredations and marauding outlaws, runaway criminals and convicts, as well as other evil-doers among white men and Indians."[4]

Because Ormsby, supported by the Richard Sides faction, had been working in opposition to Mormon rule since his arrival, it seems likely that the "other evil-doers" and crimes of "every hue and grade" included polygamists and polygamy. It may also have been referring to gamblers—specifically Lucky Bill Thorington, who was known for the vices of keeping two women and gambling. Perhaps more to the point, he assisted those who needed aid without "inquir[ing] whether they were horse thieves or Mormon tithing collectors."[5]

If Thorington, who was at the meeting, did not realize the resolution referred to him, he would receive a direct warning, by way of a brawl, three weeks later. Of course, he would receive the ultimate message when arrested by vigilantes ten months later.

Honey Lake residents strongly supported the mass meeting's resolutions, as they were fending off Plumas County efforts to annex them. Three weeks after the Genoa meeting, while Roop was still away, thirty-two Honey Lakers gathered at Manley Thompson's cabin. Thompson chaired the meeting, and the *Red Bluff Beacon* reported that the citizens of Honey Lake had determined to repudiate any actions of the Plumas County officials. In endeavoring to name Honey Lake as one of their county's townships, Plumas County had appointed officers to administer justice and assess taxes. Some at the meeting claimed not to believe that Honey Lake was within California state boundaries; others said they had "very reasonable doubts." They drew up a manifesto endorsing efforts to form the new territory comprising all eastern slope communities, specifically supporting the efforts of two individuals whom they named—Roop and Ormsby.

All the resolutions of the declaration passed unanimously. In one, the Honey Lakers decreed that individually and collectively, they would resist the authorities of Plumas County and their appointees. They announced further that on Election Day, they would prevent the polls from being opened. They appointed a "Committee of Safety," five individuals who would correspond with Plumas County and "end meetings when necessary." Atlas Fredonyer, who lived at the north end of Honey Lake, had registered a land claim at Plumas County rather than with Roop. Perhaps in part because of that, Plumas County officials appointed him justice of the peace. Among the last of the Thompson cabin resolutions was one stating that a committee would wait on Fredonyer to "politely inform him that the citizens of this valley can dispense with his services."[6]

Five weeks later, Roop chaired another Honey Lake meeting. Attendees again endorsed the eastern slope territory and directed him to cooperate with Major Ormsby and Martin Smith, a representative of Lake Valley (Lake Tahoe), to establish said territory.[7] The Honey Lakers stated that any attempt by California to bring the people of Honey Lake into subjugation before the territorial movement was decided would be resisted "with all the power we can command." The *San Francisco Daily Evening Bulletin* quoted a lengthy article from the *Shasta Courier:* "[The Honey Lakers] are emphatically angry at somebody, and indicate a state of mind suitable for 'treasons, strategems, etc.' These hot spur resolutions smell of war, and have a decided odor of treason."[8]

At that time, Major Ormsby and Judge Crane, who had yet to leave for Washington, DC, were promoting the eastern slope to Californians. In San Francisco, the *Daily Alta California* wrote: "Major Ormsby and Judge Crane both pronounce the land of Carson, Eagle, Washo and Honey Lake Valleys to be of a very fine quality. In Carson, there are now thousands upon thousands of acres of land where the grass, flowers and weeds are so high that when the cattle are lying down they are nearly hid from the view of the herdsman."[9]

The boosterism was politic, too. By including Honey Lake with the valleys 120 miles to the south, Ormsby and Crane would have been alleviating tension in a developing dispute. The US secretary of the interior, seeking to create the most serviceable entryway to California, had directed John Kirk, an engineering contractor from Placerville, to find a route for a road between City of the Rocks in southern Idaho and Honey Lake. After two months studying northern Nevada, Kirk determined that the only feasible route was south of Pyramid Lake, which would create a short, easier road to Carson Valley, directing traffic, and therefore business, away from Honey Lake. Roads to Carson Valley led to Placerville. The Honey Lakers accused Kirk of a lack of honesty and of "dastardly misrepresenting everything north of Sacramento" in order to promote his own interests. Interior officials came to conclude that Kirk's plan was not adequate. They replaced him, and the road to Honey Lake was improved. Nonetheless, most emigrants wanted to get to Sacramento or central California. Because the Honey Lake route took them too far north, the Carson Valley route continued to attract most of the traffic.[10]

For a short time, it had seemed the principal California wagon route would follow the Truckee River, as did the first train in 1844–45, but that road quickly lost favor. Wagons had to cross the river more than twenty times, passing through a long, narrow canyon, and the river eventually led into steep, heavily timbered escarpments. The Truckee's mouth is at Pyramid Lake, and, because the route did not develop, pioneers did not immediately overrun the area that was the heart of the Northern Paiute economy.

Pyramid is the deepest of the lakes in the Eastern Sierra drainage. In the 1850s it reached a depth of some 360 feet. It has no outlet, so only subsurface seepage, sun, and wind-driven evaporation and drought years lowered its surface level. Its waters hosted the Lahontan cutthroat trout, growing to ten pounds and more, and the three- to five-pound cuiui, a lacustrine sucker found only in Pyramid and the lower part of the Truckee. In the thick tules, rushes, grasses, and reeds of a nearby slough, migratory waterfowl, using the Great Western Flyway, rested before continuing their journeys. Cottonwoods and berry bushes in canyons formed by the river harbored animals, and, in the surrounding mountains, pine nuts could be collected from thin stands of piñon pines.

Even without the wagon route, American encroachment had been merely delayed. By 1858 infringements had become so pervasive that Indian agent Frederick Dodge called the state "intolerable." The Americans' actions, he declared, were inducing "acts of crime and barbarity."[11]

Dodge was directed to find reservation land for the Paiutes. For that purpose, in November 1859 the agent proposed allotting Pyramid Lake, together with parts of the deserts to the north, hills to the east and west, a bit of the slough to the east, and the lower Truckee River to the south. The suggestion was approved by the president, but the vague description of the land did not prompt a survey until 1865, when it appeared that the Central Pacific Railroad needed to be run across the southern tip of the reservation. The survey was completed that year, but there was no official executive order setting aside the reservation land for another nine years. In the interim, Anglo settlers claimed and developed farms in the most fertile areas and developed systems to use water from the Truckee.[12]

In 1858 a government report by an army lieutenant to his commander indicated that the Paiutes were friendly and industrious. He described them as an altogether superior race, intelligent, mounted, and well armed. He urged his superior to cultivate their friendship.[13]

With Winnemucca leading the Paiutes from the Pyramid Lake band and Isaac Roop and Peter Lassen leading the settlers, they had common understandings. Relations at Honey Lake had been peaceful into 1858, as both sides observed the treaty arrangement made three years earlier.

Captain William Weatherlow came to Honey Lake with Isaac Roop in 1854, helping to build Roop's cabin. He did not move to the valley until two years later, procuring land near Roop's and building his own cabin. Weatherlow, reputed to have come west with Frémont in the 1840s, was a small man with a commanding presence. In 1857 he organized the militia, the Honey Lake Rangers. Associates who rode with him reported that in any Indian expedition when he was present, Weatherlow was looked upon as the leader.[14]

It is interesting to note that Weatherlow did not always ride on the missions. This points to the fact that, unlike some other missions across the Sierra, the Honey Lake Rangers were not state funded. Still, forming it as an organization gave it legitimacy, raising their image above that of a makeshift posse or a band of incendiaries. As historian Madley observes, the widely publicized Ranger militia operations provided state endorsement, "communicating an unofficial grant of legal impunity for Indian killing, and eroding cultural and moral barriers to the homicide and mass murder of Indians."[15]

From the time of the first American settlement at Honey Lake, the Pit River Indians, a Paiute band that lived north of Honey Lake, had taken opportunities to drive off settlers' stock. They were led by Smoke Creek Sam and were outside Winnemucca's influence. Weatherlow's company was composed of sixty men, and he led groups of them against the Pit River band on a number of occasions. Winnemucca was inclined to assist the Honey Lakers. Weatherlow wrote, "Winnemucca volunteered to go out with his warriors, and aid us in fighting the Pit River tribe. He obeyed orders strictly, and fought as bravely as any white man." On one occasion they rescued emigrants in a small wagon train, killing twenty-five of the Pit River band. "By the aid of Winnemucca and his warriors, we finally scattered the Pit River tribe of Indians," said

Weatherlow, "and they have never since that time made an incursion upon thc valley."[16]

Despite Weatherlow's leadership, a number of Honey Lakers had a propensity for ruthlessness, and they would soon demonstrate it in extremely ugly incidents involving the Indians.

Equally truculent affairs were being alleged in Salt Lake City. William Drummond had resigned his post as Utah district judge, and, in April 1857, he had begun writing to newspapers, making accusations against the Mormon Church. He said that every member of the Church acted at the will of Brigham Young and that "the leading men of the Church are more traitorous than ever." He alleged that murders were common and that Mormons could not be convicted by Mormon juries with Mormon witnesses and officers. He charged that the crimes were often disguised as the acts of Indians. Specifically, he said that the survey party of Captain John Gunnison, reportedly killed by Indians in 1853, and the killing of secretary of the territory A. W. Babbitt had been done by white people. He accused the church elders of ordering those deaths, along with the poisoning of territorial judge Leonidas Shaver.

When she read Drummond's allegations, Captain Gunnison's widow wrote him asking for particulars of her husband's killing. On May 1, 1857, *The New York Times* printed her letter and Drummond's lengthy response under the heading "The Mormon Outrages." Drummond said that Captain Gunnison had been "most foully and inhumanly murdered." A group of Indians was put on trial but found not guilty by order of the church. Subsequently, Drummond put an Indian in the employ of Brigham Young on trial for the murder of Gunnison. Other Indians testified for the government, which allowed Drummond to list eight Mormons by name who he said were guilty of the associated murders. He then described how Indians had been dispatched to scalp and mutilate the bodies and steal the clothes from the victims to wear themselves. In his letter Drummond provided gruesomely lurid details of the desecration of Captain Gunnison's body.

On May 20, 1857, *The New York Times* added fuel to the fire. The first four and a half columns of its front page contained a letter written from Salt Lake City over the course of several dates between March 9 and March 30. The writer, identified only as "Vigo," said that on those days, he had found "safe opportunities" to make specific charges against the Mormons: murders, robberies, and women being "sealed" to unwanted husbands who were church officials or to their sons. He wrote of the Danites, a.k.a. the "Destroying Angels," and said that although baptisms of water served for the remission of sins, serious sins required blood. Some murders took place in the desert, he said, when "the country became unhealthy" for apostates. "Be assured that affairs here are approaching a fearful crisis," he warned. Newspapers in the West added opinions, saying that credible sources were describing Mormon treason and depravity.[17]

President Buchanan was trying to finesse his way past the nation's fixation on slavery, currently playing out in the contested elections in "Bleeding Kansas" and the Supreme Court's *Dred Scott* decision. Feeling the Mormons were in open defiance of the Constitution, he began searching for a replacement for Brigham Young as territorial governor and directed action be taken to reestablish Utah's law and order. On May 28, 1857, General Winfield Scott ordered twenty-five hundred troops from the states to be gathered at Fort Leavenworth, Kansas, and to march on Salt Lake City. Buchanan did not notify Brigham Young of any change or movement by the army, but the news spread, and Governor Young, having already anticipated such action, readied his followers to meet an armed intervention.[18]

At the beginning of July, *The New York Times* reported that there were complaints of mail, especially correspondence between government officials, being illegally opened at Salt Lake City. The contract for carrying mails had been set aside, and a new postmaster was being sent to the territory. He would be supported by the military force.[19]

Young was uncertain what he wanted the Carson Valley Mormons to do. Early in the summer of 1857, as they awaited direction, the entire fraternity reaffirmed their commitment to the church, submitting to a new baptism. In July a train of sixty-five Mormons left Carson County for Utah. In June Young had written a letter telling them they were not recalled, as they were not needed in Salt Lake Valley. That word did not arrive until August, by which time he again reversed his decision.

On August 15 Young sent his next message, recalling the faithful, instructing them to bring all the ammunition they could get. By the end of October, he had once again changed his mind, wanting them to remain at their outpost raising livestock and grains to supply Salt Lake when needed. By then it was too late.[20]

On September 15, 1857, the *San Francisco Herald* spoke of emigration into Carson Valley coming "thicker and faster" and announced that Mormon ranches were being disposed of by giving them to the newcomers. On the twenty-second, a great stirring of people and animals in the valley was announced.

The Saints had gathered some $800 and sent two men to San Francisco to purchase powder, lead, and caps. On their return, they were stopped by a group of miners at Angel's Camp, who said they would not allow ammunition to fight the government to get to Salt Lake. Luckily for the two transporters, there was a tavern nearby, and, passing out liquor, they were able to continue their journey with their cargo intact.[21]

On September 26 about 450 Mormon men, women, and children, some from Oregon and California, left Carson Valley for the City of Saints. Many had sustained substantial losses in selling their properties.[22]

Major Ormsby, whose political fortunes rose with the exodus, gave it his blessing. He relayed word that he had visited the Mormons, and they left after dealing fairly with the other valley settlers. Uncle Billy Rodgers presented a similar account to California's *Nevada Journal.* It read, in part, that the Mormons "paid up to the last dollar of indebtedness and left with the good wishes of all." He continued, commenting on the Saints' war readiness, as they had heeded Young's August entreaty: "They carried with them immense amounts of powder and other ammunition, and before their departure had purchased nearly all the revolvers in the Valley. Some members of the train had in possession as high as six of these weapons." One of the men who left in the September train was Judge Chester Loveland. Mormon rule in Carson Valley was over. The resulting power vacuum produced further attempts to bring about political coherence. The means would often include violence.[23]

Until November 1858, when the telegraph line ran over the Sierra, news from the eastern slope printed in Placerville, Sacramento, or San Francisco newspapers was haphazard and slow to arrive. Telegraph lines had been run from San Francisco to Sacramento and Marysville in October 1853. In January 1854 the system reached Placerville. After that, linked newspapers could reprint articles printed the day before in other towns.

The heading for those items included some mention of the telegraph, generally "by state telegraph line" or "by Magnetic Telegraph."[24]

Before the winter of 1858, news was carried across the Sierra by unpaid correspondents, often stagecoach drivers or mail carriers like Snowshoe Thompson. Sometimes the information came from travelers who had passed through Carson Valley and had seen something they believed newsworthy. Any news articles deemed important that arrived in Placerville were then telegraphed to the major cities, with smaller California papers printing them some days later.

In Carson Valley, the year 1857 was defined by tumult and brutality. In March news reports showed Anglo-Indian difficulties escalating to dangerous proportions. Snowshoe Thompson carried news to Placerville: Indians had stolen a horse and killed several cows; other cows had been found with arrows in them, and "one had seven." On May 23 Major Ormsby carried word to Placerville that residents feared an "Indian outbreak." Washoes had been caught stealing horses, for which they were whipped. The Indians were reported to be "greatly exasperated," and Captain Jim lit signal fires calling for a general meeting of the tribe across the Carson River. Ormsby said residents were preparing for the worst.[25]

Before the arrival of American settlers, the Washoes' history included attacks on trespassers whom they deemed to have evil intent. They were not, however, a warlike tribe. Their first response to encroachments was to take cover and keep watch. When they chose to attack, they used bows and special war arrows coated with secret medicines that would bring instant death. Sometimes, they attacked at night. If the battles took place during the day, the Washoes would release their arrows from behind rock breastworks. There was no commander to issue orders for individuals to join in a battle; each warrior made his own decision. The Hangalelti band, across the river from Genoa in the southern part of the valley, was known especially for their bravery and willingness to fight. Captain Jim, however, was not from their band, and they did not join him in this instance. The judgment not to fight prevailed.[26]

In mid-August there were two reports of Indian attacks on the overland trail. A wagon train had been attacked by thirty "Shoshony" Indians, twenty-four of whom had been killed along with a white man who was supposed to be their leader. The report said several Anglos' bodies had been seen as well. The second story came from two men who carried word of an attack at Goose Creek, west of Salt Lake, with forty-five head of cattle being stolen. In this case also, the messengers were convinced white men led the attack. They reported that both arrows and bullet balls had been fired during the skirmish and that they distinctly heard voices of three men who spoke English freely. Three white traders from the post at Gravelly Ford, on the Humboldt River, had disappeared, and it was speculated that either they were now leading the Indians or they had been killed by other white men who were now in league with marauders.[27]

Major Ormsby and Judge Crane told the newspapers a similar story: there were "bands of robbers" who had joined with Indians to perpetrate crimes. The *San Francisco Herald* commented that it was impossible to exterminate the evildoers just then, but preparations were being made to prevent a recurrence of the scenes described by the following year.

On August 23 the paper again printed a story of white men in league with Indians. That report included an incident showing how edgy emigrants were becoming: someone in a wagon train had accidentally shot another man dead while the second man was on guard duty.

On September 1, the *Herald* carried word of another massacre by Indians. A wagon train had been attacked, and six men and three children were reported killed. Also, three more men had been murdered at Gravelly Ford, and the body of one of the traders from that post, reported missing two weeks earlier, had been found. He was shot through the heart and scalped.[28]

As the summer turned to fall, the violence moved close to Carson Valley. On September 5, two men leaving Placerville were murdered. A man on the trail heard gunshots and a shout. On the summit of Slippery Ford Hill, he found a hat and a horse without a rider.

Two "well esteemed" citizens, John McMarlin, the former county selectman, and James Williams, a former constable, had been ambushed and killed after leaving Placerville for Genoa. Williams's body was missing. McMarlin had been "shot completely through" by an arrow, believed to be Washoe. The story, repeated in a number of newspapers, concluded that twenty-four whites had been massacred within the past six weeks.[29]

A couple of days later, a posse found Williams's body. Although no arrests had yet been made, the report from Placerville said that the Indians who had committed the act were well known.

Uncle Billy Rodgers employed members of the Washoe Tribe, and they at times used his residence as a rendezvous. On September 28, serious trouble was reported. He had apprehended three Washoes he accused of robbing his cabin three weeks earlier. They drew their bows and shot arrows at him, and he shot one through the thigh. The wounded man was Captain Jim's brother. The Indians escaped, and the newspaper reported that now the whole Washoe Tribe was painting their faces red. At the same time, it stated, some six hundred "Pinto" (Paiute) Indians were ready to help the American settlers punish the murderers of McMarlin and Williams.[30]

On October 6, there was a report of another attack at Goose Creek: two white people were killed, two wounded, and twenty head of stock stolen. The citizens east of the Sierra were alarmed. Uncle Billy Rodgers left for Sacramento carrying a petition to Governor J. Neely Johnson, asking for assistance.[31] On October 9, the *San Francisco Herald* told of two more men reportedly killed by Washoes. Three hundred Washoes were said to be camped within a few miles of Genoa, and they had declared their intentions to kill all white people in the valley. It reported further that the people of the valley, having received top dollar for their guns from the departed Mormons, were without arms.

On October 14, a new correspondent, Richard N. Allen, an attorney using the nom de plume "Tennessee," wrote to the *Herald.* Although he soon became a dependable commentator, this instance illustrates the inconsistent quality of reporting and how fear influences perception. He had just arrived in Carson Valley and wrote that there were eight thousand Washoes in the area. He was overestimating by four times the entire Washoe population.

Three days after Tennessee's correspondence, Ormsby reported that the Washoes had agreed to a treaty. A "captain" of the Washoes, presumably Captain Jim, had negotiated with respected settler Hiram Mott. The Washoe headman vowed to shoot any Washoe who violated a white man and asked that white offenders also be brought to justice. The action may have been influenced by the fact that the Paiutes had agreed to help the settlers, as the Washoes and the Paiutes were feuding.[32]

About the same time, Rodgers returned from Sacramento with a band of twenty-five volunteers. They were heavily armed with weapons lent to Colonel Rodgers by Governor Johnson of California. The volunteers had been recruited from San Francisco, Sacramento, and Placerville to assist in finding the murderers of McMarlin and Williams. They would be employed working for Rodgers and would protect the valley's families from hostile Indians once the passes closed for the winter. It was said that the volunteers were willing to undertake the hazards and hardships of a winter campaign. The presence of Uncle Billy's "army" helped reduce fears and tension in the valley, although by the onset of winter the volunteers' number had been reduced to seven.[33]

Besides the violence, there was another acute issue affecting white and Native people's relations. In his contemporary history, California historian H.H. Bancroft discussed how territorial officials felt helpless to prevent Indian slavery. There was a long history in the Southwest of Indians raiding other tribes to procure slaves. Hispanos did little to negate the trade after gaining control of the area, and it continued throughout the nineteenth century under American governance. There were repeated reports of Hispanos and white settlers raiding Indians or purchasing slaves from Indian slave traders. Bancroft wrote that there were few American military or civil officials who did not own captive slaves and that slaves were even found in the service of the Indian agents. California passed legislation, the Act for the Government and Protection of Indians of 1850, containing a wide range of declarations. The document had little to do with protecting Indians. Instead, it exploited their rights as individuals. For example, it legalized "expeditions against the Indians" and allowed for "the removal of Indians from lands in the white person's possession." Section 15 prohibited the sale of alcohol to Indians. Section 20 decreed that Indians who were deemed vagrant could be hired out to the "best bidder" for a term of up to four months.[34]

Another section of the law allowed a petitioner to gain custody of an Indian child if parents or friends showed that it was a voluntary transaction. The stated purpose of this law was to allow Indian minors to gain apprenticeships, but it was widely abused in the mid-1850s by traffickers of children, very few of whom were caught.[35]

The Book of Mormon taught that Indians are the descendants of Laman, the Israelite, and Mormons referred to them as Lamanites. They believed the Native Americans were fearsome and warlike because they had been cut off from God's teachings. Along with saving Indians' souls, Mormon leaders wanted to end the severe abuses perpetrated in the slave trade. Apostle Orson Pratt lectured on the issue: "The Lord has caused us to come here for this very purpose, that we might accomplish the redemption of these suffering degraded Israelites." In 1852 the Utah

Legislature passed the Act for the Relief of Indian Slaves and Prisoners, which provided that Utah citizens could become guardians of Indian children for up to twenty years.[36]

Major William Ormsby seems to have followed the spirit of the California and Utah precepts in bringing two young Paiute sisters to live with his family. Thirteen-year-old Sarah Winnemucca and her younger sister lived with the Ormsbys, learning American customs and the English language while serving as companions to Ormsby's daughter and doing light housework. In her autobiography, Sarah consistently referred to Ormsby as their friend.[37]

In the McMarlin and Williams case, Ormsby called in the Paiute girls' brother and cousin, Natchez and Numaga, the latter also known as Young Winnemucca. The young Paiute leaders verified what had been suspected, identifying the arrows found at the McMarlin and Williams murder site as those of the Washoes. Although their manner of seeking justice would have been to wait for time to prove guilt or innocence, the Paiutes agreed to help Ormsby secure suspects.

Sarah Winnemucca wrote of the incident in her autobiography. Her brother, her cousin, and a hundred Paiutes came to Genoa and brought in Captain Jim and several other Washoes.

> As soon as [the Washoes] came in the white men gathered round them. Major Ormsbey showed the arrows, and asked them if they knew them. The Washoe chief, who is called Jam, said, "You ask me if these are my people's arrows. I say yes."
>
> Major Ormsbey said, "That is enough." He said to my brother Natchez,—
>
> "Tell Captain Jam that his people have killed two men, and he must bring the men and all the money, and they shall not be hurt, and all will be right." The Washoe chief said,—
>
> "I know my people have not killed the men, because none of my men have been away; we are all at Pine-nut Valley, and I do not know what to think of the sad thing that has happened."
>
> "But here are your arrows, and you cannot say anything," said my cousin, the war-chief. "We will give you ten days to bring the men who killed our two white brothers, and if you do not we shall have to fight you, for they have been so kind to us all. Who could have the heart to kill them? Now go and bring in the men."[38]

Here, stories diverge. The newspaper accounts were carried to Placerville by a man named Haines and a Placerville resident who was moving to Carson Valley, Chauncey Noteware. Living in the West since 1850, Noteware was respected on both sides of the Sierra. He had just finished serving as the El Dorado County recorder. In 1858 he would be elected surveyor for Carson County, continuing his career of public service that would include a tenure as a probate judge and culminate with his election as the first secretary of state for Nevada. According to Haines and Noteware's account, a Washoe named Charley had been lured to Lucky Bill Thorington's ranch by Captain Jim. There, Colonel Rodgers's men and other citizens arrested him.

Charley was interrogated by McMarlin's brother, through an interpreter, but no information was elicited. The white settlers held a trial the next day. The article stated that Charley "confessed enough" to convict any man. While a vote was being taken regarding his fate, Charley ran and was shot twice, dying that night. A story three days later gave additional details, stating that Charley was present when McMarlin and Williams were killed, but that he took no part in the shooting. He said he was laying in the chaparral fixing his gun and that two others had done the killing. The story concluded, "While the citizens were deliberating as to what was to be done with the red rascal, he struck his guard a severe blow in the eye and ran for life, but was soon brought down by one who anticipated such a movement, and came prepared for it."[39]

Sarah Winnemucca's account was decidedly different. She reported that six days after her cousin gave the ultimatum, Captain Jim returned with three prisoners: two were unmarried, while the third had been married a short time, with no children. The young wife and the prisoners' mothers accompanied them. The women pleaded with the Paiutes Natchez and Numaga to intervene, insisting that the men had not been away from their families for more than a month and that they had been chosen by Captain Jim so the whole tribe would not suffer.

Sarah Winnemucca said that the prisoners were kept handcuffed in a small house overnight. The next day, with townspeople gathered, Ormsby questioned them. She reported: "Some said, 'Hang the red devils right off,' and the white boys threw stones at them and used most shameful language to them. At about three o'clock in the afternoon came thirty-one white men, all with guns on their shoulders, and as they marched my brother and cousin ran to meet them. One Washoe woman began to scream, 'Oh, they have come to kill them!' How they did cry!"

Sarah Winnemucca wrote that the crowd took charge of the prisoners to transfer them to a jail in California. She said that one of the women cried out and that the prisoners broke and ran and were shot. "I ran to Mrs. Ormsbey crying," she stated. "I thought my poor heart would break. I said to her 'I believe those Washoe women. They say their men are all innocent...' Mrs. Ormsbey said,—'How came the Washoe arrows there? and the chief himself has brought them to us, and my husband knows what he is doing.'"[40]

After the shootings, Sarah Winnemucca returned to live with the Paiutes. Biographer Katherine Gehn comments that after living with the Ormsbys and interacting with white settlers, Sarah developed an idea of their temperament. She liked them, but, it seemed to her, they tended to panic, never taking time to reason things out.[41]

According to Sarah Winnemucca, sometime that winter Captain Jim came to the Paiutes asking for payment for the murdered Washoes. He told them that Major Ormsby had informed him that the actual murderers of McMarlin and Williams had been caught. They were white men. The Paiutes refused to pay, saying Captain Jim was responsible, for he had brought the men in. They had only done what the white settlers would do for them. When the Washoes were shot, their women relations had cursed Captain Jim, and he had admitted, "It is I who have killed them. Their blood is on my hands. I know their spirits will haunt me, and give me bad luck while I live." The mother of one had also directed words at the Paiutes: "Oh, may the Good Spirit send the same curse upon you. You may all live to see the day when you will suffer at the hands of your white brothers, as you call them." The statement would prove more prophesy than curse.[42]

The acute differences in the stories of the McMarlin and Williams murders leave open the question of who killed them. What both the newspaper reports and Sarah Winnemucca's account do is expose the difficulty in applying American justice in the undeveloped community, particularly when incidents involved Indians. Forced into the mountains or small spaces, deprived of food sources, and, in instances, hunted, Indians responded by raiding livestock and attacking the white settlers. Historian Lindsay points out, "Rather than recognizing these actions as resistance to their own actions, Euro-Americans perceived them as wanton, unprovoked savagery and became that much more determined to exterminate the barbarous Indians."[43]

A month after the affair that attempted to resolve the McMarlin and Williams murders, the *San Francisco Herald* reported that everything in Carson Valley had been quiet and that the Indians were friendly if left alone. "Those who had been anxious to get up an Indian War," it stated, "have been disappointed."[44]

That was not the case to the north, at Honey Lake, where an attempt by Washoes to compensate for lost food resources was met with retaliation. Deer Dick was the headman of the Welmelti band of about three hundred who lived in the Washoes' northernmost quadrant, not far from Honey Lake. What kind of power Deer Dick wielded is unrecorded, and the only stories of interactions between the Welmelti and Honey Lakers involve violence. In this instance, a large number of the band, said by the white settlers to be one hundred, raided a ranch belonging to William Morehead, a few miles west of Honey Lake.

While Morehead was away, the Indians cleared three acres of potatoes, so that upon his return, the field was barren. Morehead, who had an unspecified disability, reported the theft to his neighbors. Six men, including Cap Hill, one of the original settlers and later elected Lake County sheriff, went after the Indians. Finding the Welmelti camp in the mountains four miles south, the Honey Lakers engaged them. The white settlers killed three and wounded another before having to retreat, first to Hill's cabin and then to a nearby log fort. They were soon joined by fifteen or sixteen other Honey Lakers, and the Washoes were forced to retreat back to the mountains. With the additional men, the Honey Lakers again attacked the Washoe camp. No one was killed, but the Honey Lakers recovered about a ton of the potatoes. Shortly thereafter, ten more recruits arrived.

With the reinforcements, the Honey Lakers moved under cover of darkness, planning a daybreak attack on the Washoes. The Indians were now in three camps, and the Honey Lakers split up to attack all three simultaneously. They made a mistake in that only three men attacked the largest camp. They had to fight their way back to the fort, carrying one of their number in a blanket after he was wounded in the leg. The fighting continued until the arrival of Captain Weatherlow, commanding some of his Rangers, along with Winnemucca and his Paiutes. The newcomers had been far to the north conducting a raid against the Pit River band.

The Washoe battle ended when the Washoes again withdrew from the valley. Eleven Washoes had been killed and fourteen wounded. One of the Paiutes, mistaken for a Washoe, had been shot by a Honey Laker. It took a number of presents to mollify Winnemucca and prevent a breakdown in relations.[45]

The reason the Washoes had raided the potato field was understandable: their world was being constricted. Indian agent Frederick Dodge, completing a survey of the Indians within the western Utah Territory, made contact with 4,077 Indians: 3,735 Paiutes and 342 Washoes. In his report he said that numbers of Washoes were destitute, telling the familiar story: "The encroachments of the emigrants have driven away the game upon which they depend for a subsistence.... They must, therefore steal or starve." Describing the winter's bitter cold and snow, the document illustrated the point: "A few days ago a 'Wa-sho' died from actual starvation and exposure in the vicinity of [Lake Tahoe], which is situated in the Sierra Nevada mountains. And another was found dead at the base of those mountains yesterday, from the same cause."[46]

In 1859 a newspaper article revealed how the Washoes and Captain Jim were attempting to adapt, confronting those they saw as trespassing. Captain Jim had told a white man, identified as Captain Ham, that he could not fish in Lake Tahoe. The newspaper writer used the common vernacular of the day in describing how white settlers were maintaining control. Under the title "The Matter Settled," the correspondent commented, "Maj. Dodge has succeeded in convincing the rascal that he cannot whip the whole world with his few hundred redskins. So he has graciously condescended to permit Captain Ham and others to catch fish, and he has also promised to return two horses he had stolen from the whites."[47]

A report five years later shows how encroachments turned into appropriation. James Nye, the governor of the newly created Nevada Territory, also served as the acting superintendent of Indian affairs. He described "spoiled" rivers and streams in the area, writing that settlers had taken possession of Lake Tahoe and that it had become a place of resort for large numbers of settlers who had virtually excluded the Indians.[48]

The Washoes' plight was exacerbated by the disordered implementation of War Department policy. In 1860, following the first battle in what came to be known as the Pyramid Lake War, soldiers were brought to the area to fight the Paiutes. On an occasion when peaceable Washoe men, women, and children were using a stream in Washoe Valley, the soldiers attacked. A Washoe woman and her child survived by hiding in the willows. She reported that the women were out cutting willows while the menfolk were fishing, when someone said horses were coming their way. Before they knew it, the soldiers opened fire, killing everyone but the concealed woman and child.[49]

Responsible Indian agents realized the devastation that was occurring, but their calls for a reservation for the Washoes went unanswered. Then, in 1865, Hubbard G. Parker, a former mine superintendent and politician in the newly formed State of Nevada, was given control of Nevada's Indian affairs. He made things worse. Serving three years, and describing his position as a "sinecure," he argued that the less done for Native peoples, the better. He described the Washoes as some five hundred individuals, a small remnant of an idle, moving tribe. His misrepresentations demonstrate the oppression caused by racist government higher-ups. Parker determined the Washoes needed no land, as their numbers were diminishing anyway. In general, he felt that the more the desert country was settled by white people, the better for the Indians. "Every white man who makes himself a farm on any of the strips of cultivable lands," he said, "adds to the comforts of the Indians more than they could get on fifty miles square in its natural state."[50]

The tribe's means of subsistence had been destroyed. Their haphazard attempts to exact payment in the Carson Valley area had been met with punishments from flogging to summary execution. At Honey Lake they had been overwhelmed in battle. In at least one incident, the army had killed innocent Washoes. In newspaper accounts of the McMarlin-Williams murders, one Washoe had been killed. In Sarah Winnemucca's account, when Ormsby attempted to adjudicate the matter, it was three tribe members killed for a crime they did not commit. The American settlers' usurpation of land and resources left no options for Washoes to sustain their precontact economy. The Ormsby-style absolutism allowed few ways for them to adapt.

The government would be of no help. Indian agent Dodge made a plea for the government to establish reservations for the Washoes and Paiutes away from the American settlers, as was government policy. His plea for land in Utah Territory was being held in abeyance. In California, where Washoe land included Lake Tahoe and from Honey Lake south to the Sonora Pass, there was no consideration. According to the commissioner of Indian affairs, writing in the US interior secretary's report for 1859, California's reservation policy "has almost wholly failed to accomplish the beneficent purposes for which it was inaugurated." While proposing instruction in husbandry for members of those bands who were settled down and while compelling others to labor, he concluded, "Neither the government nor California recognizes any right in the Indians of that state to one foot of land within her borders."[51]

Committed to maintaining the connection to their ancestral lands, the Washoes were forced to live on the margins of American society into the twentieth century. Some worked as hired ranch hands and domestics. The large landowners allowed them to live on the outskirts of the properties as long as they worked on the ranches. Other Washoes utilized the edges of the cultivated fields to gather a new type of sunflower and seeds scattered outside the fenced land. They hunted rabbits, waterfowl, and other birds that lived among the willows and cattails growing along the ranchers' irrigation ditches. Generosity in giving was part of the Washoe ethos, and some resorted to begging, seeing no shame in asking for food or clothing from the prosperous. Others began to adapt traditional skills to American commerce, acting as hunting and fishing guides or weaving artistic designs into their conventional baskets and offering them for sale.

A reservation was never created for the Washoes. Finally, under the Dawes Act of 1887, they were allowed to claim individual land allotments. However, they continued to reject government policy makers' insistence that they assimilate by becoming yeoman farmers. They turned down potential farmlands to protect their sacred piñon-pine groves, claiming their allotments together in the forest of the Pine Nut Range.[52]

At the end of the decade, the US Indian commissioner ignored his agent's conclusion that encroachments and the destruction of the game on which the Native Americans' subsistence depended were causes for the disturbances involving Indians and white settlers. The commissioner's report said that it was because the Northern California Indians were "thriftless, idle and debased" that the settlers were "excited to acts of violence."[53] In retrospect, the abusive misassessment seems little more than bureaucratic justification for taking land and pursuing aggression. Meanwhile, similarly slanted perceptions were pitting one faction of Eastern Sierra emigrants against another.

CHAPTER FIVE

Hostilities

In mid-July 1857 US troops had begun the march toward Salt Lake. Their cavalry was detained. Led by senior officer Colonel Albert Sidney Johnston, later the Confederate commander in the western theater of the Civil War, the cavalry was deployed to suppress the guerrilla warfare between proslavery and antislavery forces in Kansas. Mormon militias were able to slow the remaining troops, numbering about fifteen hundred, as they approached Utah Territory. The Mormons conducted raiding parties that stampeded the army's livestock, and they burned supply-train wagons. As the army approached, the militia diverted streams and dug canals that flooded the canyon road leading to Salt Lake. The action forced the troops to take a longer northern route.[1]

The *Deseret News,* the voice of the Latter-day Saints, supported the resistance. On July 15, 1857, it carried a lengthy editorial counseling heathen editors, politicians, chief priests, and rulers to follow the advice of Gamaliel, a Pharisee scholar of Hebrew law: "Refrain from these men and let them alone...lest haply ye be found to fight against God.' Acts V. 37 & 38." A month later, the paper's tone had devolved: "Rotten political pygmies have attained to almost supreme sway in the Government, and are fast trampling under foot the last vestige of unalienable rights." What had changed, according to *The New York Times,* was that Young had announced the approach of the troops, saying they came "not openly and boldly, but underhandedly, and sneekingly, raskaly—in the form of a mob—again to pour their intolerant persecution upon this people and break them up, and ruin them—to destroy and kill them."[2]

Rampant rumors declared that the army "vowed to hang the Mormon leaders when it reached Utah, then declare martial law and massacre the people." In response Young had declared, "I will fight them and I will fight all hell."[3]

On August 26, 1857, Orson Hyde, late of Carson County, published an editorial in the *Deseret News* expressing his faith that if armies were approaching, they best beware, for the hand of the Lord would be involved: "He will send forth his angels and gather out of his kingdom all things that offend and that do iniquity."

Six weeks later on October 4, Brigham Young promised his people, "God will fight our battles, and he will do it just as he pleases." His followers could claim the statement as a revelation when in mid-October ruinous snow and sleet halted the army outside Utah Territory. The troops were forced to take refuge near Fort Bridger, Wyoming. The Mormons had burned the fort, and the troops constructed a crude fortification nearby. In struggling against the storm, three thousand horses and mules perished. Any further advance would not be until spring, as it would take six months for the necessary number of replacement animals to be brought the seven hundred miles over mountainous terrain from Santa Fe. When the Mormon wagons from Carson County arrived in Salt Lake City on November 2 and 3, spirits were high.[4] Another piece of news was creating an entirely different reaction in other locales.

In early October, the heinous attack on an emigrant wagon train, which came to be known as the Mountain Meadows Massacre, became public knowledge. The *Los Angeles Star* used double exclamation points in their headline describing the butchery: "Horrible Massacre of Emigrants!! Over 100 Persons Murdered!!" Although details were murky, the rumors carried by emigrants caused the paper to accuse the Mormons' "Destroying Angels," the Danites, of the crime. Newspapers throughout California reprinted the *Star*'s account.[5]

In Placerville the *Mountain Democrat* wrote: "If statements of emigrants were true, and we have no reason to doubt them, the General Government will be forced to take some speedy steps to teach Brigham Young, his assassins, thieves, vagabonds, harlots and Indian allies, that Uncle Sam is powerful enough to protect his children and punish his rebellious subjects."[6] In Carson Valley, where few of the religionists remained, the anti-Mormons continued to refer to those who opposed them as the Mormon Party.

Although stories and commentaries raced through California, a reliable account of the mass homicide would not be published for two years. More than a century and a half later, discrepancies remain about who gave the orders and why. Authoritative accounts in recent years agree on basic facts. In September 1857 a wagon train from Arkansas, passing through Utah Territory, was attacked. The travelers made a corral of the train and filled dirt up to the base of the wagons, creating a fort. A siege lasted several days. Finally, the attackers, under a flag of truce, told those who were barricaded that they would be allowed safe passage if they relinquished their guns. When they did so, on September 11, the 120 men, women, and children of the train were slaughtered. The only mercy shown was to the 17 youngest children, ages two months to seven years, who were adjudged not mature enough to give testimony; they were placed with Mormon families until being recovered by the government ten months later.[7]

The Mormons accused eastern Utah Paiutes of the atrocity. The Paiutes, knowing they would be blamed, were already leaving the area. A descendant of a Paiute, who had witnessed the massacre, was told by an elder that they left, knowing they would be killed by either the Mormons or the Americans.[8]

The original story, carried west by Mormons, was that the wagon train's members had cheated the Paiutes in trading with them. They then poisoned a dead ox with strychnine and put arsenic in a large spring from which the Indians drank. The meat and water killed tribe members, which was said to provoke the attack. Outraged Californians distrusted the account. The Indians would have taken the women captive, and there had never been a battle where not even one American escaped. In other dealings the Mormons were known to be in league with the Paiutes. Other travelers through Utah had felt themselves in danger and claimed the Mormons were complicit.[9]

In fact, J. Forney, the superintendent of Indian affairs for Utah Territory, investigated the matter the following year. He stated that his original purpose was to attempt to exculpate all Anglos from participation in the massacre. He reported, though, that his inquiries left him satisfied that the Indians acted only in a subordinate role. He found the story of the Mormons unbelievable, citing in particular that a wagon train would carry several pounds of strychnine and arsenic across the country merely so they could poison oxen and Indians. Twenty years passed before a lone actor, John D. Lee, a prominent member of the Latter-day Saints who had admitted seeing the massacre and had been Forney's chief informant, was tried, found guilty, and executed by Utah officials.[10]

In California by the end of 1857, many believed the Danites were responsible. In Los Angeles, there was a mass meeting, charging the Mormons, and specifically Young, with robbery and murder. A resolution petitioned the president to punish the authors of the butchery. The *Los Angeles Star* quoted the petition's initial accusation: "Whereas, after a careful examination into all the circumstances connected with the late horrible massacre in Utah Territory, we firmly believe the atrocious act was perpetrated by the Mormons and their allies the Indians." The *Daily Alta,* in San Francisco, went a step further, charging the Mormons with concocting a system to exterminate the Gentiles.[11]

By December 1857, the *Placerville Mountain Democrat,* continuing its practice of publishing hateful anti-Mormon editorials, said that Brigham Young knew how to satisfy his followers: "He indulges them in all their degrading vices, sanctions with unction their lustful passions, and encourages them in every vile dissipation." A week later it stated that in event of a war with the Mormons, Placerville and surrounding communities would furnish men. "Companies are organizing in different parts of our country, and a number of our young men, of the true grit, are eager to have a dash at Brigham and his followers."[12]

On the eastern border of Utah Territory, replacement animals for the bivouacked troops arrived from Santa Fe in the spring of 1858. In March, with the army poised to begin its assault, Brigham Young ordered the evacuation of Salt Lake City. What would be titled the Mormon War or the Utah War would be settled without a battle. Negotiations led to compromises. President Buchanan issued a blanket pardon for sedition and treason and promised not to interfere with the Mormon religion. Young gave up the governorship to Alfred Cumming, a Buchanan appointee. On June 26, 1858, US troops marched through the city to set up a camp in desolate lands forty miles away, and the citizens returned to their homes at Salt Lake. Cumming announced that the road through Utah Territory could now be traveled in complete safety, while privately admitting to Young, "I can do nothing here without your influence."[13]

Despite the conflict's resolution, in California and the western border of Utah Territory, the confrontation and the Mountain Meadows

Massacre continued to arouse feelings. In Carson Valley animosity was directed not just at the few remaining Mormons but also at those who had befriended or supported them.

Lithographer John Gast's famous allegorical painting *American Progress* has been reproduced on book covers, in textbooks, and on posters and websites. Although a tiny work, only 12¾ inches by 16¾, it represents the monumental concept of America's westward expansion. It might also have symbolized the state of progress in Carson County in the summer of 1857. The left side of the painting shows animals, Indians, and their horses—one pulling a travois, under a dark sky. They are retreating before the march of miners, pioneers with a covered wagon, a stagecoach, ranchers, and farmers with oxen pulling a plow. An angelic figure floats above the others, a bright sky behind her. She holds a book in one hand and pulls a telegraph wire in the other.

Genoa was a year and a half from having the telegraph, which would connect it with California cities across the mountains. Even before the telegraph's completion, the valley's modes of communication and transportation were improved as the road over the Sierra was upgraded. It was reported that stagecoaches could now go uphill or down at a trot. In June J.B. Crandall's Pioneer Stage Line had established triweekly service to Placerville. Major Ormsby, one of the line's agents, had proved the road's development by driving over the steepest grade, and down the formidable Slippery Ford, with a team hauling five thousand pounds.[14]

Along with his work, Ormsby was pursuing progressive change on the east side of the Sierra. He did not approve of Lucky Bill Thorington, whose freewheeling lifestyle was countenanced by the old settlers. Thorington did not fit neatly into "civilized society." Harry Hawkins, whose father had been a neighbor of Thorington's, described how the gambler took emigrants' possessions, only to give them back: "Well lots of times, emigrants would come through and sometimes they'd lost their wagons and everything—horses and all. Well, he generally give them back to the wife and not to the husband (so they belonged to the wife not to the [gambling] husband) and let them go on, you know." Northern California historian Asa Fairfield reported an incident involving a pioneer couple who were being bullied and threatened by "hard characters." Noticing the fracas, Lucky Bill challenged and ran off the ruffians and then helped the couple continue their journey.[15]

In June a man signing himself as "S" wrote to a Sacramento newspaper, telling of Lucky Bill's hospitality to emigrants, not because of courtesy but because "he appreciated the personal benefit he was to reap from the road when completed. 'Never mind boys, you're welcome to my free hostile reception this time, but look out! When you come again, I'll make you smart for it.'" S described Thorington as "a 'character' quite by himself. He is an original; one of those geniuses who might have rendered a great and healthy service to society, if in his early days his attention had turned to something beside the speedy consumption of bad whiskey."[16]

In August 1857 the Ormsby faction's enmity against Thorington erupted. Three weeks had passed since Ormsby chaired the meeting seeking a governing body that would protect settlers from transgressors, including "evil-doers among white men." The *San Francisco Herald* published a story on August 27, claiming to give the particulars of "a desperate and bloody fight" at the inaugural celebration of Uncle Billy Rodgers's hotel. (Lucky Bill was a partner in the enterprise, which was named the White House Hotel, but was not mentioned as being in attendance for the dance celebrating its opening.)

The report said Rodgers ordered several young men to leave the hotel when they were "in company with a woman of disreputable character, formerly known in Sacramento as Miss Lamb, alias Baker, lately the mistress of the notorious Luckey Bill, alias Thorington." One of the men, identified as Sidus, obviously Richard Sides, knocked Rodgers down and left the building. The story then described Abernathy taking up the fight. Rodgers shot a gun, "grazing the top of Abernethy's head, taking his scalp completely off." Abernathy threw a rock, striking Rodgers in the eye, "destroying it completely," and Abernathy "completely mash[ed] Rodgers' face by kicking him." Young men then, reportedly, "tore the house down." The story said the town's population was determined to give all disreputable characters notice to leave. Rather than Sides and the trespassers who wreaked havoc, the disreputable individuals were identified as Thorington and Martha Lamb. The article ended, declaring, "Luckey Bill and his mistress will be the first to walk the plank. A Vigilance Committee is to be organized by [the Sides party]."[17]

On September 5, 1867, the *Placerville Mountain Democrat* published a letter from P. H. Lovell, later the telegraph operator at Genoa, disputing the original story. He suggested that the report had been issued by someone intending to defame Rodgers and other "worthy" citizens. Lovell said Rodgers and Abernathy were both fine and that the hotel was open and doing good business.

Two days later the *Sacramento Daily Union* wrote a version of the fight that differed from the original. It said Sides "was under the influence of liquor" and argued with the ticket taker at the door of the hall. Rodgers asked him to leave, but Sides, described as "a large man—young and muscular," struck the older man. Rodgers fired two shots from his revolver before being struck by a rock, causing a severe cut below his eye. Sides's partner Abernathy, who had thrown the rock, wrenched the gun from Rodgers and began beating him with it. Two of Rodgers's friends pulled him away, ending the fight.

Abernathy had a cut on top of his head, and the Sides crowd, said to be six or eight "young, able-bodied men," vowed to take vengeance the next day. Nothing further had occurred in the days since. The writer commented that perhaps the Sides contingent realized they would not look so brave "hunting down an old man of sixty in daylight, whose only offense in this case was the protection of his person, property, and the reputation of his house."[18]

The original article, in the *San Francisco Herald,* said that Sides and the others had been "in company" with "Miss Lamb." Owing to the conclusion of the piece, it is much more likely that they had some kind of confrontation with her or said something untoward about her. The *Herald* called Thorington "notorious," declaring that he and Martha Lamb, and perhaps by association Uncle Billy, were "disreputable characters" against whom "the whole population" was determined to take action. The second letter sketched a portrait of a bullying Sides. Its tenor, describing the start of the fight and the threat of action the next morning, suggests his and his associates' precarious standing with another segment of the community. It seems likely that those citizens were friendly toward Thorington, evinced by residents' comments quoted in earlier chapters. As regarded Rodgers, the newspapers had consistently painted him in a positive light. Before Ormsby's arrival, he had been mentioned more than any other settler, with reports often commenting on his status as a leader. In the *History of Nevada,* Angel identified him as "the famous pioneer and frontiersman."[19]

The conflicting reports reveal the differing allegiances of the citizenry and allow two critical points. Now in the open, the feud pitting Sides, his partner Abernathy, and the others against Uncle Billy Rodgers and Thorington was significant. Furthermore, Martha Lamb, and her relationship with Lucky Bill, was one source of the dispute.

The news that a vigilance committee was being formed by Sides, Abernathy, and others, and that Thorington and Martha Lamb would be "the first to walk the plank," is of utmost importance. The previous year, from May until August, San Francisco's Committee of Vigilance hanged eight individuals, whipped one, deported fourteen to Australia, and banished or ran off scores of others. There was strong support for the movement. A San Francisco abolitionist, speaking at the first Republican convention in June 1856, described what he had seen firsthand as a popular revolution "conducted upon original principals, in the most regular, scientific, beautiful, effective and overwhelming manner."[20]

Philosopher and historian Josiah Royce later termed the San Francisco movement "the Businessmen's Revolution." He identified it as having been composed of the city's Protestant businessmen who originally sought to punish the killers of a crusading newspaper editor and a US marshal. Like others who espoused the group's civil righteousness, he missed or overlooked its hidden economic objective of resolving city land disputes to favor the vigilante leaders. Royce's book on California, written in 1886, declared that the organization's work "was to agitate for a reform in municipal society and politics." Whatever the group's goals, the autumn elections sustained the movement by electing officials sympathetic to the vigilance movement. Royce concluded that "thenceforth, for years, San Francisco was one of the best governed municipalities in the United States."[21]

The fact that the successful reformers had been businessmen, who had taken the law into their own hands, would have interested the entrepreneur and very active civic leader Ormsby. In her book on the San Francisco vigilantes, Nancy Taniguchi points out that the men of the nineteenth century believed that "respectability counted for everything"—not just social status but in business as well, for much depended on one's word being good.[22] Ormsby certainly strove for respectability, and he would have been aware of the approval for what the men of the Committee of Vigilance had done. He formed the

Carson Valley vigilante organization, in league with the Sides clan, and he named it "the Committee."[23]

At the end of September, three weeks after the Rodgers affray, there was further indication of Carson Valley's disorder. It was just a day or so after the second wagon train of recalled Mormons left from Genoa. A man described as a German butcher was shot, suffering a nonfatal wound near the shoulder. The shooting was over who was allowed to occupy Colonel Reese's house. Although he would return, Reese may have accompanied the wagons, as he was not present at the time of the shooting. The report of what occurred appears to have been carried by a traveler or newcomer to the territory. He analyzed the situation, calling it "squatter sovereignty." He pointed out that two sets of officials had been elected, one by the Mormons and their sympathizers and one by the Gentiles. Each refused to recognize their opponents, and since neither was backed by federal troops, neither would take action. He concluded, "The result is that anarchy and crime are very common, and go unpunished. We were requested to assist in arresting some one who had shot the butcher at the Station, but when we asked for an officer, were told by the same person that 'we have neither officers or law here;' and so the matter rests."[24]

Most of the original non-Mormon settlers in western Utah had good relations with the Mormons. Henry Van Sickle commented, "While here in the vallies they were a hard working and prosperous people. They never litigate on any subject but settle all matters in an amicable manner and to this idea can be attributed much of their success in life.... I always [found] their word to be as good as their bond." But more recent arrivals resented the fact that Colonel Reese and the other Mormons had secured much of the prime land and created laws to protect their claims. As US troops marched toward Salt Lake and the war of words between California newspaper editors and church elders escalated, so too did the valley's discord. When the Mormons left and power shifted, Ormsby's campaign to create order gained impetus.[25]

There was a group of thieves in Carson Valley called the Border Ruffians. Their identity was kept secret, but it was rumored that one was the rancher and hotel owner named Luther "Lute" Olds. He and his two brothers had reportedly come west with Thorington from Michigan, and they were among the earliest settlers in the valley.

Olds had a ranch near Thorington's Fredricksburg ranch, and he owned the Cotton Hotel alongside the emigrant trail that ran through the property. At one time he served as a supervisor in Utah's Carson County, and his residence served as a polling place during elections. In contrast, the Border Ruffians reputedly used a canyon across the emigrant trail from his ranch to hide stock stolen from emigrants. Once the animals' owners had continued their journey, and the livestock had been fattened up, they would be led back out for sale to others passing through.

When the vigilantes arrested Lucky Bill Thorington, they also arrested Olds, his brother-in-law Isaac Gandy, and Calvin Austin, a hired hand who was rumored to be a horse thief from California. Charges against the three were of minor consequence. Gandy and Austin disappeared from the histories. Olds ended up living many years in Carson Valley, and his daughter owned property in Genoa well into the twentieth century. Still, Olds's reputation as an outlaw stuck in some circles. In 1940 Elzyette Knott Selby, daughter of Thorington's friend Elzy Knott, and granddaughter of the mill builder Thomas Knott, commented, "Lute Olds was a bigger horse thief than Lucky Bill could ever hope to be.... I think the Carey's were in with Lute. Their ranches were all adjoining. My mother said Lucky Bill was better than all the folks around Horse Thief Canyon." In her history of Carson Valley, published in 1972, Grace Dangberg also mentioned Olds being one of the Border Ruffians. Nevertheless, as Tennessee, living there at the time, wrote in the *San Francisco Herald*, the only crime of which Olds had ever been accused was "entertaining those 'suspected' of horse stealing."

Lute Olds had two brothers, John and David, who each had land claims in the valley. Together the Olds brothers controlled 960 acres of prime ranch land. Several years later, in 1863, David Olds was elected to the first board of commissioners representing Carson Valley in the newly formed Douglas County, Nevada Territory. He, too, was destined to become a player in the Lucky Bill Thorington story, marrying Martha Lamb three years after Thorington's death.

Near the first of November in 1857, there was a murder on the Carson River in California's Alpine County, southeast of Carson Valley. The *Sacramento Daily Union* reported: "[The murder] was committed by a gang of desperadoes who infest that region, and who thought he was possessed of some knowledge of their crimes. The citizens of that vicinity have concluded to organize for the purpose of defending their lives and property against the incursions of this gang of desperate scoundrels." Whether the suspected desperadoes were the Boarder Ruffians is not clear, but presumably the citizens said to be organizing were Ormsby and the Committee, as the group's formation had been discussed in the newspapers six weeks earlier.[26]

Another murder, one that took place across the Sierra, would have significant ramifications in Carson Valley. On Thursday, December 10, 1857, the *Daily Alta California* carried a small item at the bottom of column 1, page 1. It told of the murder of a man named Snelling, the leading citizen at Snelling in Merced County, California, the hamlet having been named after him. William Coombs Edwards had been identified as the murderer. He had escaped, and the Freemasons, of which Snelling had been a member, were offering a $1,500 reward for Edwards's capture. The murderer had fled east over the Sierra. In Carson Valley Edwards sought out Lucky Bill Thorington, a man who had a reputation for helping all who asked. Edwards told the gambler of the killing, saying it had been self-defense, something he consistently maintained.

Edwards wished to leave a sack of money with Thorington while he traveled to Honey Lake Valley, where he had friends. They were former Texans, as apparently was he. Without counting the money, which was later reported to be gold worth some $1,000, Thorington buried the sack under a willow tree on his ranch. Edwards, calling himself Bill Coombs, continued on to Honey Lake to the ranch of Rough Elliott and Junius Brutus Gilpin.

Also in December, an unnamed writer in a California newspaper again demeaned Uncle Billy Rodgers, using the appellation "Colonel" rather than "Uncle." The article concerned the men he had brought to defend settlers against the Indians, saying Rodgers's "army" had been disbanded. The announcement used quotation marks around the term *army,* seemingly to disparage Rodgers's effort. It then posed a question: "Wonder if any bills will be presented to pay for this senseless expedition?" On December 16, the *San Francisco Herald's* correspondent Tennessee responded, "I am very sorry to perceive that some evil disposed person has been misrepresenting the course of Uncle Billy Rodgers. In justice to an upright and honorable old man, I beg leave to correct some impressions you have.... In short, I know that no family in this place would feel secure if Uncle Billy's men were not here." The controversy died because it had become apparent that the treaty with the Washoes would hold. Some of Rodgers's crew had already abandoned the project, while others were dismissed. What the statement against Rodgers actually did was spur the contentiousness between the anti-Mormons, including Sides and Abernathy, who were openly enemies of Rodgers, and those like Tennessee, who, as future correspondence would reveal, opposed the anti-Mormons. By February 1, 1858, everything was reported to be quiet in Carson Valley. It was the calm before the storm.[27]

The following week the feud between the anti-Mormons and the old guard began heating up. In the paper on February 8, 1858, Tennessee scoffed that a public meeting had been held in Genoa "for the purpose of promoting moral habits among the people." He said that following it, "the people had more quarreling and fighting among themselves than they ever had before since my arrival. Today a man had his hand nearly cut off by another and tomorrow another person is to be tried for slander."[28]

It is unclear toward which individuals the irony in Tennessee's report is directed, but an educated guess would include Major Ormsby. As evinced by his actions regarding the Mormon issue, Indian disputes, and territorial government, Ormsby was a leader in such matters. Tennessee later identified Ormsby as his enemy, and the correspondent was friends with Uncle Billy Rodgers and Thorington. He was one of only a couple of men who would hazard testifying for Thorington at the vigilante trial.

Snowshoe Thompson, packing the mail and a quantity of gold from new diggings, arrived in Placerville on February 12. He reported that Ormsby had a new quartz mill that was now running in Carson County, and it was off to an auspicious start. The expressman also brought news of the knifing incident mentioned by Tennessee: "A difficulty occurred at Genoa, between two men named Thornton and Sisco, in which the latter was severely wounded with a knife, having had his hand nearly cut off." The Thornton in this story was Lucky Bill's son, Jerome. Many years later pioneer D.R. Hawkins wrote: "At a later date I saw Dr. Daggett on the same spot save the life of Cisco whose wrist was nearly severed by Jerome Thorington with a Bowie knife."[29]

At the end of February, Tennessee sent word from Carson Valley that "Chief Winnemuck" had informed the people of Genoa that two white men, whom the Paiutes believed to be murderers, had stopped with the Indians. Why the Paiutes had come to Genoa rather than give word to their neighbors, the Honey Lakers with whom they had a treaty, goes unreported. Lucky Bill Thorington recruited citizens to go after the suspects. On March 7 the *San Francisco Herald* reported: "Lucky Bill, with a posse of five or six men, had started in company with Winnemuck, the Paiute chief, in search of the two white desperadoes, of whom we made mention in Tuesday's issue." It was out of character for Thorington, whose credo was generally "live and let live," to raise a posse to track criminals. His motive seems to have been revealed three and a half months later when the vigilantes arrested him. At that time, members of the posse told their versions of what had happened, as did the murderer from Merced County, William Coombs Edwards. Apparently, Thorington led the group, at least in part, to gain an opportunity to speak with Edwards.

The posse that left Carson Valley comprised two parties: B. Cherry and Jack Howard in one; Thorington, James Menofee, and Ab. Smith in the other. They were searching for men named Stewart and Beasley. According to Cherry, he and Howard were not going expecting to find Stewart and Beasley with the Paiutes. They went to try to find the murderer from Merced County. The Masonic Lodge and people of Snelling were still offering the $1,500, and they had notified Masons on both sides of the Sierra to keep an eye out for him.

When the five posse members reached the Paiute camp, they found that the men they were after had gone to Honey Lake. Cherry reported that they were low on provisions, went directly there, and found and arrested Beasley. He said that Thorington directed them to take the prisoner to a nearby ranch, saying he would seek out friends to get money enough to buy supplies to get back to Carson Valley.[30]

Thorington left the others, riding to the ranch of Solomon Perrin, another former resident of Carson Valley. There he borrowed a fresh horse and rode to Rough Elliott and Gilpin's house at Honey Lake. A great number of the valley's residents were visiting when Thorington arrived. He sought out Bill Edwards, known there as Coombs, borrowing $15 and meeting privately with him beneath a large pine near the cabin. After a time, Edwards called Gilpin over, showing him a letter Thorington had received from Merced County. Both Gilpin and Elliott had been told by Edwards that he had killed Snelling in self-defense. The letter said that people now believed Edwards was in Honey Lake Valley. Thorington had come to warn Edwards. When Thorington left, Edwards rode with him perhaps a mile and a half, then returned.

At Perrin's Lucky Bill offered to pay for the use of the horse, saying he had no money earlier but had seen Coombs and obtained some. He got back to the others at nine or ten that night. At the Thorington trial, Cherry testified that when asked, "What luck?" Thorington replied, "'Good,' that he met up there a good many friends; that when he told them his name, they were ready to give him any amount of money... that he refused, only taking $15.... [N]othing more was said that night, only that the boys up there were a brave set of Texas boys and in this connection spoke of Elliott, Coombs, Gilpin, etc." Thorington had no idea that a killing by one of the boys would soon be the cause of the others pursuing revenge against Thorington himself.[31]

After eight days, Thorington and the posse returned. Newspapers said they had no success, never mentioning Beasley, the man Cherry said they arrested.

In Genoa the anti-Mormons' most implacable members were soon to take vigilante action as the Committee. Although the organization had been talked about since the previous September, Nevada writer Effie Mona Mack thought that they began to meet in March 1858, so it may have been that they met while Thorington was out of the valley. H. Hamlin wrote: "There were 19 members of this secret organization that had as its secret meeting place an upstairs room of the home of a Mrs. Haines, later Mrs. Singleton, and later married a third time. The home, now gone, was in Genoa."[32]

Thomas Dimsdale wrote a book in 1866 about contemporaneous vigilante actions in Montana mining camps. The book focused, in particular, on the capture and execution of Henry Plummer and his gang of road agents. The Montanans, like the vigilante groups preceding it, saw themselves as working for the salvation of the community; in the West, the line separating the two sides of the law was tissue thin. In Bannack, Montana, Plummer, the leader of the outlaws, was the sheriff; his deputies were members of his gang. One of the first men San Francisco's

Vigilance Committee of 1856 hanged was James Casey, a city supervisor. In Carson Valley the key figures who would be arrested, Thorington and Luther Olds, were prominent businessmen and owners of large tracts of land.[33]

Dimsdale stressed that secrecy was critical to the workings of a vigilance society because intelligence was as easily obtained by the criminal as by the law abiding. That Carson Valley's Committee had formed was public knowledge. And although its membership was kept secret, it was known that Ormsby and Sides took leading roles. It was likely that Abernathy, named in the brawl against Uncle Billy, and Sides's other partner, John M. Baldwin, were involved. How many of the Committee's early actions were covert is unclear, as, shortly after their first meeting, Thorington and eighteen others formed the antivigilantes, their number the exact equal of the vigilantes. The antivigilantes believed that by standing together, they could thwart the use of force by the Ormsby-Sides faction.[34]

In San Francisco there were examples from the previous year of individuals standing up to the vigilantes. William Tecumseh Sherman, at the time a banker and the head of the California State Militia, called the organization "irresponsible," and the Reverend William A. Scott of San Francisco's Calvary Church wrote a letter that was "highly critical" of the Committee's actions. Neither criticism had the desired effect. Sherman resigned his militia post when he discovered a great majority of those serving under him supported the vigilantes. Reverend Scott was hanged in effigy from a lamppost across the street from his church. A third instance of opposition resulted in a notorious confrontation. David Terry, the California Supreme Court chief justice, was one of the West's ablest and most feared men. When vigilantes attempted to arrest a witness seeking Terry's protection, the chief justice pulled a bowie knife from under his coat, stabbing a vigilante, severing the carotid artery in his neck. The vigilantes overpowered and arrested Terry. Somehow the wounded man survived, allowing the Committee to save face by releasing Terry after weeks of drama.[35]

There were minor altercations in Genoa in early April 1858, signaling a general unease. At a ball, a fight broke out in which bowie knives were used freely, although no one was seriously hurt. Colonel Rodgers was involved in another incident involving stones. Stone throwing seems to have been a fairly frequent method of combat in Carson Valley, even though Henry Van Sickle said everyone carried a gun or had one handy. This fight was with a man named Cloud who, predictably, worked with Ormsby running pack trains over the Sierra. Snowshoe Thompson, who carried the news, suggested that the incident amounted to nothing serious. In mid-month two men were said to have gotten drunk and become involved in an altercation using knives and stones, but it did not amount to any injuries serious enough to be reported.[36]

There also was news in April that the last of the Mormons wanted to leave the valley but were fearful that the anti-Mormons would not allow it. Negotiations between the federal government and Brigham Young had been taking place since February. On April 12 Alfred Cumming, appointed by President Buchanan, arrived in Salt Lake City to replace Young as governor. US troops were still garrisoned in their encampment east of Salt Lake, and, although issues were not fully resolved for another two months, the discussions ensured the dispute would not end in warfare. At Genoa Major Ormsby again stepped forward, assuring the Mormons, who wanted to leave, safe passage, and their wagons pulled away.[37]

Business between Carson Valley and Placerville was booming. At the end of April, a newspaper announced the arrival of John Child and Uncle Billy Rodgers with twenty-five pack animals, bringing the total to one hundred animals in two days. This mention of Rodgers was the last that would occur for many weeks. He left for San Francisco, from there to travel down the coast on business. In mid-June, when Honey Lakers stormed Genoa to join members of the Committee and arrest his friend Thorington, Rodgers would be far away in California.[38]

CHAPTER SIX

MILITIAS, MOBS, AND VIGILANTES

In the nineteenth century, Americans' constructs regarding Native Americans centered on the idea that Native Americans were savages, inferior to the civilized emigrants. The Indians were dangerous and to be feared. For many frontiersmen, killing Indians was a "coming of age" experience. A case in point was the incident when Joseph Walker's party surrounded and opened fire on curious Paiutes at the Humboldt River in 1833, described at the beginning of chapter 1. It was seen by party members as valuable practice. Zenas Leonard, the company secretary, noted that Walker unleashed his young charges because in such circumstances, nothing was equal to a good start. Leonard explained further, "A number of our men had never been engaged in any fighting with the Indians, and were anxious to try their skill."[1]

"The Pathfinder" John Charles Frémont wrote about his experiences crossing the Great Basin and exploring the Far West's uncharted mountainous terrain in the 1840s. He commented on fighting Indians, before he described a nighttime battle in the deep woods between his troops and a "hostile and treacherous" band in California's Shasta country. The government did not appreciate such combat, although it required "the utmost skill and courage," more, he argued, than "milder civilized warfare." He explained: "This Indian fighting is always close, incurring more certain risk of life and far more sanguinary, than in the ordinary contests between civilized troops. Every Indian fights with intention, and for all that is in him; he waits for no orders, but has every effort concentrated on his intention to kill."[2]

Beginning in the last half of the twentieth century, researchers and historians concluded that the genocide perpetrated against Indians was committed "by the white population at large as an extension of their popular will." The first California historical demographer, Serburne Cook, said, "Since the quickest and easiest way to get rid of [the Northern California Indian] was to kill him off, this procedure was adopted for some years."[3]

In 1850 the course was set for the settlers of the Eastern Sierra. James Calhoun was the Indian agent overseeing Utah Territory. Calhoun distinguished between Indian tribes, some being "great tribes," others not worthy to live. He explained to the commissioner of Indian affairs that the Paiutes, inhabiting the country east of the Sierra Nevada, existed on food consisting of "roots, vermin, insects of all kinds, and everything that creeps, crawls, swims, flies, or bounds, they may chance to overtake; and when these resources fail them, and they can find no stranger, they feed upon their own children." Spreading the lie about cannibalizing children led him to his official determination: "Such a people should not be permitted to live within the limits of the United States, and must be elevated in the scale of human existence, or exterminated."[4]

The polity had no effective strategy to deal with calls for extermination. A number of politicians, as well as many newcomers to the region, agreed with Calhoun, subscribing to the adage "The only good Indian is a dead Indian."

In their book *Sierra-Nevada Lakes,* written in the middle of the twentieth century, George and Bliss Hinkle described the difficulties confronting the men living in Honey Lake Valley a hundred years earlier. The writers noted the loose federation of settlers and Paiutes to the east, while describing the Washoes, to the south, as "thieving and treacherous" and the Pit River Indians and Modoc, to the north, as "extremely hostile." Furthermore, there were the internal dangers created by certain of those who came with the influx of settlers: road agents, professional gunmen, and rustlers. The Hinkles wrote that no other community of early California or Nevada more closely resembled the conception of the Wild West portrayed in early-day movies. Specifically, they stressed that all the Honey Lakers wore six guns and carried bowie knives and that no man rode away from his residence without his rifle.[5]

The sympathy for the pioneers in their violent dealings with Indians is reflected in the early-day histories of Northern California. In 1882 Clarence L. Smith and Frank T. Gilbert published Fariss and Smith's history of Plumas, Lassen, and Sierra Counties. They described how the colonists had to protect their families against attacks and depredations by Indians. While admitting that the Native Americans might have had reasons for their actions, the writers, with unwitting irony, dismissed white incidents of brutality and California's campaign of genocide against Native peoples:

> That the Indians on the frontier have not always been treated properly, and have frequently been grossly deceived and abused, is a fact well known to all; but this does not excuse them for their acts of barbarity and horrible cruelty, which are accounted for only by their inherent bloodthirsty disposition. Even in case the savages were simply avenging real or imaginary injuries, the innocent settler who sees his wife and children in deadly peril is comforted but little by knowing that some other white man has wronged the savages that are now seeking the death of him and his loved ones. All that he can see is that he and those who cling to him for protection are threatened with a horrible death by a fiendish, treacherous, and relentless foe. This was the condition of the pioneer settler, and it is no wonder that he fought the savage and pursued and exterminated them whenever they were guilty of committing outrages upon himself or his neighbors.[6]

A.M. Fairfield's *A Pioneer History of Lassen County, California,* written in 1912, traced the remaking of Honey Lake Valley into an American outpost and then a bustling community. While researching his book, he interviewed a number of the Eastern Sierra pioneers still alive in the first decade of the twentieth century. Their casually dismissive attitudes toward Indians and violence allows firsthand insight into the Fariss and Smith interpretation. Fairfield recorded several incidents wherein Americans happened upon innocent Indians and killed them. He reported, "In many cases, before a massacre by the Indians took place, one or more Indians had been killed for the fun of it; and the savages wreaked their vengeance as soon as possible, perhaps on innocent people.... In numberless cases a little more justice on the part of the whites would have saved a great deal of trouble and bloodshed."[7]

As with Fariss and Smith, in places the irony of Fairfield's own observations escaped him. While recognizing cases of Americans initiating the bloodshed, it is the Indians who are identified as "savages." The term was used a dozen times throughout Fairfield's book, serving generally as a synonym for *Indians.* Mirroring Fariss and Smith, and prefiguring the Hinkles, Fairfield used the casual references to Indians as "thieving" and "treacherous," whether they were committing depredations, engaging in warfare, or being abused.

Scholars attribute four main motives to genocide: convenience, when killing takes precedence over compensation or accommodation; revenge, to teach the futility of resistance or disobedience; simple fear; and "fear of pollution," or threat to the purity of the stronger group. Any of the four can be attributed at times to the Honey Lake militiamen's lethal approach to dealing with Native Americans. At different times, each might explain an instance when the Rangers happened upon Indian camps and killed everyone.[8]

In organized killing, corpses convey messages. Indians often mutilated those they killed. Honey Lakers left Native Americans they killed unburied, and scalps were collected by both sides. In one battle, at Goose Lake on April 18, 1858, seventeen Honey Lake Rangers, looking for stolen livestock, fought perhaps thirty or forty Indians. The story was told some fifty years after it took place by two participants, Fred Hines and William Dow. Even though the white settlers were outnumbered three or four to one, they held a disproportionate advantage. They were using rifles and pistols. The Indians were using arrows with stone points, although they may have had one gun, as Hines and Dow thought they heard a couple of shots. They told of one brave Indian who had not run, even though all he had to fight with was an arrow with no tip. He was shot and fell against a tree. That Indian's scalp was one of seventeen the Honey Lakers collected. The settlers had recovered only one stolen animal, but, Fairfield chronicled, "They made a good many of what they then considered good Indians, and so were well satisfied with their trip."[9]

The battle had taken place because Indians had stolen five horses and three mules from two ranches at Honey Lake. Captain William Weatherlow, his lieutenant U. J. Tutt, Rough Elliott, Junius Brutus Gilpin, Hines, Dow, and ten more Honey Lakers formed a posse that spent several days pursuing the thieves. At one point, when they were running low on provisions, Elliott and Alec Chapman, another quick-tempered man, almost fought over whether to follow the trail or turn back. Two nights before the big battle, just at dusk, they used a spyglass and saw four Indians setting nets for ducks in a lake. They thought these might be the ones they were tracking, so they crossed the lake and under cover of darkness snuck up to where the Indians were camped on the east side of a steep ledge. At dawn, when one of the Indians rose and began stirring the campfire, the Honey Lakers opened fire. One of the victims rose up when he was hit, and a posse member, using a double-barreled shotgun, shot him again. The four Indians, three men and a woman, were killed. The writer commented, "They were Pit river or Dixie valley, Indians, but not the ones they were following. The white men thought, however, that they deserved their fate, for there were marrow bones and fresh rawhides in their camp. The party then went back to camp, and after breakfast took the trail and followed it around the east side of the lake."[10]

The casual racism in the telling and the offhanded viciousness of these incidents as recounted in Fairfield's book are salient lessons regarding white men of that era in that place. A man named Harper told Fairfield of another incident that took place in 1862. Twelve or fifteen men went to Gravelly Ford, hoping Indians, who seemed to know, would show them where there were gold nuggets. After a few days of traveling, three of the Indians slipped away in the night, and Harper did not know if the party had killed the fourth or not. When the men came on a group of Indians fishing, they killed perhaps ten or twelve and scalped them. They took the scalps with them into Star City, and some of the crowd wore them on their belts around town.[11]

As for the act of scalping, it had been used by Americans when state-sponsored scalp bounties were offered in colonial times. It was in widespread use by the mountain men and trappers and carried forward into the 1850s. Historian Madley notes, "In California, between 1846 and 1873, scalping was an almost exclusively non-Indian practice, inflicted on California Indians. Scalping served as a way to inventory killing, collect macabre trophies, and express a profound disdain for victims." Madley noted that collecting Indians' severed heads served similar purposes. When the perpetrators were not seeking extermination, scalping and beheading could also serve as messages intended to terrorize survivors. In 1856 James Beckwourth, an African American and a significant figure in the western fur trade, gave a gruesome explanation for why risks were taken to scalp a dead opponent during battle: "Scalps are taken off with greater ease while the bodies are warm."[12]

Fairfield lived for many years in Lassen County, and he had an obvious affection for the land and its pioneers. At one point he uses a lighthearted tone to tell how Honey Lake's early community was perceived: "You and I, kind reader, know that very few people excepting good ones lived in the land of the Never Sweats at that time. But the best of people are sometimes slandered, and evil tongues must have been spreading false rumors about those good folks." Fairfield then told of the time when a wagon train was crossing the plains: "People who claimed to know the country said that if they went through [Honey Lake] they were likely to be robbed or killed, or at least have their horses stolen. One man in the train who had been in California before, said he did not believe the Honey Lakers were any worse than the Indians and he took the road leading to this valley." The outcome, of course, was that when the rest of the train reached their destination, they found that the man had gone safely through Honey Lake, arriving three weeks earlier.[13]

Honey Laker W.T.C. Elliott was nicknamed "Rough." It is said he was called that because he came from the mining camp of Rough and Ready. Fairfield commented: "He could be very polite and 'smooth' if he saw fit to do it." During the winter early in 1858, Rough Elliott argued with J.H. "Blackhawk" Ferry, the town blacksmith. A few days later, Elliott, who was younger, very powerful, and subscribed to a violent doctrine of honor in combat, backed Ferry over the anvil in his shop and "beat him up considerably." Later, when Elliott's dog wandered into Ferry's shop, the blacksmith went after it with a gun. Elliott was nearby. Seeing Ferry, he jumped behind a stump, and the two men emptied their pistols at one another. With Elliott trapped and out of ammunition, Ferry took up his rifle. Before he could come out of the shop, boys from the mill grabbed him, stopping the fight and almost certainly saving Elliott's life. Elliott's role in other, similar, incidents would lead most to conclude that regardless of whether his nickname came from a previous residence or he could be "smooth" at times, the name fit.

Chauncey Noteware, the state of Nevada's future secretary of state, was certainly more mannerly and trustworthy than Elliott. It was Noteware who would transcribe the testimony at Thorington's vigilante trial. Perhaps aware of the San Francisco Vigilance Committee's practice of executing the accused after secret tribunals, Thorington asked Noteware to take down the evidence. He apparently chose him because

Noteware would be seen as an unbiased reporter. After the turn of the century, Noteware composed a statement concerning Thorington. In it, speaking of himself in the third person, he stated: "The testimony was taken by C.N. Noteware at the request of Thorington, who declared at the time that he was bound to be executed by the vigilantes, and he wanted the evidence upon which he would be convicted published."[14]

The trial transcript was published in the *Placerville Tri-Weekly Register* a few days after the trial. It was read and used by Myron Angel in his account, published in 1881. Although the complete transcription seems to no longer exist, part of the testimony survives, reprinted from the *Register* by the *Sacramento Daily Union* on June 25, 1875. The witnesses' accounts and Noteware's statement, as well as Fairfield's subsequent interviews with several of those involved, allow an overview of events leading up to the trial.

When Bill Coombs Edwards killed Snelling and ran from Merced County, he moved to Honey Lake, staying with Elliott and Gilpin. Sometime in April 1858, about a month after Thorington left the posse to warn Edwards that his whereabouts were suspected, Edwards moved. He went to live with John Mullen and his hired man Asa Snow. Mullen had a few cattle and was said to be proficient at picking up other people's calves.[15]

A short time after they began living together, Edwards and Mullins committed a murder in order to steal a herd of cattle. When the Mormons had been preparing to leave Carson Valley the previous fall, the religionists sold the herd to two men from Honey Lake Valley. The cattle were said to be the finest ever brought to Honey Lake. Henry Gordier, a Frenchman of considerable means, took most of them. Noteware wrote an account of what happened next. He noted that Gordier's brother was a ne'er-do-well, an alcoholic who sponged off him. Gordier was known to have said that if he could sell his cattle, he would leave the country and his brother would never find him. Noteware reported: "Edwards then wrote to Thorington to dig up his money and put enough with it to buy Gordier's cattle and come up himself and they would buy the cattle. Thorington answered by saying that he did not have the money to do it." Noteware continued his account, saying that Edwards and Mullins devised their scheme shortly thereafter. The two would forge a bill of sale for the cattle and kill Gordier. Because the Frenchman had said he would secretly leave the country, people would think that is what occurred.[16]

Fairfield then takes up the story. Edwards and Mullen sought out Gordier. They told him he had a sick cow across the river and offered to take him to it. "They struck the river a little too high up and turned and went down it. They were riding side by side and Mullen dropped back a little and shot the Frenchman through the head." Upon taking possession of Gordier's cattle, Mullen and Edwards told neighbors that Gordier had sold out, met a friend, and left for France. Mullen's hired hand Snow moved into Gordier's cabin. Gordier's alcoholic brother contacted some of the Honey Lakers. He insisted that Gordier would never have left without telling him.

When Weatherlow and the company that had been in the fight and had collected seventeen scalps at Goose Lake returned, the community held a dance. There were three Mormon women from a wagon train, and the Honey Lakers managed to get three or four more for the occasion. Having so few women there allowed abundant time for talk. It was around the first of May 1858, and the main topic was Gordier's sudden departure.[17]

The day after the dance, one of the Honey Lakers took Edwards aside, telling him something was not right in the Frenchman's disappearance and that many of the boys believed the incident required further investigation. Edwards and Mullen left Honey Lake that day. Their flight incited even stronger suspicions.

Days earlier, men camping near the Susan River had heard an unaccountable gunshot and seen a fire. They now came forward, suggesting the area be searched. A Mrs. Coulthurst, the wife of Gordier's ex-partner, later said that she had dreamed about the location of the Frenchman's body and told the men where to look. Whether prompted by common or uncommon perception, several Honey Lakers now investigated the site of a fire near the river. There they found charred metal buttons, as if clothing had been burned, and dried blood that was deemed human. Using a hook on a pole in a nearby hole in the river, the men soon produced the decomposing body tied around a rock.[18]

The chief suspects, Edwards and Mullen, were gone, but others were still in the area. The Honey Lakers focused first on Rough Elliott and his partner, Gilpin. These men knew the accused well, having housed the one who went by the name of Coombs. When confronted, they admitted knowing that Edwards's name was not Coombs and that it was he who had killed Snelling in Merced County. However, Edwards had insisted the killing was in self-defense, and they denied knowing anything about the immediate crime. It was suggested that they could be cleared of suspicion if they assisted in investigating the case. Elliott left immediately to begin an investigation in Carson Valley. Gilpin would follow in a few days. John Neale, a cattle rancher who had moved to Honey Lake Valley the previous year, took particular interest in the case. He stayed behind to pursue the case at Honey Lake. It was mid-May.

On Thursday, June 10, 1858, the *Daily Alta California* ran a small announcement at the bottom of a column that preceded its advertising section:

> HANGING IN HONEY LAKE VALLEY.—We are indebted to Mr. Whiting, of Whiting's Express, for the information that a man named Snow was hung in Honey Lake Valley Monday last, by the citizens. He confessed having been accessory to the murder of the Frenchman, some weeks since, in the valley. He implicates two other men, now supposed to be in the lower country.—Marysville News.

The report illustrates one role of the era's press: spreading information intended to justify a deed after the fact. Snow had indeed been hanged, but he had confessed nothing nor implicated anyone. He had not been an accessory. The Honey Lake sheriff, Orlando Streshly, reported that Edwards later told him: "There was no one present but Mullen and I when we killed [Gordier] and we would not trust Snow with a secret."[19]

Fairfield would not vouch for the information that came from some of those involved in the hanging. They claimed Snow was an assumed name, that he had killed a man before coming to Honey Lake. Fairfield commented, "It may have been a case of 'Give a dog a bad name and hang him.'" He reported simply: "[Snow] denied knowing anything about the murder of Gordier."[20] Accounts of those who participated in the hanging and those involved in what came next disagreed on many points, but none said that Snow confessed anything.

Fairfield's compilation of information from those present led him to write that John Neale and a crowd from the upper end of the valley went to the Breed cabin to interrogate Snow. The investigation lasted into the night. Snow insisted on his innocence and was defiant, daring them to hang him. They took him two-thirds of a mile from the cabin to two pine trees. One of the pines had a large limb growing at a right angle with the trunk, some twelve or fifteen feet from the ground. They probably thought they could scare a confession out of him. They strung him up and let him down, but he continued to curse and defy them. They pulled him up again, let him down, and questioned him, and he maintained that he knew nothing. They pulled him up a third time, and this time when they let him down, he was dead.[21]

R. W. Young, who was part of the crowd, allowed a different slant in his view of the hanging and the victim. He noted that Snow was a very delicate man, far gone with consumption. There had been no evidence against him, said Young, except a rope under his bunk. "Some considered [the rope] looked suspicious and afterward masked themselves and took poor Snow in the dead of night and hanged him I always thot they murdered poor Snow."[22]

When suspicions about Gordier's disappearance arose and Edwards and Mullen had separated, Edwards took Mullen's horse, Bald Hornet. Mullen apparently thought the horse a liability, for it was a thousand pound, bald-faced, chestnut sorrel, a racehorse known up and down the Sierra. Getting rid of the horse seems to have helped, as Mullen left the country and was never heard from again. Edwards rode Bald Hornet to the mountains above Genoa, secretly seeking out Lucky Bill Thorington.

By the time Edwards approached Thorington, news of Gordier's murder had already reached Carson Valley. Edwards's intention was to collect the money he had left with Lucky Bill and to sell Bald Hornet. Thorington was suspicious. Noteware quoted him and gave Edwards's response: "'Edwards if you had any hand in killing Gordier, and palming yourself on me, you are the most ungrateful wretch alive!' Edwards answered him that he had no part in the killing of Gordier."[23]

Even with Edwards's denial, Thorington was reluctant to allow Edwards to stay around him. At the trial Edwards testified that Lucky Bill told him that he had befriended him once when in trouble but now thought it best that he just ride away. Part of Thorington's hesitancy to help stemmed from the fact that some Honey Lakers had been seeking Edwards and had now discovered Coombs and Edwards were the same man. Knowing Lucky Bill to have been his friend, they realized the gambler had helped him evade them all these months.[24] The same case could have been made against Elliott and Gilpin, with whom Edwards had lived, but, once they agreed to investigate Thorington's role, that issue was not pursued.

Rumor had it that the Honey Lakers now not only wanted to arrest Edwards but also wanted to settle up with his accomplice Thorington. At the Thorington trial Richard N. Allen, the attorney known as Tennessee, told the assembly, "Thorington has told me on many occasions that he was willing to go before a legal tribunal and be tried; I have heard from Thorington and Peter Vallely that the people of Honey Lake Valley had collected, and were in the vicinity for the purpose of arresting Thorington, and taking him to Honey Lake Valley, and hanging him without judge or jury, and I believed it at the time."[25]

Despite his qualms, Lucky Bill helped Edwards. The day after meeting with him, Thorington sent his son, Jerome, to Merced to collect a debt owed to Edwards. He also had Jerome ride to Marysville to alert Mullen of the excitement at Honey Lake. Jerome collected $350 and a mare in partial payment of the debt owed Edwards ($600 more was owed), but never made contact with Mullen.

Edwards testified that after his meeting with Lucky Bill, he stayed in the mountains. He came down once or twice at night to Lute Olds's hotel, where, because he was Thorington's friend, he purchased food on credit. Once, outside Olds's place, Edwards met with Lucky Bill so he could get the money Jerome brought from Merced. Jerome Thorington testified that Edwards planned to go to either Salt Lake City or Valparaiso, Chile. One of Olds's hands, Cal Austin, who Jerome said was known to have been "run off the East Fork for stealing horses in California," intended to accompany Edwards if he went to Salt Lake but did not have enough money if he chose to go to Valparaiso.

When Rough Elliott arrived in Carson Valley to begin his investigation, he received a cool reception. People believed he had come to try to arrest Thorington and take him back to Honey Lake. The third night after his arrival, a friend of Lucky Bill's named McBride approached him. Elliott reported that McBride said that Thorington was willing to give himself up, "as he did not believe they could prove enough against him to convict him of anything criminal in any Court of Justice; that

Thorington was willing to be tried by the citizens of Carson Valley, but would not go to Honey Lake Valley." Elliott attempted to convince McBride that his intentions were friendly, and, eventually, he was taken to Thorington's house.

During their meeting Thorington told Elliott he believed Edwards was innocent. At the trial Elliott testified, "Thorington told me he did not believe that Edwards was guilty of the murder of Gordier; he appeared at the time to have but little confidence in me."

Shortly after this meeting, Elliott's housemate, Gilpin, arrived in Genoa with a plan to entrap Thorington. At the trial Gilpin reported: "I tried to gain his confidence through pretense of having stolen a horse from Honey Lake Valley; I claimed his protection; in this I failed in a great measure; I had hurt my mare, or the one I was riding, and Thorington offered me fifty dollars to pay the damages...and to return the mare to Mr. Johnson to whom she belongs."

Elliott's insistence that he wished to help their friend finally won Lucky Bill over. Thorington took Elliott to meet with Edwards. The three men met at the ford of a slough near Hiram Mott's field, holding a rambling conversation that spanned several hours. Edwards commented, "There was something said of almost everything." One of the topics was raising money to get Edwards out of the territory.

Rough Elliott told of a scheme that he proposed wherein he and Gilpin would pretend to have a gun battle with Edwards and capture Bald Hornet while Edwards escaped. Then they would sell the racehorse and secure the money for Edwards. It was mentioned that perhaps a third party should accompany the two Honey Lakers to act as a witness. Elliott said, "Thorington then suggested that Barber be this third person, as it was well known that he was an enemy of his, and would give good color to the transaction and free him, Thorington, from all suspicion in the transaction." The conversation then turned. There would be danger to Edwards if Barber got too close to him. Edwards assured the others that if Barber got too close, he would kill him. Elliott said:

> When talking over this arrangement, Thorington suggested that if any man was to be killed by taking the horse, that among several men in the Valley here, say three, he would rather it would be Maj. Ormsby or Rich. Sides, no matter which; he then suggested

> that Maj. Ormsby go along anyway; that he would give money to have him killed, anyhow; Edwards then said, send him out if he wanted him killed, and he would kill him, sure; I then suggested that it would not do to create any more difficulty at present; Thorington appeared to concur with me; we finally concluded that Barber should be the man to go along, and that no killing should be done unless in case of emergency.

We do not have Thorington's version of this conversation, so it is impossible to know the tenor of his comment. Was it a serious proposal or idle talk? Regardless, the statement was to become the source of rumors spread in newspapers about Thorington trying to assassinate Ormsby. Further, it was used to justify the gambler's hanging.

Because of confusion, the plan was carried out in somewhat different fashion than was discussed. Jerome Thorington was involved as the third man instead of Barber. Snowshoe Thompson, coming from Genoa, gave an account picked up by the *Sacramento Daily Union* on June 14: "The notorious Bill Edwards who murdered Snelling has been around here the last four days, and has been pursued by a number of persons. Yesterday they found him on the trail above Daggett's and captured his horse. They shot six or eight times at Edwards, he returning their fire twice. He fled to the mountains and got away. His horse proved to be the celebrated racehorse 'Bald Hornet.'"

The plan to sell Edwards's horse would not be carried out. Rough Elliott had been keeping Ormsby apprised of the situation. Word had been sent to Honey Lake. The morning after Thompson's report, thirty riders from the lake, with others swelling the number along the way, had arrived in Genoa. There they joined forces with Ormsby and the vigilantes.

CHAPTER SEVEN

JUDGMENT

Within twenty-four hours of receiving word that Edwards was in Carson Valley, the Honey Lakers, many of whom were members of the Honey Lake Rangers, were ready to ride. Elliott and Gilpin were already there. Fairfield listed those who left the valley:

> John H. Neale, Cap Hill, William Weatherlow, U. J. Tutt, William Dow, Fred Hines, Henry Arnold, D.M. Munchie, Thad Norton, Richard Thompson, Anotone Storrff, Tom. McMurtry, John C. Davis, "Mormon Joe" Owens, John Mote, _____ Henderson, William N. Crawford, William H. Clark, A.G. Epstein, Frank Johnson, William Meyers, R.W. Young, _____ Hughes, Alec Chapman, George Lathrop, Thomas J. Harvey, Thomas Watson, John Baxter, Mark Haviland, _____ McVeagh, Mat. Craft and R. J. Scott.

Cap Hill, whose real name was William Hill Naileigh, was at times a leader in Honey Lake Valley. He was on the committee to form a government that met in Genoa in 1857, and later, when they mustered a Civil War force from the area, he was named first lieutenant, the only one from this list named among fourteen officers. He later served as sheriff of the county. Despite the assertion that Hill participated, Fairfield wrote: "There's a possibility that instead of Hill another man went, but it is impossible to tell who it was."[1]

This points up the fact that Honey Lake's leaders, with one exception, did not make the trip. Neither Issac Roop, Peter Lassen, nor Manley Thompson, who hosted and chaired meetings at his cabin, rode with the band. William Weatherlow, the leader of the Rangers, started out but "got sick" and turned back with the man named McVeagh, after one night's ride. Honey Lake sheriff Orlando Streshly did not participate. Neither did Solomon Perrin, the former Carson Valley lawyer who served at least once as arbitrator in a Honey Lake land dispute—even though conversations between Perrin and Thorington were crucial to the prosecution's case. At the trial, those conversations were described by another Honey Laker as he thought they had occurred.

John H. Neale led the men into Genoa. He was just beginning to establish himself as a leader and is the only one mentioned by name when the mob hanged Snow. Over the next couple of years, he acted as the administrator of Peter Lassen's estate and chaired at least two citizens' committees.

Those with Neale were men of action, used to violence. U. J. Tutt was Weatherlow's lieutenant in the Rangers. Earlier in the year when the Rangers were pursuing Indians who had stolen horses, Weatherlow got separated from the others. Alone, he was confronted by two Indians. He shot one dead and began wrestling with the other. A small man, Weatherlow was being bested. Yelling, he threw sand in the Indian's eyes and mouth and was attempting to bite his finger off. Still, the Indian got on top and, securing his knife, would have killed Weatherlow, but "[Tutt] ran up caught the Indian by the hair, and with one stroke of his Bowie knife almost cut off his head." Tutt and William Dow "were considered to be among the very best Indian fighters in the valley."[2]

Alec Chapman was the man who nearly fought with Rough Elliott before the battle at Goose Lake. That battle, where at least seventeen Indians had been killed, had taken place in April, two months earlier. Of the seventeen Honey Lake Rangers who took part in it, thirteen would be involved in the action at Genoa. A month after returning to Honey Lake, one of the riders, Mat. Craft, would kill another, R. J. Scott.

Illustrating the transitory nature of the force, in January 1860, a year and a half later, the Honey Lakers petitioned the government to rally military forces to "chastise" Indians who were congregating in force. Of the ninety-one men signing the petition, only a half dozen had been among those who rode into Genoa.[3]

The trail between Honey Lake and Genoa was over 120 miles of rugged terrain. To avoid detection, the men rode by night, camping in wooded areas during the day. As they came closer to Carson Valley, other men joined them. Fairfield believed they were probably Masons who knew of their coming. The murdered Snelling had been a Mason, and the organization's large reward for Edwards's capture was still being tendered. However, the Carson Valley vigilante trial was not a plot by Masons. Chauncey Noteware was a leading Mason, a senior deacon who served twenty-three years as Nevada's grand secretary. It was Noteware who recorded and published the transcript of the trial and, years later on Masonic stationery, wrote to Fairfield recounting its injustices.[4]

While the Honey Lakers were in Washoe Valley, Theodore Winters, a relative newcomer to the area, showed up, riding out from Genoa. He was a burly, walrus-mustachioed widower in his midthirties, and he was about to take a big role in vigilante business. He later carved out a niche in Nevada's ranching and horse-racing history. In this circumstance, he was seeking information about the Honey Lakers' arrival to take back, so Rough Elliott could be sure that those in town would be ready. The Honey Lakers did not know Winters and were reluctant to let him leave, fearing he was a spy. He convinced them of his mission and was finally allowed to return and alert Elliott and the vigilantes of the Honey Lakers' imminent arrival.

The riders reached Genoa on Monday, June 14, just before daybreak. Rough Elliott met them, and they tied their horses behind a long barn at the edge of Main Street. There were a few lights on in town, and Major Ormsby and others of the Committee joined them. Ormsby told them that he and his wife had been sitting up waiting all night. Elliott took charge, directing men into position.[5]

There was importance in Ormsby's coordination with the Honey Lakers and the fact that others from outlying areas strengthened their numbers. A common problem in quelling crime in developing settlements was that if the accused was well liked, they were often acquitted, regardless of evidence against them. That would have been a distinct possibility with the popular Thorington. The Carson Valley vigilantes were opposed by an equal number of antivigilante Genoans. If Ormsby and the Committee were to succeed, they needed overwhelming force so that their adversaries would not try to stop them. Ominously for Thorington, in vigilante actions, the prevalent belief was that consequences had to be immediate and severe. Writing in the era about Montana vigilantes, Dimsdale said, "None but extreme penalties inflicted with promptitude, are of any avail to quell the spirit of the desperadoes with whom they have to contend."[6]

On Thursday, June 17, the report on the front page of the *Daily Alta California* included the following:

> On Monday morning last before daylight a body of armed horse men, numbering about 100 men, charged into Carson Valley, and took possession of all the roads and trails leading from the valley into the mountains....
>
> All egress was cut off from the valley by a strong armed guard, and those wishing to pass out or into the valley are furnished with passports.

Once the roads were secure, Elliott led most of the men to Thorington's house. They surrounded it, and, as the sun rose, Theodore Winters went in. He first brought out Lucky Bill and then Jerome. Maria Thorington followed, pleading for her boy, but, it was reported, "not a word for her husband."[7]

A group went to the White House Hotel and placed two gamblers, Orin Gray and John McBride, in custody. The prisoners were taken to an upstairs room in the recently built Singleton Hotel. T. J. Singleton would give testimony at the trial and later became the second of three husbands to Mrs. Haines, who owned the house where the vigilantes usually met. The arrestees were kept under guard while the vigilantes ate breakfast.

Outside the hotel, the streets were charged. Many years later, D.R. Hawkins recounted that at age twelve he woke one morning "to find the town thronged with armed men who styled themselves a vigilance committee." They were after Edwards and had arrested Lucky Bill. He and his father were allowed to visit the prisoner upstairs at the Singleton Hotel. "[I] saw there at the far corner of the large room Lucky Bill, bound and reclining on the floor. As we approached him my father said, 'Well Bill, what is all this about?' and he replied, 'Mr. Hawkins, these men have come here to hang me and I guess they are going to do it.'"

D.R. Hawkins went downstairs and witnessed a seemingly unrelated incident that played a part in what followed. One of the Honey Lakers named McMurtry was standing on one foot, the other propped against a building wall. His hand rested on the muzzle of his rifle, with the butt of the rifle on the walkway. As he dropped his foot to switch legs, the bowknot of the string tying his holster to his leg caught on the rifle trigger, firing a shot. The bullet left just a small hole in the palm of McMurtry's hand, but blew away the back of it. Dr. Daggett was able to save the man's life, but his hand was impaired for the rest of his life. McMurtry had pertinent information regarding Thorington's visit to Edwards at Honey Lake, but the seriousness of the injury kept him from attending the trial.[8]

After breakfasting, Rough Elliott led a group out to Lute Olds's Cotton Hotel, where they arrested Olds, his brother-in-law Ike Gandy, and Calvin Austin. Gandy started to fight but was subdued by Elliott brandishing his pistol.

In the afternoon, the seven prisoners were taken from town to Sides and Abernathy's Clear Creek Ranch. The ranch was removed from Lucky Bill's friends in Genoa. It was a station with a large barn where many men could gather. Bounded by flat, treeless land, the vigilantes could be assured that they would not be surprised by Thorington supporters. Plans to arrest Bill Edwards were now made. Travel in and out of the valley was controlled, as were communications. Influenced by emotions, rumors and half-truths spread.[9]

The *Sacramento Union* of June 17, 1858, stated that it appeared Snow turned state's evidence on the scaffold, confessing that he belonged to a band of thieves and giving names of individuals in Carson Valley involved in the murder of the Frenchman. When Snow was executed, two men went to Genoa to investigate and learn the band's secrets. The investigators got in with the murderers by using signs Snow had given them.

The report went on to list those arrested: "W.B. Thornton, alias 'Lucky Bill;' his son, Jerome Thornton, aged about 17 years; Luther Olds, Orrin Gray, McWade, a gambler, and two men in the employ of Olds known as Little Ike and Colonel." The story concluded:

> It is reported that a scheme was laid for the assassination of Major W.M. Ormsby early on Monday morning by the gang of desperadoes. The Major has been active in aiding to ferret out the parties. It was arranged to waylay him on his route to Placerville, where he proposed going that morning.
>
> Edwards, who committed a murder at Snelling's ranch, on the San Juaquin River, last fall, is said to be the party detailed to

silence the Major on Daggitt's trail, leading out of the valley but the timely arrival of the party from Honey Lake detained him, and perhaps saved his life.

California newspapers that had little control over communiqués from the Eastern Sierra to begin with now had none. In the emotionally charged atmosphere, unconfirmed reports were rapidly disseminated and distorted. In their June 18 editions, the papers added erroneous detail to the original story. Focusing on the deceased Snow, one new version stated: "On Monday last, a party of about one hundred men arrived in Carson valley from Honey Lake, in search of the murderers of the Frenchman, who was murdered at Honey Lake some time since." The men reported that by means of threats to Snow, and, by hanging him up for a time, they forced him to confess the whole matter and disclose the names of his accomplices. This account said that Snow told them when and where the murder was committed and that they had thrown the body loaded with stones into a stream near Honey Lake. "The party then made search, and found the body as represented by Snow." It repeated the fiction that there was an organized band in Carson Valley "whose objects were to rob, steal, and murder…and, that the members of the band had signs, pass-words and grips by which to recognize each other." The new report also added detail to the threat to Major Ormsby, saying Lucky Bill had offered a reward of fifty head of cattle to anyone who would kill him.[10]

The story misstates the facts, alleging that the searchers found the body based on Snow's confession, when he was actually interrogated and lynched after Gordier's body had been discovered. It also raises the question of why a small band of thieves and murderers would need signs and passwords to recognize one another.[11]

The June 18 *Sacramento Daily Bee* joined in circulating untruths, saying Snow's hanging was a ruse. He had turned state's evidence, confessing he was part of a gang of robbers in Carson Valley. It continued with the regular line that there were secret signs used by two Honey Lakers to gain the confidence of the gang, that a hundred men had taken control of Carson Valley, that seven citizens had been arrested, and that a scheme to assassinate Major Ormsby had been averted by the arrival of the Honey Lakers. It quoted a Mr. Alden as saying, "The inhabitants of the valleys breathe freer at present than they have done for two years knowing that there was an organized band of robbers and murderers amongst them and that as they have got the leaders in their hands it will be a means of breaking up the organization." The article commented ominously, "[The arrested] were placed under strong guard to await a hearing before Judge Lynch, and a People's Jury."

There is no other mention of a man named Alden residing in Carson Valley. Richard *Allen* was the attorney who served as a correspondent for the *San Francisco Herald,* but that quote would not have reflected his feelings, as he was a friend of Thorington's, testifying for him at the trial, and he later identified Ormsby as his enemy. Moreover, Alden's comment would have been contradicted by many other territory pioneers.

Years later, Elzy Knott's daughter disassociated Thorington from that Olds and his employees, saying that her mother thought Lucky Bill was better than any of those men. The antivigilantes also would have taken exception to Alden's statement, although it is a reasonable assumption that Olds was one of them, and perhaps so too were a couple of others swept up in the dragnet. Harry Hawkins's son D.R. Hawkins later noted that only four men in all of Carson Valley were glad of Thorington's arrest and that all four had had business differences with him. Another Genoa resident, D.H. Holdridge, commented that he did not even know the names of anyone who participated and that, in fact, "very few went in with the Honey Lakers in capturing and trying Lucky Bill." In their history written in 1882, Fariss and Smith reported: "The majority of the old residents of Carson and Eagle Valleys, where [Lucky Bill] resided are firmly convinced of his innocence."[12]

The other untruths, specifically that Snow testified that he was part of a gang and that there was a gang at all, were disproved by testimony at the trial and the subsequent statements of those involved. The rumor that Ormsby was fingered for assassination undoubtedly sprang from Rough Elliott's account of the plan to secure Bald Hornet. The suggestion that Edwards might be in a position to *ambush* Ormsby was unfeasible on two counts: Edwards was on the run and being sought by others besides Elliott, including Northern California Masons and B. Cherry and Jack Howard from Carson Valley, and Ormsby was working with Elliott and would not have been traveling to Placerville with arrests imminent. He and his wife stayed up through the night when the Honey Lakers were due to arrive. Communication in and out of the valley was controlled by the vigilantes, and it may be surmised that the persons transmitting the misinformation were attempting to lay the groundwork for Judge Lynch.

Jerome Thorington was used to bait Edwards into being captured. One Honey Laker wrote: "They told Jerome Thornton they would give him his liberty if he would go out to woods and bring in Edwards or Combs as he called himself. Jerome said if he was guilty of any wrong that he would suffer the penalty but that he would not betray a friend. His Father begged him to go saying that Edwards Evidence would clear him."[13]

Fairfield said, "It has been told that they promised to let Lucky Bill go, too, but the Honey Lake men say they made no such promise. It is said that Jerome did not want to betray Edwards; but his father told him that Edwards testimony would clear him and finally the boy agreed to do what they wanted him to."

Just before dark, Jerome left for the hills to find Edwards. At the same time, Elliott, Gilpin, Dow, Theodore Winters, and eight others departed for Lucky Bill's river ranch, where Martha Lamb and her baby lived. The cabin was divided in two, the front being a living room and the back a bedroom.

Jerome brought Edwards to the ranch. Edwards later told the Honey Laker Hines that as they got close to the ranch, he began to get suspicious. He put his pistol inside his shirt and cocked both barrels of his shotgun. As Edwards entered the house, Elliott, on one side of the door, and Winters, on the other, hit him with clubs. The shotgun, carried before him, received the impact of one blow, breaking both barrels from the stack. The other blow landed on his head. The *Placerville Mountain Democrat* succinctly reported, "Theodore Winters gave him a lick over the head with a club, knocking him down, and then the party secured him without difficulty."[14]

Edwards was tied and bandaged, and William Dow reported, "The first words Edwards spoke were 'I deserve it.'" The interview with Dow took place more than fifty years after the event, and his memory may have been colored by the wistfulness of age. In fact, a man wrote to historian Fairfield for Dow in 1914, saying, "Mr. Dow's mind is not so good. He realizes it himself, he said you would have to get what information you wished from him soon." Closer to expectations of what the killer might have said appeared in the *San Francisco Herald:* "Edwards said he only wished to live to kill five men, viz: Maj. Ormsby, R. Sides, Wade, Buckner and J.L. Carry, prominent citizens, and who had taken active part in breaking up and arresting the band."[15]

The men stayed at the ranch that night. The next morning Edwards, unnoticed, managed to get free of his leg bindings and run. He was caught by Elliott, who jumped on him just as he leaped into a nearby slough. Both men were pulled out of the water, and, shortly after, they rode back to Genoa. There blacksmith G.W. Hepperly fashioned irons using a chain and whatever else was at hand, including an old frying-pan handle, and Edwards was secured.[16]

While others tended to Edwards, Rough Elliott gathered a crowd with his tale of the capture, escape, and recapture. D.R. Hawkins wrote, "I saw Elliott at that time take from his pockets and exhibit two purses of gold which I understood he had taken from Edwards at the time of the capture. One of the purses was nearly as large as a Bologna sausage."[17]

Rumors were a consistent aspect of vigilante actions. In San Francisco in 1856, there were numerous instances when, hearing their security was threatened, the vigilantes detailed 100 or 200 men to guard the interior or patrol the exterior of their downtown headquarters. During one anxious time, 200 vigilantes filled sandbags through the night, stacking them at the building's front and rear entrances, after which the site was commonly referred to as "Fort Gunny Bags." In a Montana people's court action in 1863, the fact that the arrestee's sympathizers had left the area "did not mean they were gone for good, only that they might be out there on the trails somewhere, regrouping."[18]

The first night at Clear Creek Ranch, an excitement roused the vigilantes. A report circulated that Uncle Billy Rodgers had gathered 100 men and was coming to rescue Lucky Bill. The prisoners were locked inside rooms in Sides's ranch house. Guards kept watch through the night. The rescuers did not show; the report had been the consequence of rattled nerves. Rodgers was still far across the Sierra.[19]

Snowshoe Thompson's report to the *Sacramento Union* was that there were 150 citizens at the vigilante trial at Sides's ranch. Fairfield noted that few of Lucky Bill's friends made the ride out to Clear Creek. Despite any rumor, the other antivigilantes were in hiding, fearing they might be next.[20]

The trial was held in the barn. Carson Valley's John Cary served as judge. Cary was one of the earliest settlers on the eastern slope. He had sold mill and ranch properties to Thorington in 1854 and was said to have business differences with him. In 1859, the year following the lynching, Cary was made a judge in another people's court, organized so the citizens might avoid resorting to "a Lynch Court, under the excitement of some recent outrage."[21]

B.L. King, owner of a brewery and place of public resort in Eagle Valley, and John Neale of Honey Lake served as associate judges. Rough Elliott acted as sheriff; his housemate, Gilpin, assisted as deputy. Like the San Francisco Committee of Vigilance of 1856, a jury of eighteen vigilantes was called, with twelve of their number required to find a verdict. A list of jurors was never compiled. Fairfield reported that six of the jurors were from Honey Lake. By their own statements, we know that William Dow, from Honey Lake, served, as did Joseph Frey, an eight-month resident of Genoa. Emanuel Penrod, who owned a ranch in Eagle Valley adjoining the Clear Creek Ranch and was said to be a partner to Sides, Abernathy, and Baldwin, also declared his participation. Men named Williamson and Taylor and two brothers named Hale, without further identification, were said to be on the jury. The other eleven, though the object of much speculation, remained unnamed. When asked, D.R. Hawkins responded merely, "They were selected from the mob."[22]

This was not a normal trial. Any spectators allowed inside the barn had to have been friendly to the vigilantes. Fariss and Smith noted: "The judges, jurors and spectators sat in the courtroom, armed with guns and revolvers."[23]

Noteware took down the testimony. He said that Edwards served as a witness. "[The prisoners] were tried by the committee at the Clear Creek ranch, having first secured the arrest of Edwards, who was their own witness in the trial of 'Lucky Bill.' Edwards himself—not being on trial—convicted on his own confession."

On June 18 the *Sacramento Union* reported: "The cases were being tried secretly; hence nothing is known outside the jury room." The secrecy sprung leaks that gave further impetus to speculation. The same day the *Sacramento Daily Bee* concluded its own rumor-filled account by apparently quoting John Child, soon to be named, under Utah jurisdiction, as probate judge for Carson County: "Mr. Childs says, that Lucky

Bill, L. Olds, and Edwards will certainly be hung, and that the rest will probably be banished, except Jerome Thornton, who, owing to his youth, and doubtless being under fear of his father, has been compelled to participate in their crimes."[24]

Someone else got word out as well, perhaps giving hope to his allies that Thorington's fate had not yet been sealed. On the nineteenth, the *Union* reported: "From Carson Valley.—J.A. Thompson, of the Express, writing from Genoa, Carson Valley, says the prisoners were being tried, but the people had not got through examining witnesses. Edwards, being sworn, stated that Lucky Bill had no hand in the murder of Goddard nor any one in the Valley."[25]

As for the trial itself, Orin Gray, McBride, and Ike Gandy—identified as "Little Ike" in some news reports—were each acquitted, as there was no evidence against them. T. J. Singleton, at whose hotel the accused had been held, testified that a man named Bannen told him that he feared there was a plan to rob or injure him the previous September. Bannen suspected that McBride, the hotel manager—D.E. Gilbert—and a man named Hawes were involved. Bannen said it might be conjecture, "but he had been in the habit through life of watching men, and if they made a false step he was apt to detect it." Three moves had been made that night that aroused his suspicion: one was the losing of a watch, "which was to be the means of getting him out of doors; another, McBride did not, as was his custom, lock the door upon going to bed; the other movement I don't remember."

The jurors apparently felt there was more conjecture than evidence in this hearsay, and it was peremptorily dismissed. This seems to have been the extent of testimony about gang behavior at the trial. The gang of the news reports had proved nonexistent.

Owing to his youth, Jerome Thorington was also released, although he admitted helping his father help Edwards. Lute Olds was found guilty of assisting Edwards, "harboring a fugitive," according to the *Daily Alta*. Olds was fined $875 and banished from the country under penalty of being shot. Calvin Austin was similarly banished, being fined $220. He had not assisted Edwards, but he had planned to travel with him when he escaped. These cases being resolved left only the fate of Lucky Bill to be considered.[26]

Thorington's testimony, if it was taken, does not still exist. In fact, of those accused, only Edwards, who had already admitted his own guilt, and young Jerome Thorington had their testimony recorded. Chauncey Noteware wrote the testimony of eight other witnesses: L.M. Breed, B. Cherry, T.J. Atchison, W.T.C. Elliott, J.B. Gilpin, T.J. Singleton, Richard Allen, and P. Vallely. Fairfield said that John Reese was allowed to speak for Thorington, but if he did his statement has been lost.[27] In his history, Myron Angel wrote that he had read all the testimony recorded by Noteware: "Not a thing appears there implicating Lucky Bill in anything except the attempt to secure the murderer's escape. The absence of any knowledge on the part of the accused of the guilt of Edwards, is a notable feature in that testimony."[28]

Edwards's testimony regarding Lucky Bill's knowledge of the crime still exists. It substantiates Angel's account: "Thorington had no knowledge of the murder of Gordier, that I know of; I had no conversation with Thorington concerning the murder, previous to the death of Gordier; he made no arrangement with me in regard to purchasing Gordier's stock when he visited Honey Lake; he told me his business was hunting horse thieves and murderers, and that he came to my house to borrow money on which to return to Carson Valley."

Later in his testimony, while telling of Lucky Bill sending Jerome to Merced County to try to collect money owed him, Edwards said, "At the time Jerome was sent I denied to Thorington the murder of Gordier."

Rough Elliott, the prosecution's other leading witness, corroborated Edwards's statements in his testimony: "Thorington told me he did not believe that Edwards was guilty of the murder of Gordier."

L.M. Breed, at whose cabin the Honey Lakers had met to interrogate Snow before lynching him, raised the issue that seems to have been taken to insinuate guilt on Thorington's part. The testimony deals with Thorington visiting Edwards at Honey Lake in March, after leading a posse to track two criminals.

> L.M. Breed, sworn.—Reside in Honey Lake Valley, about a half mile from McMurtry & Perrin's. Two or three weeks previous to the murder of Henry Gordier, W.O. Thorington arrived in Honey Lake Valley. He called at the residence of McMurtry & Perrin, and

> wanted to procure an animal to go and see Henry Gordier's cattle; he thought of buying them; he got an animal and went away; on his return he offered to pay for the use of the animal, remarking that he had no money when he procured it, but that he had seen Coombs [a.k.a. Edwards] since he had gone, and obtained money, and now had plenty; McMurtry or Perrin asked him if he bought Harry Gordier's stock; he said no, but that he had made arrangements with Coombs to purchase them.[29]

The insinuation taken from Breed's testimony was that at his meeting with Edwards, Thorington conspired to murder Gordier. This evidence was not substantiated by either of the supposed principals: Perrin was not at the trial, and neither was McMurtry, the man on the street in Genoa whose rifle had gone off, causing the serious wound to his hand. So Breed's hearsay appears to have been the key evidence that convicted Thorington of being Edwards and Mullen's accomplice.

Further insinuation was supplied by B. Cherry. The relevant part of his testimony was that when they were together on the posse, Thorington remarked that he would like to go to Honey Lake and see Gordier's stock. When they learned that the men they were chasing had gone to Honey Lake, no further mention of Gordier was made. Instead, when the opportunity arose, Thorington left the others so he might get money to buy supplies for the return ride to Carson Valley.

J. P. Gilpin testified after Breed and Cherry, telling of his role in discussions with Thorington about Gordier's cattle. He told of meeting Thorington through Edwards in Carson Valley about a month before Thorington came to Honey Lake with the letter of warning. Gilpin knew that Edwards, who was living with Elliott and him, had killed Snelling, in self-defense, or so Edwards had claimed. Gilpin said he saw enough of the letter Thorington brought to know it concerned the Snelling affair. He said Thorington stayed an hour or an hour and a half, saying, "I used every endeavor to prevail upon him to remain over night, and go down and see Gordier's cattle; I was the first man to propose to Thorington to go in with Edwards and purchase Gordier's stock and ranch; and they spoke to me when down here as though they would buy them when Edwards should have seen them." Gilpin also said that when Thorington left, Edwards went with him, returning in about an hour.[30]

When Thorington rode to see Edwards, he conducted two items of business. He borrowed fifteen dollars, and he gave Edwards a letter saying his whereabouts were suspected by those chasing him. Gilpin was encouraging Thorington to go in with Edwards to buy the cattle and Gordier's ranch. Cherry's testimony and Breed's hearsay both stated that Thorington had gone to see Edwards intending to talk about Gordier's cattle. Thorington never looked at the cattle. Noteware reported that Thorington said he did not have the money to invest.

Could saying he was going to Honey Lake to talk about the cattle have been a ruse Thorington used in order to contact and warn Edwards? The innuendo that was allowed to stand was that when Lucky Bill met Edwards, they planned the murder of Gordier. Knowing parties suspected Edwards's whereabouts, would Thorington have wanted to back him in such a scheme? There is no record in Thorington's history of his ever being involved in stealing stock or of having committed a murder. During his testimony, Edwards said that he and Thorington made no arrangement regarding Gordier's cattle and that Thorington did not know that he had killed Gordier.

Fairfield apparently did not have access to Noteware's trial transcript when he wrote his history. He used Honey Laker William Dow's recounting of trial testimony: "Dow says Edwards testified that while Lucky Bill was in Honey Lake valley he helped plan the murder of the Frenchman." Because Edwards's testimony still exists, we know this statement to be flagrantly false. William Dow was one of the jurors.[31]

Another of the jurors was Emanuel Penrod. As mentioned earlier, his claim to fame was that he was one of the original locators of the Comstock Lode. Unfortunately for him, he sold his interest before the extraordinary strikes made millionaires of mine owners.[32] When Penrod lived in Eagle Valley as Sides's neighbor, he co-owned a mill with Rough Elliott. Fifty years after Thorington's death, Penrod, using his own versions of grammar, spelling, and punctuation, wrote his account of the trial in a letter to Fairfield:

> The actions of this Court has been called in all the Historys and writings of Nevada a Vigelants Comity, formed untel after these hangings, when there was Comity Organised, but never had any work to do.

> I must say in the work of bringing to Justises there Murderers, Rufe Elliott Did some of the best Detective work ever done; what ever Rufe was after this, he did a sharp piece of Detective work in this.... He brought to light a murder for gain in which a Rancher who thought he was selling for cash, when his life was the price. i write this only to show that the Hanging was not by a Vigalance Comitty as has been reported.[33]

Regarding Thorington, Penrod said: "[He] was given every show with in the reach of justice. And Luckey Bill Expressed himself satisfied with the jury, and expressed himself during the trial that his luck was gonen that the cards was stocked on him."

Penrod had begun the letter by giving his assessment of the proceedings: "As i was one of the jury who tried him, and so heared all the evidence.and I must say that he (Luckey Bill) had as fair a Trial as any one-ever had."[34] Of course, Noteware's trial record does not support Penrod's contentions. In no reasonable trial would hearsay and innuendo, contradicted by sworn testimony, be evidence to convict a man and generate a death sentence.

The assertion that Thorington was the leader of a gang had been disproved. In fact, no evidence was produced to support the claim of a gang's existence. The only crime of which Thorington was guilty was the same for which Lute Olds was convicted: harboring a fugitive.

Historian Frederick Allen calls attention to a weakness in people's courts. Both the gathering of evidence, which should be collected over time to establish grounds for an indictment, and the hearing of the testimony were abridged, many times compressed into a few hours. Additionally, when the evidence was uncertain, cases needed to be broadened.[35]

Thorington was sentenced to death, although there was no evidence of his involvement in the murder. For him to be executed, other offenses had to have tipped the scale. He was a gambler who was flagrant in rejecting others' notions of civil obedience. His business concerns had created enemies. In assisting Edwards, he had stood against the Masons. In his dealings with the Mormons, he had stood against members of the Committee. He had two wives. Finally, there was testimony that he had suggested killing Sides or Ormsby. This last offense added the fear of allowing Thorington back into the community to the emotional contagion of the moment. This state of affairs allows the death sentence to be better understood, as does the fact that it had been preordained. Using the third person, Noteware wrote: "The jury was out sometime, occupying a room in the upper story of the Clear Creek ranch building. During their deliberations they sent for Mr. Noteware to read them certain portions of the evidence. While so reading he heard noise of carpenter work. He looked out the window and saw the cross beam—or gallows being made for the hanging of 'Lucky Bill.'"[36]

CHAPTER EIGHT

ENFORCEMENT

On Saturday morning, June 19, Lucky Bill Thorington was brought shackled from the barn, guarded by J.M. Baldwin and a man named Squires. Fairfield reported that R.W. Young watched an exchange between Rough Elliott and Jerome Thorington: "Young says that just before Lucky Bill was taken away to be executed Elliott went up to Jerome, standing near-by, and offered him his hand saying 'I'll bid you goodby.' The boy threw back his hand and said he would never shake hands with any man who helped murder his father." Dow said that he heard Thorington tell Jerome to let whiskey and gambling alone and to take care of his mother, that he, Lucky Bill, was the cause of her affliction. Young reported that Lucky Bill said "a cool fairwell" to Maria and "made a great racket with his chains" when Martha Lamb arrived.[1]

Young also heard Thorington comment on the provisional nature of justice in the region: "When the time came, they placed him in a wagon with armed guards of either side and drove to the gallows which was erected for this purpose while the trial was in progress. Before he was hanged he told some friend present to tell Billy Rodgers that if he had been here this would not have happened."[2]

There are several versions of Lucky Bill's last moments. The first newspaper account reported: "Thornton made no confession, but took things cool, putting the rope around his neck. His last words were, 'If they wanted to hang him, he was no hog.'"[3]

The descendants of Carson Valley pioneers focused their accounts of the hanging on young Lawrence Frey, the teenage son of one of the jurors, who drove the wagon from beneath the gallows. Elzyette Knott Selby said he was haunted all his life by the act and that he had been tricked into it. "They drew straws to see who'd do the hanging. They played a trick on him alright.... The one who drew the short straw had to drive the mules and because he was a kid the older ones arranged that he was the one to draw it."[4]

Grace Dangberg reported that young Frey and several other youths, to whom Thorington was a hero, joined the crowd following the vigilantes on the way to the site of the hanging. The Committee members forced Frey up into the driver's seat and had him take up the reins in the wagon on which Thorington stood. "When the weeping teenager hesitated," Dangberg wrote, "Lucky Bill came to the rescue with his unfailing gallantry: 'Drive out, Boy,' he said."[5]

Angel's Nevada history presented a more direct account, noting that it took place on June 19, between three and four in the afternoon. "Lucky Bill, whose scaffold was built while the trial was going...was placed in a wagon with the fatal noose around his neck, when, the team being started, he was dragged by the tightening rope out from the rear of the vehicle, where, with body swinging back and forth and twisting round and round, he slowly choked to death."[6]

On June 22, 1858, a report from Placerville spoke of the reaction to the Thorington hanging: "There is considerable excitement in our city this evening: knots of citizens are discussing the events of the last few days." A few days later, another account noted the "intense excitement" in the streets.[7]

There were a number of reasons for vigilance committees to attempt to control news. Avoiding disturbance in the streets, as was happening in Placerville, was a motive; after all, an avowed goal of such associations was to attempt to bring about order. Moreover, their proceedings were easier to undertake if they were able to galvanize public support. There might be other reasons to manage information also. The first hangings by the San Francisco vigilantes, in 1856, were delayed so the news would not be transmitted until after the mail steamer left. That guaranteed that if there was to be federal retaliation from the east, it would take extra weeks to arrive.[8] The news was also used after vigilante actions to exonerate those who had taken part. That proved true in Carson Valley. For some time before Thorington's arrest, members of the Committee had sought to bring him down. After the trial, Carson Valley citizens pointed accusingly at Ormsby as the ringleader. Those supporting Ormsby sought to use the newspapers to change the narrative.

On June 26, the *Placerville Mountain Democrat* published a letter written on the twenty-first. It was signed "Jerry." The writer was J.F. Long, a surveyor who had moved across the Sierra from Placerville. He was a friend of Ormsby's and had laid out the Carson City town site where the major was subdividing and selling lots. In the letter, Long apologized for not sending news sooner. "Excitement, the most intense and absorbing, has been prevalent here for the last week, scarcely paralleled by that of the Vigilance Committee of San Francisco in 1850." He commented that it was well known that the valleys east of the Sierra had been "infested with thieves" and had been a "lurking place for all fugitives" from California justice. He gave his synopsis of what had occurred at the trial, then got to the essence of his communiqué: "Thorington and some of his friends have endeavored and in fact have made some people believe, that Major Ormsby has been the sole cause of all the excitement, because Thorington and Major O. were enemies, and Major had influence &c." Long answered the charges, saying that he knew Ormsby had nothing to do with the affair. He then adjusted his argument, explaining that in view of the fact that Thorington offered money to have Ormsby or Sides or Barber killed, "who can blame Major O. for wanting to see Thorington properly punished?" In summarizing his defense, he said that the verdict was "severe and terrible—but what better could the people of this valley do?" It would have been madness to turn Thorington loose, he submitted. Without laws or a prison, he closed, "Then I repeat, what could they do?"

The editor of the *Mountain Democrat* responded with a columns-long editorial. It began with the statement that Lucky Bill was well known in Placerville. Although he associated with the lawless and dissolute, he was known to have integrity in financial matters. The editor commented that many of those connected with the hanging were known as "gentlemen of great moral worth, opposed to mob violence." He went on, reflecting that without courts and with the Mormons in open rebellion against the government (a favorite topic of the *Mountain Democrat*), the trial may have been as fair as circumstances permitted. The conundrum was raised by Long's letter. The arrest would make the accused more embittered and revengeful. It would make him more dangerous. How could he be released under such circumstances? Consequently, those who put him on trial were almost compelled to find him guilty.

The editor explained that this is "the strongest argument against the action of all such organizations." He ended by saying, "We hope that the necessity for other action by those citizens may never again exist, and that a Territorial government will soon relieve them from their present anomalous and embarrassing situation."[9]

False statements intended to bolster the vigilante action had continued to appear in the papers after the execution. On June 22, 1858, the *Sacramento Daily Union* reported that the stage run by Crandall, which had employed Ormsby the previous year, carried news that Thorington had a bill of sale for Gordier's cattle. The bill would have proved that there had been a deal between Edwards and Thorington, but it was never produced.

"Jerry" Long again wrote to the *Mountain Democrat* ten days later. He stated that evidence had been taken down that would prove Lucky Bill's guilt and the existence of the gang of thieves and those harboring murderers in Carson Valley. The only record that was forthcoming was Noteware's record of the trial, which, rather than prove Thorington's guilt as an accomplice, presented testimony by Edwards: "I had no conversation with Thorington concerning the murder, previous to the death of Gordier." And "At the time Jerome was sent [before Gordier's body was found], I denied to Thorington the murder of Gordier." The record contained as well what would seem to be Rough Elliott's substantiation: "Thorington told me he did not believe that Edwards was guilty of the murder of Gordier."[10]

The morning after the lynching, Sunday, June 20, the men from Honey Lake rode out from Genoa. In their midst, the murderer Bill Edwards rode Bald Hornet. Fairfield reported that Edwards was not tied, and he rode along talking just as the others were. Theodore Winters, Walter Cosser, and Samuel Swanger were appointed as a committee to see that Edwards was hanged, but the Honey Lakers said they never accompanied them.[11]

Many Carson Valley residents believed Edwards was not hanged but instead was set free. Noteware wrote, "A committee took Edwards to Honey Lake for execution—but there was good reason to believe that he was never executed but that he was allowed to escape—an effigy being hanged in his stead." Regarding Walter Cosser from Carson Valley, one of those who was assigned to view the hanging, Henry Van Sickle reported: "He says that all who went from this valley were barred from any participation in the alleged hanging of the aforesaid Bill Edwards, and that he did not believe the said (E) was ever hung by said mob.... [T]he whole affair has a suspicious odor, when we consider the haste with which Lucky Bill was hung against whom there was no positive evidence."[12]

Honey Laker R.W. Young, who in other statements to Fairfield seemed a reliable observer, gave a matter-of-fact account, as if he had witnessed the Edwards hanging: "Edwards pulled off a ring from his pocket and $480.00 (as I understood at the time) from his pocket. And handed them to Ruff Elliot and requested him to send them to his mother which Elliot promised to do.... I have been creditably informed that Elliot never sent the things as he promised the dying man. When Edwards was hanged it affected me so much I could not look at him." Fairfield noted that Elliott ended up with Edwards's money and Bald Hornet, turning the racehorse over to Cap Hill in its old age.[13]

Although the Honey Lakers said no Carson Valley men rode with them, on June 29 Samuel Swanger, Ormsby's clerk and real-estate partner, came into Genoa with a remarkable story. He claimed that not only had he attended the hanging, but a deposition had been taken and Edwards had changed his trial testimony. On July 3 a letter from a man signing himself "Quiz" was printed in the *Placerville Mountain Democrat* relaying Swanger's information: "Swanger returned from Honey Lake Valley last evening and informed me that Edwards was hung Wednesday, June 23d, 1858, between 6 and 7 o'clock P.M. Before he was hung he made a full confession and the following statement, under oath." The statement said that Edwards had been sworn and deposed by John Neale and included reversing testimony from the trial: Thorington first proposed to Edwards that he should murder Gordier, after which Thorington would buy the Gordier stock below its value; when Edwards arrived in Carson Valley, after the murder, he told Thorington he had done it; Edwards had not told Snow about the murder, but Snow had previously shot a man; Mullen had killed a man for money; Edwards had killed Snelling in Merced County, but it was in self-defense; the only murder Edwards was guilty of was the killing of Gordier.

As was typical, after its appearance in the Placerville paper, Swanger's story was picked up and printed in other newspapers. It was almost certainly a fabrication, concocted to justify Thorington's hanging. If true, the story would have reversed the trial testimony of Edwards and neatly tied up all loose ends. It was the version of Gordier's murder that the Honey Lakers and the Carson Valley vigilantes hoped would come out at the trial: that is, that Thorington first proposed the murder, he was told of it immediately upon Edwards's arrival in Genoa, and Snow had formerly killed a man, which would have helped excuse Snow's lynching. In one statement, all the actions of those involved would have been justified. Edwards had even been sworn and deposed.

Swanger's statement was never substantiated. L.M. Breed and a man named Chas. C. Walden, each of whom Swanger said certified his account, left immediately for Canada, as did a number of others who had participated in the hangings. Swanger said that Neale and another Honey Laker, Z.N. Spaulding, were both witnesses to Edwards's confession and hanging. Each of them remained for years at Honey Lake, and there is no documentation that either ever acknowledged the Swanger statement. Similarly, none of the early histories—those by Angel, Fariss and Smith, or Fairfield—refer to Swanger's account. None report that Edwards changed his trial testimony. Two of Fairfield's primary informants, Honey Lakers Fred Hines and William Dow, rode with Edwards all the way back from Carson Valley, and neither mentions anything about a confession. R.W. Young says nothing about Edwards changing his story. And neither does Sheriff Orlando Streshly, who did not ride to Genoa with the others but who said he was at the hanging and buried Edwards. According to Streshly, "[Edwards] requested me to take his body up to My place & bury him at the side of the road, about half way between his mining claim & Richmond & I did so."[14]

Neither the Genoans, who believed Edwards was set free, nor the Honey Lakers, who said they witnessed the hanging, repeated Swanger's story. Curiously, the one Genoan who believed the story was the man who vouched for Thorington at the trial, Richard Allen, "Tennessee." He wrote to the *San Francisco Herald* that he *had* believed Thorington innocent. Now, because Edwards's purported eleventh-hour confession declared that Thorington participated in planning the murder, Allen was compelled to say justice had been served. Although he was an adamant opponent of lynch law, he concluded, "If people were ever in any country justified in taking the law into their own hands, it was here and in this case."[15]

The news accounts claimed one hundred men had entered Carson Valley with the Honey Laker party. This seems to have been an exaggeration, but there were a large number who took part in the action. Thirty-two men had started out from Honey Lake, but two had turned back. Others were said to have met with them as they rode. Fairfield speculated that they were probably Masons who joined the group at Washoe Valley. Elliott, Gilpin, and Theodore Winters, as well as more Masons, met the group in Genoa. The Committee's original membership had been nineteen, so the total of those with the vigilantes would have been over sixty, perhaps well over, depending on the uncounted numbers who joined as they rode and the Masons who met them in town. Many years later D.R. Hawkins, who was twelve years old at the time, said the town was "thronged with armed men."

Uncle Billy Rodgers was gone, and, with the principals arrested, there was no one who could rally the antivigilantes and the faction in the valley who supported Lucky Bill. In fact, many of the antivigilantes were in hiding. It was later reported that when his friends took Lucky Bill's body down from the gallows, they did it at night, secretly burying him on his own ranch. Elzyette Knott Selby described her father Elzy Knott's actions after Thorington's arrest: "He was with a bunch of men who hid in the daytime up in Genoa Canyon. At night they came down to visit their families, but they always knew where each other was, and in case of trouble, had their own signals to let each other know." She also said her pregnant mother was so frightened over her father's danger that she miscarried, "her fear causing her to lose the baby." Elzyette's uncle said, "After Lucky Bill was killed Elzy had to hide out for several days with a bunch of other fellows." The Committee had won control of the valley.[16]

CHAPTER NINE

FALLOUT

Friends of Thorington and those who he had helped were outraged over the lynching. Fairfield told of a woman who called "the vengeance of Heaven down upon the heads of those who hanged him." To the east, Mormons reacted sharply. Although US troops passed through Salt Lake City on June 26, they set up camp in a distant mountain valley. Non-Mormon Cumming had been installed as governor, but the Mormons continued to monopolize the territorial government, maintaining control. Thorington had not belonged to the church, but he had been politically aligned with the Mormons. He had been a business partner with the Mormon John Reese, and there was sentiment that his killing was because of his polygamist lifestyle.[1]

Honey Lakers Dow and Hines told of two instances wherein the religionists demonstrated acute reactions to the hanging. Dow was in Salt Lake City in the summer of 1859 and went to the ranch of a man named Coon. The rancher related the story of Lucky Bill's hanging, saying he got the information from Colonel Reese. When Dow let out that he was from Honey Lake, Coon quizzed him, saying he must have known something about the hanging. Dow said that he heard about it, but he was busy at that time. The rancher didn't seem to accept the answer, asking if maybe he was involved. Dow repeated his denial. He was certain that if he had been found out, the Mormons would have taken revenge, killing him before he got away. Fellow Honey Laker Hines had moved to the Humboldt River where he had established a trading post, and that same year a large group of Mormons stopped there. "They cursed and abused the Honey Lakers for the part they took in the hanging of Lucky Bill, but Hines said it was too big a crowd for him and he kept still."[2]

With Lucky Bill's death, Jerome and his mother took control of the Thorington properties. In July they sold their interest in the White House Hotel to D.E. Gilbert, beginning a process of gradually selling off their holdings. At some point, Maria's mind snapped, and she lived in asylums until her death around the turn of the century. Ignoring his father's last admonition, Jerome became a saloon keeper, dying an alcoholic in San Francisco at age thirty-seven.[3]

Whether her life with Lucky Bill was as a polygamist wife or a married man's mistress, Martha Lamb had been painted as a fallen woman. The anti-Mormon faction had threatened to make her "walk the plank" with Lucky Bill. Instead, she continued living with her young son, William Thorington, in Carson Valley. In November 1859 she sold the 320 acres claimed by George Lambe five years earlier.

On July 1, 1861, Mrs. David Olds was granted a divorce from her husband. Lute Olds's brother was a commissioner for the newly formed Douglas County. The petition for divorce stated: "That being so married to the petitioner the said David Olds—at the county of Carson and the Territory of Utah, on or about the first day of February 1861 did commit adultery with one Martha Lamb. And the said David Olds at divers times since the first day of February 1861 has committed the said crime of adultery with the said Martha Lamb."[4]

Shortly thereafter, David Olds and Martha Lamb married, and they left the valley. In 1866 they moved to Round Valley in Inyo County, California, took up ranching, and lived there the rest of their lives. Eighty-three-year-old Martha Lamb Olds died in 1914, five years after her husband. The front-page obituary in the *Inyo Register* commented: "Whatever the unknown future holds in reward for the upright, kindly and personally honored in this life must surely be hers." There are ironic footnotes to the relationship between her and Lucky Bill. Antithetical to the role Masons played in Thorington's fate, the Eastern Star, the Masonic appendant body, had taken charge of the tributes to Martha, as her burial was in the Order's cemetery. In addition, Nevada historian Sally Zanjani points out that "Lucky Bill would have been amused" had he known that their grandson Cecil Thorington became a sheriff.[5]

Lucky Bill's close friend and partner Uncle Billy Rodgers abandoned the valley shortly after the hanging. Moving farther from the developing civilization, he became the first American settler of Ruby Valley in Nevada's Ruby Mountains. There, in the employ of the US Indian Agency, he selected land for a Shoshone reservation. It was never approved, even though he demonstrated that the high-desert land was productive, building a cabin and growing vegetables and grain. His name was raised occasionally, as in 1862 when he was induced to pack into the Rubys to find a mystic mountain lake dreaded by the Shoshones. In Carson Valley, Uncle Billy would now be seen in a heroic light, identified in the first Nevada history as the "famous frontiersman."[6]

In July 1858 Utah Territory's new governor, Alfred Cumming, appointed John Child as probate judge for Carson County. Cumming was pursuing a policy of "conciliatory adjustment," attempting to pacify Brigham Young and the Mormons through judicious compromise.[7] Although a non-Mormon, Child was one of the old settlers untroubled with living under the Utah territorial government. He had arrived in Carson Valley from Placerville in 1854 and owned a store on the Carson River three miles below Genoa. He ran a pack train in partnership with Snowshoe Thompson, and, in the fall of 1859, they started a Genoa-to-Placerville stagecoach line. His commerce and transportation interests were in direct competition with Major Ormsby's, and that fact may have played a part in the chaos over governing that followed. He said he had not sought the job and had no idea why he was chosen: he had not even come to Carson County through Salt Lake City.[8]

On October 30, 1858, Child called for a county reorganizing election. Candidates ran on two tickets: the anti-Mormon Party, composed of Ormsby allies, the vigilante faction, and its sympathizers; and the Mormon Party, still called that although there were few active church members left in Carson County. The Ormsby faction, believing the Mormon Party would win most races, planned disruptions, such as creating voting irregularities and running candidates who would refuse to serve if elected. Ultimately, protests about illegal voting caused the votes from the precincts outside Carson Valley—including Eagle Valley, Washoe Valley, Gold Canyon, and Humboldt Sink—to be thrown out. The results of the races in the two Carson Valley precincts, allowed to stand, were closely contested. The Mormon Party won all but two offices. The anti-Mormons elected were the Clear Creek Ranch owners and Committee members Richard Sides, who tied for second in the race for selectmen, and L.B. Abernathy, as sheriff. The latter won fifty-eight votes to fifty-five for his opponent. The election did nothing to ease the discord in the valley. Historian Angel noted that the people paid little attention to the results, and the positions became "mere sinecures."[9]

The telegraph line across the Sierra was to be completed at the end of November. Ten days beforehand, the *Daily Alta California* commented that soon news "will be dispatched by lightning from Carson Valley." It added that the connection would be "the first link in the great chain which will shortly bind the continent."[10]

At seven o'clock on the evening of November 30, 1858, Colonel F.A. Bee, whose company had constructed the telegraph line from Placerville, sent the first message out of Genoa. He commented that it was especially important to Carson Valley because of its isolated situation. He lauded the new line as having "brought the mountains into connection with the sea." The *Sacramento Daily Union* characterized the terminus as "the eastern side of the dreaded Sierra Nevada," perhaps alluding to the heavy winter snow in the range. The largest gathering ever held in the town took place in Genoa on the first of December, as settlers from the surrounding valleys joined in celebrating the telegraph's arrival. Major Ormsby, on behalf of the citizens, presented a city block in the center of town to Bee's company, and the celebration lasted through the night.[11]

The telegraph wire, run across the summits of the Sierra, soon became a problem. Instead of cutting poles, Bee's company had attached the wire to trees alongside the roadway. The trees swaying in mountain winds caused the wire to stretch until, by the following year, portions of it lay on the ground. Teamsters sometimes cut out pieces of the downed line to repair wheels on their wagons. Angel reported that in early November 1860, the wire had been cut, and news of Lincoln's election and his first message had to be carried across the Sierra by the telegraph's stand-in, the Pony Express.[12]

The advantage in sending news instantaneously might or might not have helped to capture an escapee accused of murder. The sheriff was Abernathy. His reactions might have stymied the recapture, irrespective of communications. In mid-November, days before the line's completion, Alexander Chauvan escaped from Genoa and made his way through Placerville before news of the killing crossed the summit. Chauvan had slain a young man named Fredrick Dixon over a game of cards. On November 20 the *Placerville Mountain Democrat* reported that there had been a trifling argument, and when Dixon stepped outside, Chauvan drew his navy revolver and fired. The shot grazed Dixon's neck. He started to run, begging Chauvan not to shoot again. Chauvan, who had been drinking, stood against the doorframe to steady his aim and shot Dixon in the back.

The killer was arrested, taken to Genoa, and set free. The newspaper commented, "[Chauvan] was an active member of the Vigilance Committee of Carson Valley, which may account for his release. A foul murder has been committed, and the murderer has been allowed to go free, through the partiality or carelessness of the officers having him in charge."[13]

The consensus was that partiality, rather than carelessness, was the cause. In discussing the escape, the *Sacramento Daily Union* castigated the sheriff by adding, "as might have been expected."[14]

The vigilantes rejected Governor Cumming's conciliatory approach toward Mormon officials. Despite having Abernathy in the position of sheriff, the vigilantes wanted the results of the October 30 election expunged, and they pledged to do something about it. On December 11 Ormsby chaired a meeting at Sides's Clear Creek Ranch. The gathering elected John Cary as president and Dr. B.L. King as one of the vice presidents. They wrote a lengthy memorial that rejected the attempted reorganization of Carson County. The statement called Utah's laws repugnant and issued a threat that any attempt to enforce those laws would be dealt with by the Committee. A group of ten, including Ormsby, Swanger, Theodore Winters, D.H. Barber, Walter Cosser, Sides, and Abernathy, was formed to take the county records from recorder Stephen Kinsey. Hearing of the meeting, Kinsey sent the records to Governor Cumming at Salt Lake, telling him they were not safe in Genoa. He charged that the Committee's ten-person deputation was mandated to obtain the records by force if necessary.[15]

The Committee's last item of business on December 11 was to acknowledge that those present supported the actions of the vigilance committee at the Thorington trial in June: "Resolved. That this committee recommend the people to sustain the award of the jury impaneled at Clear Creek Ranch on the 16th of June, 1858: pledged our lives to the faithful execution of its awards."

One of the specific decrees that followed stated: "Resolved, That the Sheriff is hereby directed to exercise strict vigilance with regard to the deportment of L Olds; and at the expiration of the time allowed for his stay, in case he does not conform to the spirit of resolution No. 1, then to summon to his assistance such men as he may deem necessary, and arrest his person and proceed to award to him the verdict rendered by the Jury, at Clear Creek Ranch, the 16th day of June, 1858." The sentence had been banishment under penalty of death.[16]

Lute Olds went on to live many years in Carson Valley. Twenty-three years after the banishment directive, Angel wrote that an unsuccessful attempt was made to collect the fine but that Olds continued to live in Carson Valley. Fairfield's account differed from Angel's on the payment of the fine. He quoted local resident Joseph Frey as saying that a month or two after the trial, the vigilantes acted again. Frey's account said that Theodore Winters and a group of men confiscated Olds's cattle and put them in Hiram Mott's corral. Suspecting that Olds would try to recover his herd, Winters directed Frey to ride to Washoe Valley and bring back fifteen or twenty of Winters's friends. When he got back with the Washoe Valley contingent, there were thirty or forty men gathered. They waited at Mott's ranch, but Olds never appeared. Frey believed in the end a cattleman named Douglas paid the fine, probably taking Olds's cattle for security.[17]

Whether the fine was paid or not, Olds never surrendered his ranch. When an election was held after Nevada Territory was created in November 1861, one of the polling places was Olds's residence. There were several factors that would have influenced his having remained in the valley. One was the formation in the winter of 1858 of a group with some of the members of the antivigilantes. Calling Ormsby's Committee the "Junta," they formed the "Law and Order Party," the same name used by those who opposed the San Francisco vigilantes in 1856. Recently appointed judge John Child had been on a large committee of arrangements, along with Thorington, Ormsby, and Sides, when they petitioned Congress to organize their own territory in 1857. He now led the new party members as they vowed that they would obey the laws of Utah until such time as they were successful in creating their own territory. Child gave a statement to the *San Francisco Herald* saying that the Committee had warned him not to attempt to enforce Utah's laws, and, whether for that reason or not, he put off holding court for some nine months.[18]

Another circumstance lessened interest in the Olds case. The Gold

Canyon diggings were proving more profitable. Ormsby had purchased a store at the mouth of the canyon in the fall of 1857, and business there was starting to boom. In the spring of 1859, Captain J.H. Simpson led his large contingent of the army's Topographical Corps across the Great Basin, mapping a more direct wagon road for the California Trail. He commented that the Gold Canyon area was yielding an average of $15 a day per placer miner but that two men, with one rocker, had made $155 in one day. This was at a time when California placer miners were giving up, as earnings had fallen to $3 to $5 a day.[19]

Ormsby had other interests as well, which would have distracted him from the Olds issue. While consistently pushing for an ordered society and incorporation, he used disorganization to his advantage. He was earning profits and gaining power while boosting nationalism, regional prestige, and civic pride.

In early June, Simpson arrived in Eagle Valley's new town, Carson City, named by Ormsby for Kit Carson. Newspapers were reporting on the importance of the place. A Marysville paper described the new town as a trading center for the surrounding communities and for those as far away as the Humboldt Sink. The town was composed of a dozen frame houses and two stores, one of which was owned by Ormsby, who was also dealing in real estate. In order to promote the town, organizers were giving away lots with the condition that the new owner build immediately. In addition, Ormsby was building a hotel. Its second story included a hall that by May 30 was completed and "ready for a ball." As often was the case, there was a political subtext to Ormsby's actions. The hall would serve as the meeting place for organizing governance. Ormsby and the town's founder, Abe Curry, were determined that Carson City would develop into the seat of territorial administration, and, for that purpose, they set aside a large midtown block of property. As planned, the territorial government set up there when Nevada Territory was formed in 1861. When Nevada became a state in 1864, Carson City was named its capital, and the state capitol building was constructed on the site.[20]

In his report to Washington, Simpson noted a social evening in Carson City: "Spent a very agreeable evening at Major Ormsby's, where I for the first time since I left Camp Floyd, encountered the society of ladies."

Simpson had government business in San Francisco. When he arrived in Genoa, he was visited by Major Dodge, the Indian agent, whom he lauded as courteous and refined. Dodge happened to be traveling to San Francisco as well, and he offered Simpson a mule to ride over the Sierra and a share of a pack mule.[21]

Accompanying Dodge were three Indians. Simpson identified the leader as "one of the head-chiefs of the Pi-Utes, Won-a-muc-a the younger." The man Simpson identified was Numaga, called "Young Winnemucca" by white settlers. Sarah Winnemucca identified him as her cousin, a nephew to the old headman. Numaga and Old Winnemucca were said to be unfriendly, and Numaga was perceived as almost as much a tribal statesman as the elderly headman. Two years earlier, Numaga had acted for Ormsby when the settlers wanted Washoe Indians to answer for the McMarlin and Williams murders. Frank Soule, a reporter and writer of a popular history, *The Annals of San Francisco,* met and described Numaga in a news article, saying he projected "a strong will and decision of character." The physical description included that he was "six feet in height: straight as an arrow, with a depth and breadth of chest which denote great physical strength, and a quiet dignity and self-possession of manner which stamped him as a superior man; his forehead was not high, but broad and expansive, and beneath his prominent brows shone two keen black eyes...observing every passing object with cool, calm look."[22]

Numaga would be a key figure in the Pyramid Lake War the following year. Why Dodge and Numaga were traveling together went unstated, and although Simpson noted that the Paiutes accompanied them to Placerville, and Numaga later talked of having been to San Francisco, Simpson made no further mention of them when the Americans continued on to the city.

That morning, on the way to Genoa, Simpson crossed the hill above Clear Creek, questioning a not uncommon vigilante tactic of intimidation. He commented: "Noticed along the road the gallows on which the vigilance committee hung 'Lucky Bill,' last June or July, a reported horse-thief and murderer. Was astonished that the relic of such a season of popular agitation and excitement should be left to be harped upon by every passer-by." The initial San Francisco vigilante victims in 1856 were dropped from the second story of the vigilantes' downtown offices and allowed to dangle for a time as a public display and warning. In Montana "five of the victims were tied to the crossbeam of an unfinished store at the very center of the main street of the territory's largest city, their bodies left dangling for a day like pennants of conquest." Two other Montana vigilante victims, in the 1860s, were hanged from a tree behind a way station. They were left several days with hand-lettered signs, identifying their roles in crimes, pinned to their backs.[23]

It had been a year since the Thorington hanging in Carson County. The Committee's advertisement, leaving the crossbeam standing, had had a negligible effect. Amid the Ormsby faction's ongoing challenge to the jurisdiction of Utah Territory, and with the Law and Order Party following the lead of John Child, each entity was stymied, and lawlessness persisted.

Elzy Knott's wife, Mary, lost a child shortly after Thorington's hanging. In the early spring of 1859 she was again pregnant. Her child would be born fatherless. Knott had won a bridle while playing cards against a nineteen-year-old, John Herring. The *Placerville Observer,* writing from Genoa on March 10, reported that Herring had used violence to take back the bridle from a young employee of Knott and threatened that if he told of it, he would kill him. Hearing of the incident, Knott went to Herring's house, meeting the boy's mother at the door. She refused him entrance, warning him that her son was armed. Seeing the bridle on the floor of the front room, he rushed past her. Herring stepped out of the back room, leveled a double-barreled shotgun at his face, and fired, killing him instantly.

Knott had been followed to the house by his father and one of his employees. The father later testified that Herring had stood with the gun "aiming at Elzy so long that I almost thought he would not shoot." Knott had not drawn his own pistol that he carried in his belt. The shotgun blast and the father's shouts brought others. Herring ran out the back door, running toward the mountains, a pursuer fired his pistol, and Herring stopped and surrendered.

The Knotts were one of the earliest of the Carson Valley homesteading families. Elzy's popularity was attested to by the funeral that the newspaper said was "attended by the largest assemblage that has ever convened at any one time in this valley." Citizens then met in a saloon to decide what to do about Herring. Without a jail to keep the prisoner, the citizens agreed to form another people's court. It was first proposed that Judge Child hear the case. He felt his appointment as probate judge did not qualify him to hear a murder case, but he agreed to act as a chief judge, assisted by the respected early-day settler Hiram Mott and an attorney, Frank M. Procter. The Placerville newspaper reported that the community had agreed to set aside the strife between the vigilance faction and the antivigilantes and act in unison. This was evidenced by one of Child's antagonists, Committee member Abernathy, heretofore irresolute in his duties as sheriff, attending the proceedings to keep order. The unity agreement notwithstanding, the trial reinforced the divide between the two sides.[24]

Impaneling a jury, hearing the evidence, and the deliberations took four days. The Committee vigilantes were prevalent on the jury, and it acquitted the boy on the grounds that he was in his home and Knott had no right to enter. Speculation was rife among Genoa's citizenry that the boy had been set free because his father was a vigilante supporter, while Knott, Thorington's good friend, had been an adamant antivigilante.

A week after the trial, the *Sacramento Daily Union* printed a letter from Elzy Knott's father. He argued that his son had not attempted to draw his gun and that Herring had paused, premeditating Elzy's murder. He pointed out that, without formal authority, the common practice in the valley was to recover stolen property by retrieving it oneself, and he decried the Committee members exercising their influence in the case because Elzy had been strongly opposed to them. He said that some of their most influential men had spoken against him, and he noted that before the verdict vigilantes had assured the Herring family that they would escort the boy to safety. His father's arguments were to no effect. Elzy Knott had been killed, and Herring was set free.[25]

John Reese, for all he did to establish the American settlement in Carson Valley, was not much longer to reside there. When Simpson's Topographical Corps expedition crossed the Great Basin, John Reese had acted as a guide. Reese, who had repeatedly made the crossing, advised Simpson regarding areas that needed to be circumvented because of alkaline water or wagon-obstructing sand. Simpson again utilized Reese on the corps' return across the Great Basin, which began at the end of June. His contributions were so valuable that Simpson named a 180-mile tributary of the Humboldt the Reese River. In his *History of Nevada,* Angel noted that afterward, Reese had returned to Salt Lake City to live out his life as a relatively poor man.[26]

Simpson had stopped again in Carson City before undertaking the return trip, noting that he once more socialized with the area's leading citizen. Major Ormsby, his wife, and others interested in his expedition visited that evening. Simpson's report was not published until the following year. By that time, relations between the Paiutes and the whites had completely broken down, and Simpson added a footnote about Ormsby: "This gentleman, I notice by the papers, has since been killed by the Pi-Utes, against whom he was operating with a party of citizens."[27]

There were several critical things that occurred leading up to Ormsby's death. One was a serious setback in Indian and white settlers' relations because of an incident in April 1859: Peter Lassen was murdered. Lassen had long been a liaison between the two entities. He understood the Paiute language and was a trusted friend to Winnemucca and the other leaders. His loss would cause a breakdown in the longstanding peaceful relations.[28]

Lassen and two others, Edward Clapper and Lemarkus Wyatt, had started out to rendezvous with a Captain Weatherlow-led party, prospecting in Black Rock country. In an area 140 miles northeast of Honey Lake, without making contact, the Lassen group camped alongside a creek in a small canyon surrounded by high walls on three sides. The original account, told by a Honey Laker and carried in newspapers, said a Paiute Indian had come to the camp that night and spoke with Lassen in the Paiute language, letting him know there were six more Paiutes in the area. The next morning both Clapper and Lassen were shot and killed. The Honey Laker concluded his story by asserting that the advance party was going to trail the Indians and chastise them.[29]

Years later, a more detailed version was told by a man who had employed Wyatt for two years. He said he had heard the story repeatedly. Wyatt, described as illiterate but honest, reported that the Paiute had come into their camp asking for powder, caps, and bullets for his muzzle-loading rifle. Although Wyatt and Clapper protested, Lassen gave them to him, saying no harm could come from it since all Paiutes knew "Uncle Pete." In the retelling, the circumstance implies that this was the man who killed Lassen.

In both versions, at daybreak a shot was fired, killing Clapper. Lassen, searching to see where the shot came from, was also shot and killed. Wyatt, a heavy-set sixty-year-old, started running for the horses picketed in a meadow. A third shot passed through his pants leg without hitting him. The horses had pulled their pickets and stampeded, but Wyatt's mount, a "fine black pacing horse," came back to him. He said it was miraculous because the horse had always been hard to catch and it was the last he had hoped to catch. With only the picket rope to guide the horse, Wyatt escaped riding bareback, day and night, the 140 miles to Honey Lake.[30]

Lassen was the region's favorite son. Fariss and Smith's history noted that he was "a pioneer whose kind heart and simple integrity had won the love of all." Masonic lodges throughout California published tributes to his memory. At Honey Lake, the killing created great excitement, but by the time a relief party reached the scene of the killings, eleven days had passed, and there was no murderer's trail to follow. Because of the circumstances of the killing, militant Honey Lakers suspected the Paiutes and demanded retribution. Others doubted their reasoning. Paiutes and the citizens of Honey Lake were confederates, and Lassen was the tribe's ally. The authoritative Weatherlow said that he did not believe the killer was a Paiute. The tribe held Lassen in high esteem. Moreover, Weatherlow noted, Paiutes continued visiting Honey Lakers as before. He accused the Pit River band, whom the Honey Lakers had fought and who hunted in Black Rock country where the white men were slain.[31]

Pioneer Honey Laker Fred Hines agreed with Weatherlow's assessment regarding the Paiutes. He told of an incident when Lassen had camped with Hines and a third man and insisted it was fine to leave his horses to graze. The next morning Lassen's horses had wandered away, but, in the afternoon, Paiutes brought them into camp. Hines said it was not the only time Paiutes assisted Lassen in that way. Historian Fairfield said that *Hutchings California Magazine,* from June 1857, supported Weatherlow's contention that the Pit River band was to be suspected. The periodical told of an incident in 1851 when Lassen led a group of thirteen white settlers and a group of Indian Valley Indians, saving women kidnapped after Pit River raiders had killed members of the Indian Valley tribe. Lassen killed three of the raiders before his group routed the renegades, something, Fairfield surmised, the defeated Pit River band would not have forgotten.[32]

Major Dodge, the Indian agent headquartered in Genoa, rode to Honey Lake and Pyramid Lake to investigate the murders. He came to a different conclusion. A dispatch from Genoa on May 20, 1859, and printed in the *Daily Alta California* the next day, said Dodge had visited Honey Lake and Pyramid Lake, investigating. The article concluded: "Maj. Dodge is not satisfied that the murders were the work of Indians, as in the camp occupied by the murdered men was found two sacks of flour, some dried beef and about half a keg of whiskey, which articles would undoubtedly have been carried off by the Indians."

The account of the *Hydraulic Press* from Nevada County, California, reported more of Dodge's summation. It said, "The Major thinks he has good reason to believe the murders were committed by white persons." The report added, "The Pah-Utah chiefs have promised to discover the guilty, at any cost."[33]

Weatherlow vehemently denied that it could have been white men who did the killing, as he and those in his party were the only white settlers within hundreds of miles. He demanded Dodge retract the charge and said the Indian agent had promised to do so. He later said he did not know if Dodge kept his word because the agent had not been back to Honey Lake.[34]

The *Daily Alta California* account had included an important remark: "Major [Dodge] will use his utmost endeavors to ferret out the perpetrators of this dreadful murder. Maj. D. met the venerable Pinto chief Nenamuca, together with about 3,000 of his tribe, in council at Pyramid Lake."[35]

The "Pinto chief Nenamuca" was one of the Paiute leaders, either Winnemucca or Numaga, a.k.a. Young Winnemucca. Every spring, bands gathered at the lake to fish for the plentiful cutthroat trout, or the "cuiui," a lacustrine sucker unique in the world. Along with the fishing, Dodge described the tribe as being "in council" that particular spring, and the tribe had reasons to be meeting. The first wave of California prospectors had begun crossing the Sierra for the Comstock and its environs. Comstock reporter Dan DeQuille noted, "The newcomers from California not only prospected in the neighborhood of Virginia [City], Gold Hill, Silver City, and all the hills surrounding these towns and the Comstock, but scouted out in all directions to the distance of from fifty to one hundred miles. They generally went in parties of from five or six to a dozen or more men."[36] Weatherlow commented that the newcomers, knowing nothing of the treaty with the Paiutes, often treated the Indians with contempt and cruelty. Additionally, the Indian Appropriations Act of 1851 mandated that Indians be moved onto farming reservations. The previous October, the superintendent of Indian affairs for Utah Territory had directed Dodge to select suitable reservation lands for the Paiutes. Dodge certainly would have announced the government's pending policy to the Indians, leading them to understand that their way of life was now to be severely restricted. The federal policy, together with newcomers' intrusions, ruined the alliance that had been nurtured by Winnemucca, Isaac Roop, and Lassen. At the same time, negligible legal authority fomented disorder in the settlements.[37]

CHAPTER TEN

Disorder

In the spring of 1859, episodes of violence were routine at Honey Lake. Fairfield tells of men drinking and gambling and arguing. In one instance, two men had to be kept from shooting each other. In another, fights broke out during a dance, primed by too few women and too much whiskey. A large body of men accompanying Colonel F. W. Lander's US Wagon Road Expedition had arrived at Honey Lake. At the end of the dance, the brawl began. It was between some fifteen of the visitors and an equal number of Honey Lakers. One of the Honey Lakers started it: "Bass took him by the nose and threw him down the stairs.... They began to fight all over the house and outside, too."

Fairfield writes, as well, of a killing and its associated "trial." A Honey Laker named Van Hickey, whom the residents thought of as disreputable, argued with his partner, Thomas "Old Tom" Harvey, as they rode alongside one another. Harvey was one of Weatherlow's Rangers and had led some of the group when they went after Washoes in the Potato War. Harvey reined up a bit, dropping behind, and then rode back up beside Van Hickey and shot him. Only five men attended the citizens' meeting to try the case; a witness, who had been riding with the other two, was not among them. Harvey pleaded self-defense. When only one man voted for conviction, Harvey went free.[1]

In Carson County, a similar killing was heard in a people's court. A man named Hammack sat as judge at the beginning of the case, but, after a time, Ormsby replaced him. The two men were substituting for John Cary who, with the county government's disorganization, had been chosen by the anti-Mormon faction as the people's court judge. The court was created with the intention of dispelling the notion that criminal proceedings were haphazard or unfair.

The case involved William Sides, charged with murder. He was the brother of Richard Sides, Ormsby's associate in forming the vigilantes.

William Sides had the same hot temper as his brother and a bad disposition.[2] A diarist's account of the incident read:

> APR. 29. Bill Sides murdered a man named "Pike," at Gold Cañon. Stabbed him twice. Row over cards.
>
> APRIL 30. Sides brought to Eagle Valley.
>
> JUNE 2. Sides liberated on bail after a week's mock trial. He paid Musser $700 to clear him. Trial put off till fall. Got bondsmen in $2,500.

With Hammack on the bench, testimony was presented that the victim had made the first assault. No explanation accompanied news, sent by telegraph on June 7, that pursuant to the people's court's adjournment, Ormsby was chosen chief judge, and a resolution was passed. Sides was released on $2,500 bail. The case would again be taken up three months later, on the first of September. A second resolution was also passed, requesting that the press not publish the evidence in the case.[3]

A twenty-one-year-old, casually educated newcomer, named Peleg Brown, was a juror in the trial. He wrote, "It was proved to bea willfull murder there being to jeurors bribed in consequence he was bailed.... He has already left the valley I think it doubtful if he come back any more." In correspondence to the *San Francisco Herald,* Tennessee noted that over the past eight months, three homicides had been committed, commenting, "2 of the guilty were active members of the Vigilance Committee, and the 3rd, at his trial, was saved by the influence of that patriotic association." He concluded that reformers were not always "the purest and best."[4]

On August 29, 1859, final word on the Sides murder case was presented in the *Sacramento Daily Union:* "William Sides, the man held to bail by a People's Court in the sum $2,400 for killing Jessup, alias Pike, at Gold Cañon, June last, has left the territory for the Atlantic states."

Should Ormsby have acted as chief judge in a case where the defendant was one of the Sides brothers? The fact that the evidence was to be kept confidential seems to imply that the community should trust Ormsby's judgment, and a percentage of them did. Two years earlier, when he insisted the Washoes be prosecuted for the McMarlin and Williams murders, Ormsby's wife declared, "My husband knows what he is doing." Subsequent incidents proved she had not been speaking for herself alone.

Circumstances for Ormsby, as well as for everyone else in the vicinity, were about to radically change. There is a small plateau near the head of the right-hand fork of Gold Canyon. On a mild day at the end of January 1859, James Finney, a.k.a. "Old Virginny," for whom Virginia City would be named, led three other miners up to clear snow away and prospect it. At the mouth of a ground squirrel's hole, they found bits of gold and began digging around it. They called the area Gold Hill to distinguish it from the canyon. A few others followed them, and, in early spring, as they dug deeper, they found chunks of decomposed quartz speckled with gold. At about ten feet deep, they found gold-infused, reddish quartz, the first manifestation of the Comstock Lode. Connected ore bodies spread for two miles north from Gold Hill to what was about to become Virginia City. Both areas contained gold and silver, more gold concentrated in the south, massive silver deposits in the north.

The gold-seeking miners had been plagued by black sand and heavy iron-ore pebbles from which they needed to cull the gold. Now, at the north end of the lode, they were digging in bluish-black sand or mud and discarding it. At the end of June, when samples were assayed at Grass Valley, they discovered that the blue sand was rich in silver. There was measured excitement, but Californians were skeptical. The year before, a sixth of the state's voting population had abandoned it for rumors of a gold strike at the Fraser River in British Columbia. On July 1 a newspaper in Nevada City, California, the *Nevada Journal,* reported the rich assay of the Comstock ore, but gave odds of ten to one that rather than continue mining, the discoverers intended to sell provisions to those who followed.[5]

Still, the finding caused miners to flood the area in the initial Comstock rush. Angel described the formerly bucolic area as "suddenly populated with an excited, vigorous, energetically enthusiastic throng, that houseless camped at night on the ground, and through the day rushed about the vicinity over the hills and country."[6]

In June 1859, the movement to separate from Utah had been reignited. This time it was the miners at Gold Hill who had assembled to establish governance. The rapidly expanding population included prospectors, speculators, adventurers, and schemers of all types. A new legal authority seemed a necessity. The miners set forth basic rules. Banking games, brandishing weapons, assault and battery, robbery, and murder were outlawed, warranting punishments that ranged from fines to floggings and banishment for the lesser offenses and death by hanging for murder. That they were influenced by the earlier attempts to break away from Salt Lake City was evinced by their having Judge Crane give a speech accounting for his efforts representing Carson County at the US Congress. The chair appointed five delegates to a constitutional convention to be held the following month in Genoa.[7]

Attorney J. J. Musser chaired the Genoa convention that comprised fifty representatives from the Eastern Sierra communities. It ran from July 18 to July 28. The result was a constitution, taken in large part from the state of California, and a lengthy declaration of cause for separation from Salt Lake City. The list of grievances included that the Mormons of eastern Utah were attempting "to reduce us under an absolute spiritual despotism" and that the religionists had managed, by their legislation, "to defeat justice, protect criminals, and render the laws and the authority of the United States, in Utah Territory, void and of no effect."

The declaration also contained more general accusations, asserting that the Mormons had attacked peaceful emigrants, commandeering their property. In addition, the statement echoed charges that had followed the religionists from the eastern states in the 1830s. Because they communicated openly with the Indians, believing they were part of God's people, it declared they had poisoned the Indians against the Gentiles, instigating "open war." Once they had established their constitution, the convention delegates called for a September 7, 1859, election to submit it to the voters.[8]

Meanwhile, on the fifth of September, federal judge John Cradlebaugh convened the Utah Second District Court in Genoa, its first session since William Drummond abdicated. Cradlebaugh was to be assisted by G. W. Hepperly, sworn as a deputy US marshal. Hepperly was the blacksmith at Honey Lake who fought against Rough Elliott. He did not serve long as Cradlebaugh's deputy, if at all. He is not mentioned in court reports, and he had already located a claim on the Comstock. He was first replaced by the vigilante Theodore Winters and then shortly thereafter, when Winters and his two brothers began acquiring interests in valuable Comstock mines, by Warren Wasson.[9]

Wasson would serve through the years in a number of important roles in the region. Something of his nature was displayed in an incident that took place the previous fall, when Wasson was squatting on land claimed, but not developed or fenced, by John Reese. The Utah Assembly required that land had to be enclosed within two years of its being claimed.[10] Wasson was returning with lumber to continue fencing the property for his use when he was confronted by John Trumbo, who was married to John Reese's daughter. Trumbo was the brother of Major Ormsby's wife and had formerly been in business with Ormsby in Sacramento. Trumbo, accompanied by Reese's teenage son, confronted Wasson, and an argument ensued.

Angel tells the story, commenting that Trumbo was armed probably as a bluff, but, because of the ethic of "a line drawn in the sand," the situation spiraled out of control. "Trumbo, seeing that he could not well back out without being charged with cowardice, opened his batteries upon Wasson—firing at him several times without effect." Simultaneously, Wasson coolly took aim and fired his Colt navy revolver, shattering Trumbo's thigh. Reese's son ran up to Wasson unnoticed and fired an ancient pistol at his head. The pistol, loaded only with shot, peppered the side of Wasson's face with leaden pellets. Wasson, with five bullets left in his gun, let the boy alone and went to aid Trumbo. He took the wounded man to his home. Trumbo lingered between life and death for a time before finally recovering. It having been a fair fight, there was no blame toward Wasson, and, although Trumbo was lame for life, all was forgiven between the parties.

Wasson, after serving with Cradlebaugh, was appointed US marshal of Nevada Territory in the Lincoln administration, later serving as assessor of internal revenue for Nevada. He also held three military commissions, serving on the staffs of Nevada's first two governors (one a Republican, one a Democrat) and, trusted by the Paiutes, served a long period as an acting Indian agent.[11]

Even without competent, strong men as US deputies to assist him, Cradlebaugh may have succeeded in his role as a sobering agent in Carson County. He was known as "the fearless Cradlebaugh," arriving with a reputation of being Brigham Young's most dangerous adversary. Early in 1859, he investigated the Mountain Meadows Massacre and other homicides in the eastern part of the territory, confronting untrustworthy grand-jury members and a prosecuting attorney who seemed to be protecting Mormon officials. One of the Saints claimed that in speaking of Mormons accused of capital offenses, the judge said if one were convicted, he would hang them before the governor had time to issue a pardon.[12]

At one point, Cradlebaugh had ordered the arrest of the Provo mayor and a bishop, causing the citizens to take to the streets. A Mormon sheriff deputized two hundred citizens to defy the judge, and guerrilla warfare seemed imminent. General Albert Sidney Johnston, who would be the Confederate commander of the western theater in the Civil War, sent eight hundred federal troops from their outpost in the mountains the fifty miles to Salt Lake to defend the judge. Attempting to calm the situation, Utah governor Alfred Cumming asked Johnston to remove the guard. The general refused. US attorney general Jeremiah Black then ruled that Johnston did not have the power to supersede Cumming's order, which resulted in the unprotected Cradlebaugh being transferred. An anonymous writer sent word from the army's encampment to San Francisco, saying, "The only civil officer—Judge Cradlebaugh—of whom the Mormons are afraid, they have managed, with the assistance of Judge Black and other powers, to transport to Carson Valley."[13]

During his time in eastern Utah, Cradlebaugh had issued almost a hundred murder warrants, although none of those would be enforced until some fifteen years later. Isaac Roop spoke for Honey Lake and Carson County, in writing about Cradlebaugh, explaining that because of his stand against Salt Lake legislation, he was given utmost respect. Roop added, though, that Cradlebaugh's endeavors in Carson County were blocked by Utah officialdom's enactments.[14]

Cradlebaugh impaneled a grand jury that yielded no major indictments. Instead, it submitted a report that cited the Mormons' attacks on immigrants and the impossibility of living with them because of their discordant religious and political sentiments. The jurists added their voices to those asking Congress to render territorial status to Carson County.[15]

In addition, Cradlebaugh was one of the early-day judges subscribing to a "no duty to retreat" philosophy. The first week of his tenure, he released two defendants who had killed armed opponents. Beyond his reputation, his political success in Carson County lay in the fact that he favored neither Ormsby's Committee nor Judge Child's territorial government. Upon his arrival he utilized Committee member Theodore

Winters as his deputy, and the day that he opened his court he acknowledged Child as qualified to be judge of the probate court.[16]

Genoa convention chair J. J. Musser and those advocating the creation of a new territory submitted the new constitution to the voters on September 7, 1859. By then the reports from the diggings had substantiated the extraordinary discovery. According to a report sent to Sacramento, "The richest vein that was ever heard of has been found in this miserable desert by two lucky Irishmen."[17]

Owing to the excitement over the mines and consequent surge of newcomers, confusion plagued the election. In the end its results were not preserved. One news report quoted an unnamed commenter who said he had heard nothing about voting on Election Day. The interviewee supposed there were some who had voted for the new territory, but he wondered how were they going to collect taxes. He said, "There was a determination on the part of all the folks about Genoa to resist the bogus tax collector as they would any other rogue who had attempted to appropriate their property. Had it not been for the coming of Judge Cradlebaugh, the whole thing would have resolved itself into a Vigilance Committee or organized band of robbers."[18]

Musser did not issue a certification of the vote until December 12. He explained the problem, stating that the Board of Canvassers had failed to meet. Still, he had received the votes and stated: "I do hereby certify that a *large majority* of the votes cast on that occasion were in favor of the Constitution, and also that Isaac Roop was elected Governor of the said Territory by a *large majority.*"

Although a segment of the population accepted Musser's certification, others, primarily the Law and Order Party, backed Utah's ongoing attempt to restore its authority.[19] Supported by Governor Cumming, Judge Child took another stab at organizing the government. He separated the evolving population centers into ten precincts and called for an election to fill the county offices. On his Election Day, October 8, 1859, a month after Musser's, three of the ten precincts opened polls. The results were to no effect; with 70 percent of the county not voting, elected parties refused to accept their positions. One result of interest reflected Committee member Abernathy's negligence as sheriff: out of 186 votes cast for county sheriff, candidate Abernathy received 1.[20]

Some months after the failed election, Child sent a letter to two of the vote winners in the balloting for selectmen, writing, "I urge upon you the necessity of appearing immediately and taking the oath of office, from the fact that with the population now within the limits of Carson County it is indispensably necessary *that we should have some law*."[21]

Reelected to lobby Congress for the provisional government, Judge Crane died of a heart attack at Gold Hill at the end of September 1859. A special election resulted in a vote to send Musser to Washington as Crane's replacement. Musser took a 250-pound block of silver ore to present to the Washington Monument Association, a gift from the Comstock's Ophir Mine, which its owners were soon to tout as the greatest silver mine in the world.[22]

Roop had taken the oath of office as governor for the newly named Nevada Territory. On December 12, 1859, the provisional government met, listened to a speech by Roop, and adjourned, lacking a quorum. Three days later, Roop issued a message. He said that with Musser having the territory's "implicit confidence" in representing their wishes to Congress, and because of the recent mining discoveries and totally unexpected influx of population, he felt it best to avoid fully organizing a government. Instead, they would rely upon the sense of Congress and reconvene in July 1860, after Congress concluded its first session.[23]

Musser's efforts were given limited consideration in the Thirty-Sixth Congress in Washington, DC. It was consumed by slavery and ever-increasing sectional tensions: investigating John Brown's raid on Harper's Ferry, dealing with the splitting apart of the Democratic Party, and pursuing doomed efforts to pass legislation that might keep the country together. Consequently, the eastern slope remained under disputed legal authority and without regulated public order.

The rush to the Comstock and development of the mining industry's hinterland contributed to ever-worsening relations between white settlers and Native Americans. Within a few months, the mining population in the territory had jumped from fewer than two hundred to being counted in the thousands, and the boomtown Virginia City sprang into existence. Anthropologists Martha Knack and Omer Stewart state that the change occurred so rapidly that it produced a contact history unique in North America. They point out that it was so sudden and complete, the Native people lost the opportunity to respond before they understood the threat.[24]

In January 1859 Indian agent Dodge issued his report on the Carson Valley Agency. He noted that Indians and white settlers could not live together, listing wrongs owing to the pioneers' occupation of the country. He added sarcastically, "And like other tribes, when brought into contact with the humane and christianizing influence of the white men, they have acquired a taste for whisky." He recommended the creation of a reservation, noting, "If you conclude to make a home for these Indians, it will require immediate action so far as making the selections is concerned, and defining the boundaries; for I am informed that as soon as the snow disappears, there will be quite an emigration to these valleys."[25]

In November 1859 Dodge wrote to the commissioner, suggesting that the valley surrounding Pyramid Lake, as well as the Walker River valley in the south, areas not yet claimed by white settlers, be set aside as reservation lands for the Paiutes. The commissioner approved the suggestion, and the surveyor general of Utah Territory closed those lands to settlement. That fall cattlemen sought to use the fertile grasses around Pyramid Lake for grazing. Winnemucca and the other headmen agreed to allow the encroachment if a few head of stock were paid to the tribe.

Soon there were three thousand cattle at the lake, many more than had been agreed upon. The grasses were all being eaten, destroying forage needed for the Indians' animals. When confronted, the herders refused to pay the Indians, accusing them of stealing stock. They refused to remove the cattle, threatening to raise a force of white men in Virginia City and "wipe out the Indians." In February 1860 Winnemucca traveled to Virginia City in an attempt to gain remuneration. Authority was undeveloped in the burgeoning boomtown, and it does not seem that anyone came forward to help him defend his rights. Without such advocacy, the statements of Indians were generally dismissed. Across the Sierra, California's Indian Act of 1850 had given legal force to the edict that "in no case [could] a white man be convicted of any offense upon the testimony of an Indian, or Indians." Whatever the circumstance in Virginia City, his appeal for assistance was ignored.[26]

Of course, the encroachments at Pyramid Lake were just a fraction of what was occurring. The burgeoning mining industry now required that the Native people's resources be wholly taken up by white settlers. Washoe and Paiute lands redoubled in value, serving as the mining hub's agricultural hinterland. The newcomers claimed all farmable and grazing land, including high mountain meadows that they put to use in summer for cattle and sheep forage. At the same time, timber companies began removing the eastern slope's forests, denuding the mountains—using the Carson River to transport logs and clear-cutting and fluming Lake Tahoe's old-growth pines. The extractive industries were forcing all Indians into smaller, more restricted areas, allowing fewer means of survival.[27]

The severe winter of 1859–60 arrived early. A foot of snow fell on November 4, and storms that followed covered the ground in the valleys with three to four feet of snow. In the Sierra there was ten feet of snow. Fairfield said fog came in on the first of December, and the Honey Lakers did not see the sun for six weeks. Where there was grass, the frost was so thick that cattle died, unable to eat it. Isaac Roop sent word to a newspaper in December that Washoe Indians were starving to death by scores. In one cabin he found three children dead or dying. He said the white settlers were trying to help: "They have sent out and built fires for them, and offered them bread and other provisions, but in many instances the starving Indians refuse to eat, fearing that the food is poisoned. They attribute the severity of the weather to the whites."[28] The fear of poisoning was reasonable, as it had been used by white settlers pursuing mass murder in Northern California. Among other instances: poisoned sugar had been left on the roadside near present-day Redding, killing Achumawi Indians in 1856, and strychnine mixed with flour had been left for the Pit River Indians in 1857.[29]

Late in the fall of 1859, sixty tons of Comstock ore reached San Francisco. It proved to be as rich as reported, inciting unparalleled fervor. As soon as the severe winter storms of 1859–60 began to relent in the Sierra, the rush was on. By March 1860 the roadway from Placerville was a combination of packed snow and mud. A thousand Californians were crossing to the Comstock. On April 5, with the road jammed, another big storm brought a couple feet of snow. Wagons and animals were forced to retreat back to lower elevations for a wait that cost the would-be mining barons and adventurers a number of precious days.[30]

In early May the flow of traffic stopped, and some people already in the territory fled back to California. The Paiute Indians and white settlers were at war.

CHAPTER ELEVEN

At Pyramid Lake

In the winter of 1859–60, Honey Lakers held a dance. A man named Jack Demming was in attendance, and Fairfield commented, "It is also said Jack Demming killed a good many Indians when there was no excuse for his doing it." There was a Pit River Indian at the dance, and the Honey Lakers said that Demming mocked the man because he wore a high-crowned Mexican hat. Finally, Demming jammed the hat down over the Indian's eyes, and everyone laughed as he struggled to get it off. The Indian was humiliated, but there were too many Honey Lakers for him to do anything about it.

In mid-January Demming visited a distant neighbor and stayed the night. He was on snowshoes and the next day visited another settler, using a small grindstone to sharpen a couple of axes and borrowing a couple of books, Lorenzo Dow's *Sermons* and Dr. Kane's *Arctic Explorations.* By the time he got to his cabin, darkness was falling. He saw blood in the snow and irregular tracks. Everything from inside, except the homemade furniture, was gone. His brother was missing. Demming put the things he carried inside the door, called for his brother, and went for help, three or four hours away.

The following day ten men returned through deep snow to the cabin. Signs showed that the previous afternoon, Demming's brother had been in a nearby meadow trying out a pair of snowshoes he had made. As he neared the cabin, murderers used a shotgun from the cabin to shoot a load of buckshot, knocking him backward some twelve to fifteen feet from the snowshoes. They then dragged the body inside and threw him into the cellar. Everything from the house and two horses had been taken. The things Jack Demming had set inside the door were also gone. That meant the killers had been close enough to have heard him and returned. He was lucky he had not met his brother's fate.

Indeed, some settlers said it was Jack Demming the Indians were after and that they were sorry when they found they had killed his brother.[1]

By January 15, two days after the murder, nearly one hundred Honey Lake settlers signed a petition addressed to Roop, asking him to call out the military forces under his command as governor to chastise the Indians. Roop sent U. J. Tutt, Weatherlow's lieutenant, and a group of fifteen men to track the killers, with the instructions not to engage them. Although the population was clamoring for vengeance, Roop was seeking to deal with Winnemucca under the terms of their treaty. Tutt reported back on January 24, saying his group had tracked the Indians into a Paiute camp. Roop immediately sent Weatherlow and Old Tom Harvey as commissioners to contact Winnemucca and demand redress. Again, illustrating the changeable notions of a moral code, Harvey is the man, in an incident described previously, who had gone free after shooting, without warning, and killing fellow Honey Laker Van Hickey.

Weatherlow and Harvey were met on their way to Winnemucca's camp by thirty mounted Paiutes who surrounded them and prevented them from going farther. They were detained overnight, and Fairfield wrote that it was probably at this time that the two were saved by a young Indian named Pike, whom Harvey had raised. Pike talked the other Indians into letting Harvey go, but Harvey insisted Weatherlow be released as well. He reminded Pike that Weatherlow had treated Pike fairly in the past. The Indians had another council, and, the next morning, they allowed both men to leave, instructing them to return to Honey Lake. Undaunted, in heavy fog, the two Honey Lakers rode to the Truckee River and followed it down to Pyramid Lake.

Circling the lake, they happened upon Winnemucca's camp. The headman had apparently reached the end of his patience with the white settlers. Weatherlow and Harvey reported that he acknowledged they were warranted in making the demand, but he made excuses and refused to interpose to prevent depredations against the white settlers. Moreover, he demanded that the white settlers pay for having taken the Paiute land at Honey Lake. He wanted $16,000. Weatherlow and Harvey said it was blackmail and that the Paiutes were also demanding one or two cows a week from the herders grazing cattle at Pyramid. This was early February, and it must have been shortly thereafter that Winnemucca traveled to Virginia City, attempting to get compensation for the grazing.

Weatherlow and Harvey concluded that the relationship with the Paiutes had dramatically changed, saying, "We believe that the Pah-Utes are determined to rob and murder as many of our citizens as they can, more especially our citizens upon the borders."[2]

On February 12, the day after receiving the two commissioners' report, Roop sent a request to the commander of the Pacific Division of the US Army, asking for troops or arms or both. In particular, he asked for a four- or six-pound field piece to drive the Indians from their strongholds. He said the tribe had killed seven Americans within the past nine months, and he declared, "We are about to be plunged into a bloody and protracted war with the Pah-Ute Indians."[3]

There was no response from the Pacific Division, and tension remained high. The war came soon enough. It would not be between Paiutes and Honey Lakers, though; the trouble began farther south.

By the end of April 1860, a large number of Indians had gathered at Pyramid Lake. Winnemucca's payment demand for Honey Lake land had been rejected, as had his request for adjudication of the issue of Americans grazing herds at Pyramid. There had been three "Indian Wars" across the Sierra in California in 1859. The *Daily Alta California* reported that several thousand Indians had been killed. The wars were actually massacres, part of the state's extermination campaign. For example, fifteen "battles" in which the Eel River Rangers engaged resulted in more than 400 Indians killed and 600 prisoners captured, while 1 militiaman was killed and 3 were wounded. How much the Indians at Pyramid Lake knew of the extent of the American campaign is unrecorded, but they had received word of a February massacre carried out at Humboldt Bay, 250 miles to the northwest. There a volunteer militia had slaughtered, in gruesome fashion, between 80 and 250 Wiyot reservation Indians. They had begun by killing old men, women, and children one night, on Duluwat Island, when the Wiyot men were away. Now, two months later, the Paiutes feared that the proffered reservations at Pyramid Lake and the Walker River valley might be traps.[4]

The rush of Americans with mining or business interests had resumed, and Virginia City was bustling. Months later, a citizen wrote that the Paiutes staying around Virginia City suddenly disappeared. A few Washoes remained, and they had compelling information. They said the Paiutes were preparing to fight the white settlers. The writer commented that there had been nothing to lead the citizens to believe that such was really the case. Because the Paiutes were known to gather at Pyramid Lake to fish each spring, the number there in 1860 had not been suspicious; also, because the Washoes and Paiutes were often feuding, the Washoes' warnings were not deemed credible.[5]

The Indians gathered at Pyramid Lake were from all parts of the territory bordering the Eastern Sierra and what soon would be designated the State of Nevada. Wa-he, Winnemucca's brother, came with the Walker River Paiutes. A Shoshone headman, married to a Paiute, brought his band from near current-day Battle Mountain. Sa-a-ba, Winnemucca's brother-in-law, brought a group from Smoke Creek. A man who was half-Bannock and half-Paiute brought his followers from Powder River. Others came from above Mason Valley and Antelope Valley. Mo-guan-no-ga, known to the white settlers as Captain Soo, was a headman from Humboldt Meadows. He would start the war. A little man, named Chiquito Winnemucca, who would play a major role in the battle, led his band from Black Rock country.[6]

Historians who focus on the catastrophe of genocide inflicted on Native Americans identify violence as a precondition for America's new social structure. Ned Blackhawk says, "The history of Indian-white relations, particularly throughout the eighteenth and nineteenth centuries, reads like a series of constant wars." Benjamin Madley quotes a young Mojave Indian who recited the arguments that had induced war on the Colorado River in 1859: "If we let the whites come and live here, they will take your wives. They will put you to work. They will take your children and carry them away and sell them. They will do that until there are not Mojave here." Brendan Lindsay lists the trespasses against the Modoc Indians that caused them to declare all-out war in Northern California some years after the Pyramid Lake War. They included broken promises, broken treaties, lies, double-dealing, theft of land, and attempts to exterminate them. The Indians at Pyramid Lake likely tallied a similar list as grounds for marshaling their warriors. Some of them had previously fought white settlers on the Humboldt and Snake Rivers, lending them confidence. Most of the leaders were advocating for war.[7]

Winnemucca, who was a leader among leaders, kept his own council, not revealing his feelings one way or the other. Numaga was also well respected, and his word generally carried great weight. Angel dramatically noted, "Among all that assemblage of the Pah-Ute tribes there was one, and one only, among the chiefs, with sufficient sagacity to foresee the evils that would result to his people from war; one only who at the same time possessed the courage to throw his influence in opposition to their will, and declare for peace. The name of that warrior was Numaga."

Angel's account stated that Numaga went from band to band arguing against war but was continually met with silence. So, for three days, he lay by himself, facedown, silent and fasting, until the council met. Numaga would speak last, after the various headmen recounted the wrongs done to their bands and called for war.[8]

Newsman Frank Soule, who heard Numaga speak at a later time, described the power in his manner of speaking:

> [He] began in a slow, deep, guttural tone.... By degrees the speaker grew more earnest, his voice rose and fell in almost measured cadence, his eyes flashed, nostril dilated, and his whole form seemed to expand with the pent-up fires of hidden emotion. The men of his tribe sat in breathless silence, broken only by occasional grunts of approval from one or two of the principal ones. Our own party were also impressed with the earnest, commanding tone and manner of the orator, and each observed him in respectful silence. As for myself, I instinctively felt as if in the presence of a great mind—albeit untutored by the schools—a commanding and controlling intellect, and the scene, to me at least, was fraught with an interest which will long fix it in my memory.[9]

Numaga had dealt with white settlers more than the others had. He had traveled to San Francisco, Sacramento, Stockton, and Marysville. Now, he asked, "What hope is there for the Pah-Ute? From where is to come your guns, your powder, your lead, your dried meats to live upon, and hay to feed your ponies with while you carry on this war. Your enemies have all of these things, more than they can use. They will come like the sand in a whirlwind and drive you from your homes." A newcomer rode up, bringing news that Captain Soo had led a group of nine men to the big bend of the Carson River and, after killing five whites, had burned down Williams Station. Numaga replied, "There is no longer any use for counsel; we must prepare for war, for the soldiers will now come here to fight us."[10]

Williams Station was a "grog station" and trading post in the desert on a big bend of the Carson River, thirty-six miles northeast of Virginia City. The three Williams brothers were not held in high regard. It was said that they cheated both Indians and pioneers passing through. In speaking of the slayings, a *Sacramento Daily Union* correspondent stated, "[The Williams brothers] were stock dealers, and who have, it is said, had trouble with the Indians and murdered some of them. [The Indians] could have killed a large number of other settlers in the same vicinity, but it appears they disturbed no one else."[11]

An Indian informant said that after Captain Soo's men killed the proprietors and burned down the station, they were going to ride to Buckland Station and kill Samuel Buckland. Fearing that the white settlers would soon be coming after them, they thought better of it and rode back to Pyramid Lake. The informant was asked why they had left the ranch of C.M. Davis untouched, as it was closer than Buckland's. He said that Davis was a good man who did not abuse Indians, but that Buckland would scold and whip Indians."[12]

It was unclear at the time what sparked the killings of those at the station. In a letter, Indian agent Dodge suggested that an Indian's horse that had been stolen when it was left grazing might have been the cause for the attack. Sarah Winnemucca told a different story. She said that her brother Natchez, who would be second only to Numaga as a leader in the coming battle, was involved. In her telling, two young Paiute girls had been kidnapped by the Williams brothers. Indians searching for the girls questioned the station keepers, but they denied seeing the girls, who at the time were hidden in a cellar. One morning a Paiute came to the station and agreed to trade his horse for a gun, powder, and lead. The white men refused to give him the lead, so the Paiute gave back the gun and powder and went to the barn to take his horse. The station owners set their dog on him. In the commotion, the young girls yelled in answer. Natchez and the girls' father and others went to the station and found the girls. Seeing their condition, the Paiutes killed both brothers and set fire to the house. Sarah Winnemucca protested: "Three days after the news was spread as usual. 'The bloodthirsty savages had murdered two innocent, hard-working, industrious, kind-hearted settlers.'"[13]

At the end of April 1860, days before the carnage at Williams Station, Major Ormsby's brother, a physician named Dr. John Ormsby, wrote to the *Daily Alta California* from Carson City. Dr. Ormsby had come west with William in 1849 to Sacramento and had later moved to Sonoma County. What precipitated his visit to the eastern slope was not clear. Regardless, involvement for the Ormsbys was a family trait. He wrote, commenting on the territory's economic and political situation. He said that Carson City was rapidly building up and that a portion of the population was made up of well-respected men with capital. He also issued the same complaints his brother made regarding problems that plagued the territory. He listed ne'er-do-wells, including bankrupts, convicts, gamblers, loafers, and roaming thieves, as congregating there, creating uncertainty in those who wanted law and order. There was another observation in the correspondence: "Word has been received this morning that the Indians have killed a man and boy, and burnt a house near the sink of the Humboldt; whether it is true, or not, I cannot say; I fear, however, it is too true. In this case, as, no doubt, in most of other cases of difficulties between the savages and white men, the wrongs commence on the side of the whites."[14]

The urgency of the murders and destruction of Williams Station swept aside discussions of a possible attack at the Humboldt Sink. The *Sacramento Daily Union* reported, "The Pony Express dispatched their horses and riders and through them we have received the horrible news." As word of the "massacre" spread, emotional contagion spurred contrasting reactions: panic in those fearing that the killing and burning was a beginning that might soon reach their community or outrage and demands of retribution.[15]

White Americans fighting against Native Americans had advantages that made battles asymmetrical. Along with superior firepower, in organizing battles they had the advantage of writing, enabling them to disseminate information widely and accurately, issue warnings, call up troops, and detail battle plans. The immediacy of the telegraph increased the discrepancy, as tribesmen were still carrying messages on foot or on horseback. The Anglos' other marked advantage was a hierarchal political system that allowed them to form and command large army units, something the Indians, with their various bands, could not match. In this instance, all that was cast aside.[16]

Across the Sierra, in California, information arrived piecemeal. The news from Virginia City on May 9 told of excitement and disorder. "Self-elected captains" were calling for volunteers to fight the Indians. There were fistfights as potential combatants, claiming to act under martial law, attempted to appropriate horses. Although some of the volunteers were men of principle, one report said, "There has been a vast deal of talk, noise, and confusion, collection of rifles, muskets, revolvers, and knives, and an immense punishment of whiskey. Could the Indians be as effectually consumed, peace would soon be restored." This was the last attempt at irony, humor, or sarcasm.[17]

The following day, word from Carson Valley was intermittently relayed by telegraph. The first dispatch to reach Sacramento read:

> It is reported that one of the Williams was found alive, and called out to his brother, "Pah-Utes." He soon died.
>
> SECOND DISPATCH. Genoa, May 10th—5 P.M. Lafawn, formerly of Genoa, has just arrived from Smith's ranch, on Walker's river, and reports from three to four hundred Pah-ute warriors, most of them mounted, and all well armed with guns. They threaten to drive the whites from Walker's river, and then clean out Carson Valley...
>
> THIRD DISPATCH. Carson City. May 10th—10 P.M. G. Clark has just arrived from the scene of the massacre.... He left the Sink of Carson at seven last night. He met one company of rangers, at Miller's Station, of thirty men, one company, three miles this side, of twenty-five men, Judge Cradlebaugh's, of twelve men, and Major Ormsby's, of thirty total, ninety-seven. Total number of rifles on the ground, two hundred, with provisions for four days.[18]

The third dispatch, while not entirely accurate, previews the difficulties for those who were seeking to organize the mob. Many of these volunteers were new to the area, and they did not know each other. In addition, as was reported in Virginia City, liquor flowed when men were volunteering.

News that shook the region came later the same day: "From the meager dispatches received yesterday, it appears that Major Ormsby's command was led into an ambuscade and attacked about ten miles south of Pyramid Lake."[19]

William Ormsby was a man in a hurry, secure in his opinions and well respected. Initiating, organizing, meting out justice, he was a plenipotentiary of American empire. Determining a need to answer the Paiutes' actions, he hastened the settlers' response. Pioneer Albert Adams Knott said, "When Major Ormsby got all excited and asked everyone to go to war against the Indians, he came on down to Genoa and got them all stirred up to go get their muskets."[20]

Ormsby recruited some forty men. Judge Cradlebaugh enlisted fourteen more from Carson Valley, and Captain Archie McDonald led thirty-three from Virginia City. The McDonald Company set out on May 9 in the afternoon, camping for a time and reaching Williams Station the next morning at ten. Ormsby's party had already buried the dead and moved on. McDonald found Ormsby late that evening, and they were then joined by Cradlebaugh's group.

The next morning, they followed the Indians' trail of discarded articles and the tracks of horses and cattle driven off from the station. After reaching the lower crossing of the Truckee River in the afternoon, they were joined by a party from Silver City, the mining town being established just south of Gold Hill. The large, and growing, contingent set up camp in a grassy area, and other stragglers found them. Strong winds rose, described in Virginia City as "preceded by a booming sound, hollow and threatening, and directly strik[ing] as if they had been solid." The strong gusts continued through the night, and three inches of snow fell. Ormsby attempted to get the entire group to decide on one commander, but there was no agreement, and so most would follow Ormsby, although he had no real authority. Twenty-six of those from Virginia City continued to ride with and heed McDonald—the others from his group having abandoned the undertaking.[21]

The next day broke clear with a cold wind. The company had to wait for the snow to melt before again taking up the trail. Judge Cradlebaugh decided that a general war against the Paiutes was not the same as protecting the community, and he and most of those accompanying him returned to Carson Valley. That left 105 or 106 men, most on horses or mules, with several stragglers on foot. They carried muskets or shotguns. Lord commented, "The Pi-Utes had been so inoffensive and placable that the idea of their offering any organized or stubborn resistance never entered the minds of the one hundred and six avengers who constituted the irregular posse and intended to administer even-handed justice to the offenders by putting to death as many of the tribe as fell into their hands."[22]

Years later, one of the company, Charles Foreman, at the time new to the area and employed by Wells, Fargo, and Company in Virginia City, criticized their readiness, saying they were poorly mounted, with only a few rifles, little ammunition, and few provisions. He decried the fact that they lacked structure and discipline, remarking, "The command consisting of several independent companies went into battle in that disorganized condition."[23]

The irregular battalion followed an Indian trail a number of miles along the east side of the Truckee River. They were on a plateau, five hundred feet above the water. In that area, after bending from its easterly direction to run north to Pyramid Lake, the river cuts a path through treeless, high-desert lands. With the heavy winter, the river was deep, running fast. About fifteen miles from their starting point, the company would do battle near present-day Nixon, on the Paiute Reservation. The scene was afterward portrayed in a participant's account of positioning for the battle:

> We kept advancing until we reached a point where Pyramid Lake and Valley were both in full view. On a low, sandy ridge to our right we discovered a party of Indians, numbering about one hundred and fifty, all mounted, drawn up in a solid body, with four or five chiefs charging backward and forward in front of the Indians. They showed great skill in the handling of their horses. So soon as they perceived us they raised their warwhoop. From their position, they were able to count us, man by man, as we marched down the deep trail. We marched down into a narrow valley, some three to five hundred yards in width, the Indians being all the time in sight. We traveled about three-quarters of a mile in this valley, until we came within eight hundred yards of the Indians.

The Indians' skill in handling their horses would be matched by their fighting strategy. Beginning with taking the high ground and inducing the white settlers to attack up the hill, they would outgeneral them.

The volunteer militiamen were ordered to dismount and tighten their saddle girths. The Indians were "yelling like demons." The volunteers were still trying to regulate themselves. Illustrating the confusion, one report said that it was then agreed that "the whole force should be placed under the command of Major Ormsby," which was not the case.[24]

Moments later, one of the party called out that on the treeless hill, an Indian, who had ridden out from the others, was waving a white flag. One of McDonald's men had a "globe-sighted" rifle, and McDonald used it to examine the Indian, who rode "an elegant black charger" and remained just out of shooting range. McDonald determined it was not a flag but "a polished battle axe glistening in the sun." He ordered the marksman to fire at the Indian, who he felt was "brandishing it in defiance." The shot missed, and the Paiute wheeled around and rode back, rejoining the others. The decision caused considerable criticism after the battle. The *Sacramento Daily Union* correspondent wrote, "As far as I have heard, the greater number insist that it was a white flag; and the previous conduct of the Indians, as far as I have been able to learn, would indicate that they had no desire to war with the settlements in this vicinity."

Another editorial in the same paper stated, "From [a survivor's] statement it appears the Indians were disposed to communicate with the whites, as indicated in the white flag waved by the Indian on the bluff. There is no room to doubt as to its being a white flag the Indian waved, as they do not possess bright battleaxes." The editorial writer concluded that because the Indian was fired upon, "contrary to all the usages of civilized nations," the white men were responsible for inciting the fight.[25]

The battle was joined, regardless of whether it was a white flag or a weapon. A large number of Indians on foot now appeared on the hill between the two groups. Ormsby wanted to charge them, but McDonald thought the company should retreat to a cluster of cottonwoods where they would be protected on one side by the river and by the open plain on the other. Ormsby made the decision for his men: he gave the command to charge. He led thirty men up the hill, with others trailing behind. The Indians scattered, running in small groups in different directions, seeming to disappear. The horses running uphill through deep sand became fatigued. Some horses could not get up the slope and, becoming unmanageable, broke back to the timber along the river. When the disordered assault reached the hilltop, Indians reappeared from behind sagebrush and depressions in the ground and began firing. Other mounted Indians had appeared in the southeast, attempting to cut off the path on which the white men had come.

The Ormsby group's horses, some now wounded, stumbled back down the hill. Ormsby and McDonald conferred, agreeing to retreat to the stand of trees by the river. On the way they came to a deep gulch, and, taking cover there, they were able to hold off the Paiutes' advances for some ten minutes. Other Indians, on foot, reportedly the Pit River band, now appeared, attacking from the rear. McDonald reported: "A great panic seized our men, and a majority of them broke for the river; the others saw that they had to follow." Control of the men was now nonexistent. A survivor commented, "Major Ormsby displayed great courage, but had lost some of his presence of mind."[26]

A number of Americans who had been pushed to the river tried to ford it. They were driven back to the same bank by the rushing currents. Chiquito Winnemucca now led his Black Rock band in an onslaught from the trees to the north. Numaga waved at the band to stop, attempting to gain time to talk peace with Ormsby or other leaders. Chiquito refused to obey. He and his warriors charged past Numaga, continuing their attack.

Another of the American survivors described one of the major battle scenes:

> The Indians had now surrounded us entirely, the main body of them advancing from below us, under cover of trees. We then succeeded in rallying our men at a spot about one hundred yards from the Truckee river, and got them to, dismount. So soon as they were dismounted some tried to mount again, but were threatened to be shot by Captain McDonald if they would attempt to run. Here the main fight took place, the Indians closing in around us within sixty yards, they and we firing all the time.[27]

With ranks depleted by casualties and desertions, the Americans' positions were soon overrun. For those who remained, fighting was to the death. Soon, the entire company was in retreat. Their flight reflected the fact that this was a mob, not a trained unit.

In stark contrast, a *Sacramento Daily Union* correspondent spoke in awe of how Winnemucca directed the Paiutes. The Pyramid Lake headman had chosen the premier position for his warriors, and he himself stood on a nearby hill. The correspondent wrote: "Observe the consummate generalship of this old Chief; he displays a hundred horsemen in the center, who provoke a charge and retreat only to expose his enemies to the deadly crossfire of his hidden infantry. Notice his reserve, with weapons in hand, ready to sustain any weak point." The writer added an anecdote, saying the headman was some seventy years old: "I had the pleasure of an introduction to him last Summer, by Major Dodge, the Indian Agent. He is over six feet high, with gray hair, and withal the 'mildest mannered man that ever cut a throat.'"[28]

Some eight miles south of the battlefield, the trail leading out followed a narrow neck of land for a half mile and then uphill to the open spaces. Ormsby had left men atop the hill to secure the line of retreat, if it became necessary. Seeing the entire company in full retreat and ruthlessly pursued, the guards broke and ran. The restricted trail allowed only a few to pass at a time. The rest were trapped. "The Indians overtook them in force; rode in among them; beat [their horses] with their hands, bows or guns...thus causing them to fall back further among their pursuers." At that point the white settlers were routed and killed. Those who had escaped were chased for miles back over the plateau, with slow or injured horses and the mules run down. The killing stopped only when night fell. Seventy-six members of the command were killed or afterward unaccounted for.[29]

There are several stories of Ormsby's last minutes. As he tried to rally the men in a dried riverbed, he was shot through the cheek by an arrow. One account said that one man held him while another pulled the arrow out, but the barb remained and the tip's poison then began to work. Another version said he pushed the arrowhead through his mouth and pulled the shaft back out his cheek, causing the wound to bleed profusely. Subsequently, he was shot twice more, in the arm and shoulder. He directed those around him, "Go on boys, you can do no more for me!" or told them "to see if they could not cut their way through and get away."[30]

Captain R.G. Watkins, a one-legged man who had tied himself on his horse, led a small contingent from Silver City. He later wrote a letter describing how he encountered Ormsby after the major was badly wounded. Watkins told him he would try to rally the men once more.

Ormsby dissuaded him, saying it would be of no use; he needed to look out for himself. All Ormsby asked for "was strength to face the foe when he received his death shot." Watkins confessed, "The Indians were gaining on us rapidly; one look at them and thought of self conquered valor, and the next moment, with a few parting words to Ormsby, I was on my way to Carson."[31]

Indians told how the injured Ormsby had retreated on a mule to a trail leading up a hill: "He was half-way up the trail when his saddle turned, throwing him upon the ground." He started to walk up the hill but looked back and saw that his closest pursuer was a Paiute he knew. "'Don't kill me,' he said, raising his hand and calling the Indian by name. 'I am your friend, I'll go and talk with the whites and make peace.'

"'No use now,' replied the Indian, 'too late.' And he shot Ormsby with arrows twice more, killing him."[32]

Sarah Winnemucca had an alternate version of that part of the story: "My brother had tried to save Major Ormsbey's life. He met him in the fight, and as he was ahead of the other Indians, Major Ormsbey threw down his arms, and implored him not to kill him. There was not a moment to be lost. My brother said, 'Drop down as if dead when I shoot, and I will fire over you;' but in the hurry and agitation he still stood pleading, and was killed by another man's shot." Natchez himself said that although he had shielded him for a moment, Ormsby "died with twenty hands at his throat."[33]

"Indian Massacre," roared California's newspaper headlines. Editors worried that it was the beginning of deadly hostilities against white settlers in western Utah. The *Sacramento Daily Union* said the fight "shows the determined intention of those Indians to wage a war of extermination against the whites." And it bemoaned the "slaughter" of the well-armed Californians, declaring, "Those savages have struck California a heavier blow than she has ever before received from a hostile quarter."[34]

The telegraph, an instrument introduced to advance American incorporation of the Eastern Sierra, now was put to use to facilitate warfare. Messages from the eastern slope telegraphed to Sacramento rallied US military, California volunteers, and militia units. One of the first transmissions requested arms and relayed the important information that a California deployment could follow the road across the Sierra and through Carson Valley: "There is no danger of parties to our relief being interrupted by the route. The Indians are about Pyramid Lake and the Truckee. Whatever is done should be done quickly. If the Indians knew our condition we should doubtless be attacked at once."[35]

As regular army units and large numbers of volunteers from communities across the Sierra responded, the editorial writers calmed down and began contextualizing events leading up to the battle. A paper in Nevada County, California, titled an article "Our Chickens Coming Home to Roost." It suggested the Indians were answering the outrages perpetrated by white settlers, mentioning specifically the slaughter at Humboldt Bay. The *Sacramento Daily Union* chronicled how the Paiutes had lived up to an agreement regarding restitution of stolen property, while the white settlers had not. It decried white people trespassing, poaching, and illegally laying claim to Pyramid Lake lands. Another article questioned why those stations near Williams Station had not been destroyed if the Paiutes were seeking a general war. Still, in acknowledging the Indians' victory, the editorial concluded that if the white settlers did not now vanquish them, there would be no safety on the frontier.[36]

In the first week of June 1860, 547 volunteers and 207 US Army troops joined to fight the now somewhat more than 300 Paiute warriors. The second battle was fought near the first battleground, south of Pyramid but up on the plateau and the steep mountainside. Once again, the Paiutes used a superior knowledge of the landscape in a defense lauded by witnesses as amazing. When the white troops formed a mile-long line and advanced northward, the Indians concealed themselves and held off the advance as their women and children escaped to the desert. Finally, the warriors themselves escaped, and the white men lost contact with them.[37]

In August 1860 Colonel F.W. Lander of the US Wagon Road Expedition faced trying circumstances when he attempted to negotiate with the mistrustful Paiutes. Nevertheless, a meeting with Numaga was arranged. Lander was in his fourth year leading the effort to improve the emigrant road. He was an impressive man, six-foot-two, two hundred pounds, and said to be imposing but gracious. A civil engineer, he turned down Lincoln's proffer to be the Nevada Territory's governor. He later served as a brevet general in the Civil War, and when he died from a wound suffered at Edward's Ferry in 1861, President Lincoln attended his funeral.

Lander reported about the meeting that Numaga "said he would look hard at me and when the sun was low would be ready to talk." When he began, Numaga explained that he might have spoken in anger earlier, for he saw men with Lander who had killed his young warriors. Lander said, "Now he had sat upon my blanket, had eaten of my meat and at last had smoked the pipe, and was quiet so that he could talk calmly." Lander agreed to listen, but could make no promises. White settlers had been killed also, and the government might seek retribution. Numaga was glad Lander made no promises; he was bitter over promises made and broken. He desired peace but told a familiar story. The white settlers had come into Paiute land, taking the best valleys and fishing sites, driving the Indians away.[38]

Numaga also raised the subject of the elderly, women, and children massacred on the reservation at Humboldt Bay. The Paiutes would rather die fighting than allow such a fate.

Lander noted, "It was difficult for me to reply to this.... I believe that the knowledge of these murders has had much to do with the present war." Lander knew that although the Paiutes were short on provisions, Numaga could sustain the fight. That intelligence was widely acknowledged. Three months earlier, on May 28, 1860, the *Sacramento Daily Union* had reported, "[Numaga] is well acquainted with the movements and numbers of the whites east of the mountain, and... has been deliberately preparing for a desperate conflict in defense of the territories and rights of his tribe." Lander turned the discussion to the terms of an armistice. After an hour of talk, they resolved to take an agreement to their respective leadership. There would be a truce, provided each side refrained from acts of hostility for a year. Within that time, they would get the treaty confirmed. Helping the cause, Warren Wasson was named acting Indian agent the following month. In December 1860, he met with the tribe, giving clothing to the men and sewing materials to the women. It is said that when an old man arrived late to the meeting and all the clothes had been given out, Wasson removed his own shirt and pants and gave them to him.[39]

Although some Paiutes joined fighting that continued in Northern California and Oregon, the truce prevented more warfare in Nevada Territory. Even so, in the following decade way stations were periodically raided, stock driven off, and some station agents killed. The federal government answered by establishing more than two dozen military posts near population centers and along the travel routes.[40]

The truce was an unequivocal defeat for the Paiute way of life. Like what happened to the Washoes, the failure of relations between them and the denizens of Carson Valley and Honey Lake Valley created a setting of continual struggle for the Native people. The government did not recognize the Indians' right to continue utilizing their traditional lands, declaring California Indians had no right to specific land.[41]

In 1879 army captain Richard Henry Pratt established the first off-reservation boarding school for Indians, Pennsylvania's Carlisle Indian School. Pratt's previous experience included educating Native American prisoners of war, and he is remembered for a phrase expressing the government's ethnocentric philosophy: "Kill the Indian, and save the man." As more boarding schools were created, attempting to rid Indian students of their traditions became an integral part of the system. Nevertheless, even as their heritage was denounced as savagery and their circumstances were radically diminished, neither Eastern Sierra tribe chose to assimilate.[42]

The Washoes, written off and without reservation lands, lived on the margins. Some tailored traditional practices to the American market. They acted as guides or sold game, fish, and pine nuts. Others worked as ranch hands or domestics. Some learned the trade of masonry, constructing, for example, the buildings of the Whittell estate on the shore of Lake Tahoe. A number of Washoe women adapted their skills for weaving utilitarian baskets to crafting decorative baskets for sale. At the end of the nineteenth century and into the twentieth, Datsolalee, a.k.a. Louisa Keyser, mixed traditional weaving and innovative design to create the *degikup* style of basketry, influencing generations of indigenous weavers. Her baskets, as well as others created by her Washoe counterparts, are now in museums and collections around the world.[43]

Paiutes Winnemucca and Numaga had cultivated relationships with white settlers as they occupied and settled on Paiutes' land. Associations with Lassen, Roop, and Weatherlow at Honey Lake, and with Ormsby and the agent Frederick Dodge in Carson Valley, were especially strong. Things changed in April 1859 with the killing of Lassen, the liaison who spoke the Paiutes' Numic language. That same year, word spread of the discovery of the Comstock's massive gold and silver deposits, the

Anglo population expanded, and difficulties multiplied beyond the two sides' capabilities to control their respective communities. Relationships abruptly switched from personal alliances to collective behaviors colored by societal prejudices.

The trusted and effective Paiute agent Warren Wasson served in his post for only two years. Numaga died of tuberculosis in 1871. Problems were ongoing, irrespective of who represented the government or the Paiutes. They were exacerbated by federal agents who did not try to protect the interests of the tribe.

In 1867 the federal government rejected the Nevada superintendent's proposal to remove the Indians from Pyramid Lake so the land could be used for what he saw as more productive purposes. In 1869 Hubbard Parker, the former supervisor who had previously vetoed finding reservation lands for the Washoes, unsuccessfully attempted to have the island in Pyramid Lake withdrawn from the Paiute Reservation so he could use it to raise cashmere goats.[44]

Mirroring many previous peace treaties, and foreshadowing others to come, the treaty between the white settlers and the Paiutes was frequently broken. American accusations of Indians pursuing "savage war" are difficult to sustain when compared with white settlers' attacks. The largest massacre of the era was Mountain Meadows, perpetrated by Mormons against Gentile Americans. White men carried out large-scale massacres against Indians as well. The butchery of Humboldt Bay reservation Indians, beginning with the women and children, is a blatant example. Between 1860 and 1870, in the Eastern Sierra region, 30 white people and 287 Indians were killed in interracial conflict. As Knack and Stewart point out, "The killing of Indians characteristically occurred in large aggregates of 15, 30, or 50, when a camp was attacked by an organized group of whites whose sole purpose was to slaughter all the natives they found."[45]

White settlers established farms and ranches on large tracts of the irrigable land on the Pyramid Lake Reservation after its designation. In 1861 Nevada's territorial governor wrote the secretary of interior, saying that he had instructed the agent to warn off the white settlers. The occupiers, though, were outside the territory's authoritative restraints. In 1924, with the white settlers still living on the properties, Congress passed legislation allowing them to purchase the land at an established price. Although some owners did not complete payments, and their holdings were deeded back to the tribe, other white settlers continued passing on their holdings from generation to generation.[46]

At the turn of the twentieth century, maintaining the country's agrarian values, the federal government sought to turn Nevada desert into arable land for white farmers. The Truckee River was dammed, and water, previously feeding Pyramid Lake, was diverted to irrigate potential farmland. The Lahontan cutthroat trout was eventually driven to extinction. By 1967 the water had fallen ninety-four feet, threatening the lake's existence. The tribe filed suits against the Department of Interior, eventually winning a Truckee River operating system that greatly increased water appropriations for the lake. Lahontan cutthroat were discovered in smaller bodies of water, and they were reintroduced into Pyramid Lake. Eventually, Congress provided moneys for the restoration of the fishery. The agreements dramatically reduced the number of court battles but did not extinguish them, as disputes over the river and lake have continued into the twenty-first century.[47]

Conclusion

This study focuses on the violent imposition of white American values and institutions during the pioneer settlement of the Eastern Sierra. The events took place in the era preceding the railroad and existed within the larger context of the Far West's incorporation. Wagon-train emigration was at its height, and Carson Valley and Honey Lake Valley served as gateways on the California Trail. The first decade of their development was plagued by inconsistencies in leadership and governance, leading to the settlements' inability to establish equitable justice systems.

The Eastern Sierra homesteaders were not inexperienced emigrants from the East but individuals who had lived in the West, in either Salt Lake City or California. Isolated from seats of government, the white settlers refused to submit to the distant, constituted authorities.

In Carson Valley, opposing local factions vied for jurisdiction, disputing one another's attempts to create civil order. Honey Lake Valley's leadership was uneven, often absent in times of trouble. The communities' refusal to pay taxes meant inconsistent or nonexistent policing and ineffective courts. With no means to bind over suspects, the accused were dealt with summarily, precluding fair trials. Transience in the populations and the reactionary, violent nature of some parties in both places added to the difficulties.

The citizenry in each valley included individualists who were indifferent to federalization, as well as people actively seeking national assimilation. The differences notwithstanding, they successfully produced charters that answered their needs regarding homesteading. Overlooking Native American rights to the land, they first provided for the survey of property claims, then designed instruments to ensure ownership lines were honored. In Carson Valley, they elected magistrates and sheriffs, although several of those elected proved untrustworthy or ineffective. At Honey Lake, disputes were to be settled by an arbitration committee of citizens, and their constitution included a noteworthy regulation. In a period when some California politicians and newspapers were calling for the extermination of Indians, the Honey Lake directive stated that anyone misusing or maltreating Indians would be referred for punishment to the board of arbitrators. In practice, the local militia regularly violated the ordinance without consequences.

The communities lacked routines to cope with unexpected crises, and when problems arose the settlers turned to violence. The lynch mobs, as well as the impromptu militia mobilized against the Paiutes at Pyramid Lake, fed off rumors. The newspapers reporting on the actions printed false statements and cited evidence that never materialized. In all cases, emotional tension raised the stakes, sustaining outrage and provoking the responses.

Mobs need leadership to provide direction for their aggressive behavior. None of Honey Lake's leading citizens participated in the hangings of Snow and Lucky Bill Thorington. It was a newcomer to Honey Lake, John Neale, who directed the crowd. A year later, he served as a delegate and chaired the committee on credentials at the Genoa constitutional convention. He then disappears from the histories, mentioned only as running cattle at the upper end of Honey Lake Valley.

Two other key players in the Thorington affair were ruffians, at times lawbreakers. The Eastern Sierra citizens embraced the idea that personal honor required men to stand their ground and that homicides were sometimes necessary. Richard Sides, at whose ranch the Thorington trial and hanging took place, and Rough Elliott, who led the Honey Lakers, were physically imposing men, epitomizing these tenets. The nature of their character encouraged others in potentially violent situations, as their bravado and bullying added to the emotional contagion. Each man's remaining years shed light on their character. Sides exhibited a disregard for morality and probity. Elliott crossed and recrossed the line between the legal and the unlawful.

After Mormon elder Orson Hyde had been recalled to Salt Lake City in the fall of 1856, Sides and a man named Jacob Rose took possession of Hyde's sawmill in Washoe Valley. Sides developed a ranch alongside it. When Hyde demanded payment for the property, Sides and Rose ignored him. Their response prompted the issuance of "Orson Hyde's

Curse." In 1862 Hyde wrote an open letter to the two men, saying they would be "living and dying advertisements of God's displeasure" and would be visited "with thunder and with earthquakes and with floods, with pestilence and with famine until your names are not known amongst men."[1]

In fact, a mountain dam ruptured in 1880, causing a flood that did wash away the old mill and bury the Sides ranch in sand. Although not of biblical proportions, another, more immediate affliction befell Sides. With the discovery of the Comstock Lode, he, Abernathy, Baldwin, and a man name Belcher filed a mining claim: five hundred feet between the celebrated Ophir Mine and the Gould and Curry Mine. Finding no ore near the surface, they gave up their claim. In January 1872, John Mackay and his partners, James Fair, James Flood, and William O'Brien, gained ownership. The four became known as the Bonanza Kings. The heart of the Comstock Lode lay beneath the property. Sides and his associates had let one of the richest mines in the world slip away.[2]

Elliott was the Honey Laker to claim leadership in the Thorington affair. He served as a detective in bringing charges against Thorington, organized the arrests in Genoa, and acted as the sheriff at the trial, in which he was a witness as well. Elliott was amply rewarded for his roles. As a reflection of his character, he reportedly kept a ring and money that he promised Edwards he would send to Edwards's mother. He kept Edwards's racehorse, and he reportedly went to Merced County to collect reward money offered by the Masons.

In 1862 Elliott bullied a man into a fistfight. When the man landed the first punch, Elliott pulled out a knife and sliced the man's throat. Elliott dropped out of sight, living in the woods for a few weeks. The victim recovered, and Elliott escaped punishment. In 1863 Elliott was elected captain of thirty Honey Lakers when they engaged in a four-hour shoot-out with a one-hundred-man posse led by Plumas County officials. Only one man was wounded, shot in the leg, before a truce was effected. Called the Sagebrush War, or the Boundary War, the gun battle was fought for standard Honey Lake reasons: disputed jurisdiction and Honey Lakers' refusal to pay taxes. Elliott appeared in court frequently in the 1860s, once as the plaintiff, seven times as the defendant.[3]

In 1874 Elliott, who was the proprietor of a hotel in Reno, was involved in a shooting affray. He suffered a head injury while shooting one robber, capturing another, and scaring off two others. He had arranged with the town sheriffs to arrest the four suspected criminals, but law enforcement was late to arrive, and he fought the miscreants alone.[4]

In the spring of 1888, an Inyo County court found Elliott guilty of murdering John B. White, his second wife's uncle. His first wife, Richard Sides's sister, had divorced him and remarried. His second wife, formerly known as the widow Baker, had also divorced him. Fearing violence from Elliott, Mrs. Baker-Elliott had asked her uncle to protect her and her children. In a confrontation on her ranch, Elliott stabbed White to death. Elliott's death sentence was appealed, and two subsequent trials resulted in hung juries.

Ironically, after the first trial, vigilantes in Inyo County met, planning to take Elliott from jail to lynch him. When the threat became known, he was transferred some 250 miles to Bakersfield, California, where the trials that ended in hung juries were held. Finally, in February 1891, with a fourth case pending, the Inyo County Board of Supervisors requested its dismissal. Costs to the county, and witnesses repeatedly required to travel to testify, had become too burdensome. The editor of the local newspaper had previously commented, "Elliott is a curse on Inyo County; pity he was not hanged on the day he murdered John B. White."[5]

William Ormsby, while claiming to regulate moral probity, allied himself with Sides and Elliott. It was he and Sides who organized the vigilantes, and they joined Elliott and the Honey Lakers in hanging Thorington. The following year, Ormsby allowed Sides's brother, accused of murder, to escape without redress.

Ormsby rejected Utah's jurisdiction while pursuing various administrative controls and extralegal actions. He realized that national interests were connected to Eastern Sierra resources: raw materials, productive soil, and valuable metals. Confident in his own abilities and full of personal ambition, he chaired committees and acted as a spokesperson for the territory. The area's leading newspaper, the *Territorial Enterprise*, noted that Ormsby was in the thick of "everything of moment," political or financial.[6]

Ormsby had progressive tendencies. Contrary to many of the settlers, who feared or hated Indians, he formed an alliance with the Paiutes. In an apparent act of goodwill, he and his wife took in thirteen-year-old Sarah Winnemucca and her sister, and the girls lived with the Ormsbys for a number of months in Genoa. On the other hand, Washoes died when he demanded that headman Captain Jim bring in tribe members to be charged with murder, although the community lacked the means to administer justice. Similarly, he sought to rebuke the Paiute Tribe before understanding members' grievance with the Williams Station owners and without differentiating between those who committed the act and the rest of the tribe. He made no attempt to contact the Paiutes' leaders. Instead, in an atmosphere of crisis, he rallied others to follow him in taking military action. Lacking strategic, operational, and tactical structure, his command was doomed to fail. As to his myriad goals for the region, he did not live to see them succeed.

Carson Valley's vigilance committee and their people's court were measures intended to deliver justice. Each failed. Over the course of several months in 1858 and 1859, three men who supported the vigilantes committed murders. Two were shootings over card games, and the other was a killing over a bridle. In each case, the killers were allowed to go free. There was a similar occurrence at Honey Lake when Old Tom Harvey, one of the Honey Lake Rangers, went unpunished after he killed his "disreputable" partner in cold blood. On two occasions, Elliott summoned other Honey Lakers to stand against Plumas County officials attempting to carry out their duties. In like manner, at Carson Valley, Sides twice mustered large groups of anti-Mormons in standoffs against the sheriff's posses. In all instances, the actions weakened the region's already unavailing efforts at law and order; often the violence complicated problems rather than resolving them.

The lynching of Thorington is a glaring example of a measure intended to bring order that instead caused widespread disunity. Another case in point was Ormsby's attempt to punish the Paiutes for Williams Station, which led to the Pyramid Lake War.

Even when violence apparently achieved goals, it raised other issues or led to efforts at retribution. Honey Lake's response to outlying bands of Indians raiding their stock was the formation of the Honey Lake Rangers. Cultural chauvinism colored the Rangers' actions, and at times they answered Indian transgressions with indiscriminate killing of innocents. The Paiute leaders who gathered with their bands preceding the

Pyramid Lake War would undoubtedly have listed the killings as among what Numaga called "the great wrongs, that rise up like the mountains before you."[7]

In some instances, retribution was circular. In 1857 strychnine-laced flour was used to poison Pit River Indians who made several raids, driving off Honey Lake stock. After Weatherlow and his Rangers, assisted by Winnemucca and the Paiutes, defeated the Pit River band, the raids on Honey Lake livestock stopped. The band's inaction did not last, however, as their warriors played a key role in the rout of Ormsby's forces during the Pyramid Lake War.

A last comment about violence involves the role of newspapers. As in the roles discussed earlier, they wielded marked power. They played a significant part in fostering white settlers' negative sentiments regarding "the other." This study traces the newspapers' provocations regarding both the Mormoms and the Indians in particular. The 1857 verbal war between Mormon leadership in Salt Lake City and Far West newspapers is one example. Recalled to Salt Lake City, the Carson Valley Mormons left at the end of September. In doing so, they avoided what was escalating into something more than jingoistic language. In San Francisco, in mid-October, the *Daily Alta California* accused the Mormons of devising a system "to exterminate Gentiles." Other papers declared Uncle Sam needed to punish the rebellious religionists. By the end of December, the *Placerville Mountain Democrat* reported a predictable outcome of such instigation: companies were organizing that were eager to clash with Brigham Young's followers.[8]

The newspapers' treatment of Indians was generally derogatory too, and editors were quick to advocate for aggression against them. After the first Pyramid Lake battle, the papers called for volunteers to fight the "savages." The *Sacramento Daily Union,* a comparatively progressive paper, editorialized that white transgressions might have instigated the war, but nevertheless, for the region's safety, the white people needed to "vanquish" the Paiutes.[9]

The Native people's total loss had been sudden. Historian Ned Blackhawk comments, "In the span of one generation, from the Rocky Mountains to the Sierras immigrants became settlers, settlements became towns, and Indians became outsiders." A decade after the discovery of the Comstock's wealth, a local newspaper illustrated the point, announcing, "Let [the Indians] fully understand that they are safe while on their reservation, but when they absent themselves there from they are liable to be shot down like deer."[10]

Ultimately, the resolution of each Anglo community to determine their own fate was overwhelmed by the sweep of larger forces. With the Civil War at hand in 1861, some of those living along the Eastern Sierra returned to their home states to join one side or the other, but many were caught up in an excitement of a different sort. The Comstock Lode's gold and silver deposits proved to be fissure veins—sheets of ore extending far underground. The deep, hard-rock mining industry that evolved required a large labor force, experimentation leading to new technology, and for corporate enterprise to raise immense sums of investment capital. Roadways over the Sierra were widened and improved so heavy equipment could be hauled from San Francisco. Processing necessitated a quartz milling industry, with dozens of on-site mills. Timber removal became another Eastern Sierra industry, as the forests were clear-cut, used to build systems of wood supports to secure the mines' shafts and tunnels hundreds of feet underground. The environmental degradation was recognized but accepted as a matter of course. By 1875 the *Territorial Enterprise* reported that the Consolidated Virginia, a leading producer among dozens of mines, was consuming six million feet of lumber per year. It commented, without hyperbole, that the Comstock Lode would be "the tomb of the forests of the Sierra."[11]

Congress did not create a new territorial regime for Carson Valley until the nearby mines revealed the extent of their riches. The region then became important enough that its plea for federal recognition was answered. In the spring of 1861, President Lincoln sent officials to reorganize a large portion of the western Great Basin as Nevada Territory.

Other actions by the federal government followed. In 1862 Congress passed the Pacific Railway Act, promoting the building of the transcontinental railroad across the Sierra. Two years later, on October 31, 1864, Nevada was admitted as the Union's thirty-sixth state.

In the 1850s, California had been unwilling to become involved in Honey Lake's political turmoil. It was not until the Sagebrush War that the citizens secured enough attention to spur the state to act. In 1864 California created the new county of Lassen. The town of Susanville, at the head of Honey Lake Valley, was named its county seat. The place-names honored the area's two respected leaders. The county, like Northern California's Lassen Peak, was named for Peter Lassen. Susanville was originally named Rooptown, and, like the Susan River, it was named for Isaac Roop's daughter.

Mining and the railroad redesigned the eastern slope. The clear-cutting of Lake Tahoe's forests caused silt to cloud its heretofore pristine waters, requiring a half century for it to regain its clarity. Lumbering wastes polluted the Truckee River; mining wastes polluted the Carson River. New towns, Reno and Truckee, were created as the Central Pacific Railroad cut its route in between Carson Valley and Honey Lake Valley. The railway diminished the valleys' importance as transportation hubs. In Nevada Territory, other railroad towns sprang up, including one named for the Paiute Winnemucca. By 1870 the territory's ranchers were shipping thirty thousand animals a year to be butchered in California.[12]

Over two decades, Comstock mines sank shafts more than three thousand feet underground. Resource extraction, by capitalized investors, became the region's focus. The adjoining towns of Virginia City and Gold Hill, built atop the Comstock Lode, totaled nearly twenty-five thousand inhabitants. Carson City, realizing Ormsby's vision, became Nevada's capital, building the statehouse and state prison and hosting a US Mint. The fertile Carson Valley provided livestock, dairy, and agriculture, serving as an exploitable resource base for the mining industry. Similarly, Honey Lake's commerce centered on agriculture, and Susanville became the heart of lumbering operations.

The Far West and the entire national economy benefited from the dislocation of the Eastern Sierra Indians and the exploitation of the land. Each white community had engaged in its version of conquest. Each had overcome fitful starts at administering justice. Disputes in the valleys now regarded water rights or property lines and were brought to a Nevada district court or California Superior Court. In other parts of the West, new resources were discovered and new markets developed. The suffering caused by the disorder and violence in the Eastern Sierra was passed over as America's vision of a federated empire advanced.

Notes

Introduction

1. For a short discussion of social order and vigilantism, see David A. Johnson, "Vigilance and the Law: The Moral Authority of Popular Justice in the Far West," 558–61. For a short overview of similar circumstances in the Eastern Sierra, see Frederick Allen, *A Decent Orderly Lynching: The Montana Vigilantes,* xv–xx.

2. James F. Downs, *The Two Worlds of the Washo: An Indian Tribe of California and Nevada,* 5, 52–53; Martha C. Knack and Omer C. Stewart, *As Long as the River Shall Run: An Ethnohistory of Pyramid Lake Indian Reservation,* 27; Ned Blackhawk, *Violence over the Land: Indians and Empires in the Early American West,* 8–11.

3. Myron Angel, *History of Nevada,* 50–51; Chauncey N. Noteware, former Nevada secretary of state, to A. M. Fairfield, n.d., California Section, California State Library, Sacramento.

4. *Sacramento Daily Union,* May 28, 1860.

5. Eliot Lord, *Comstock Mining and Miners,* 67–68.

6. In 1845 O'Sullivan issued what amounted to a call to arms against Mexico. Earlier, in speaking of the territory encompassing California, a Spanish official had said one cannot "put doors on open country." Albert Hurtado, "Their Flag, Too," 46. O'Sullivan argued America could. He said that an "imbecile and distracted" Mexico was unable any longer to hold the distant province of California. He offered cultural context for expansion: "Already the advance guard of the irresistible army of Anglo-Saxon emigration has begun to pour down upon it, armed with the plough and the rifle, and marking its trail with schools and colleges, courts and representative halls, mills and meeting-houses." O'Sullivan concluded by predicting that the Atlantic and Pacific would soon be joined, "so that a hundred years hence two hundred and fifty, or three hundred millions—and American millions [are] destined to gather beneath the flutter of the stripes and stars." John O'Sullivan, "Annexation," 5–6, 9–10; "John O'Sullivan Declares America's Manifest Destiny, 1845."

7. Robert K. Hitchcock and Charles Flowerday, "Ishi and the California Indian Genocide as Developmental Mass Violence," 73; Benjamin Madley, *An American Genocide: The United States and the California Indian Catastrophe, 1846–1873,* 207, 253, 320–21, 174.

8. Brendan C. Lindsay, *Murder State: California's Native American Genocide, 1846–1873,* 16, 30–31; Hitchcock and Flowerday, "Ishi and the California Indian Genocide," 72; Madley, *American Genocide,* 222, 175.

9. Although not identified as such in the 1850s, the propagandistic tactics were used for psychological effect and are similar to those defining current-day terrorism. See David P. Stewart, "Terrorism and Human Rights: The Perspective of International Law," report, Middle East Institute, 2018, 6–9, http://www.jstor.org/stable

/resrep19954.8. The random killings on the eastern slope echoed those across the Sierra, in Northern California. Madley describes the circumstance as the "institutionalization of California's killing machine," pointing out: "By the spring of 1854, Indian killing was so common that it sometimes required no provocation." Madley, *American Genocide*, 230, 228.

10. See Tim Wilson, "Rightist Violence: An Historical Perspective" (The Hague: International Centre for Counter-Terrorism, 2020), 2, https://www.jstor.org/stable/resrep23578?seq=1#metadata_info_tab_contents. Kathleen Belew, in discussing the modern white-power movement in America, explained that white supremacists sometimes attempt to subvert or overthrow state power. Nonetheless, throughout US history, because white supremacy undergirded it, "vigilantes most often served the white power structure." Things changed in the 1980s when white power made the state its target. Kathleen Belew, *Bring the War Home: The White Power Movement and Paramilitary America*, 106–7, 3. Even the Ku Klux Klan saw itself as part of, and serving, the white-dominated national culture. Elaine Frantz Parsons remarked that the Klan's purpose "was to promote white political, economic, and social interests over those of their black neighbors." The Ku Klux was organized in some areas, in others not, magnifying an inconsistent view of authority. That perspective was certainly buttressed by government responses that, Parsons noted, were "often half-hearted." Elaine Frantz Parsons, *Ku-Klux: The Birth of the Klan During Reconstruction*, 9, 303.

11. *Chico Record*, November 25, 1856.

12. Allen, *Decent Orderly Lynching*, xvi, xvii. Vigilante actions persist in the twenty-first century. Vigilantes periodically patrol the US-Mexico border. In 2014 a group, armed with military-style weapons, kept federal agents from collecting grazing fees from a Nevada rancher. In 2016, led by the same individuals, now dubbing themselves Citizens for Constitutional Freedom, they seized the Malheur National Wildlife Refuge in Oregon. They held it for forty-one days, resulting in the death of one of their members and the arrest of a number of others, costing taxpayers $1.2 million. Michael J. Makley, *Open Spaces, Open Rebellions: The War over America's Public Lands*, 101–7.

13. Nancy J. Taniguchi, *Dirty Deeds: Land, Violence, and the 1856 San Francisco Vigilance Committee*, xi, xv, 3–11, 236–39. The histories referred to as presenting favorable opinions regarding the San Francisco vigilantes include noted nineteenth-century California historians: Hubert Howe Bancroft, *Popular Tribunals* (1887); and Theodore H. Hittell, in the third of four volumes of his *History of California* (1885–97).

14. Henry Steele Comager, ed., "Constitution of the Committee of Vigilantes of San Francisco, May 15, 1856," in *Documents of American History*, 338–39.

15. Michael Green, *Nevada: A History of the Silver State*, 75.

16. By 1862, authorities were pursuing forms of passive violence against Indians. In Nevada, territorial governor James Nye was urging the establishment of systems that would train the Native peoples and "transform them from savages to men and women adapted to all the employments necessary to self-subsistence." "Report of James Nye," annual report of the commissioner of Indian affairs, 1863, 418–19, in *Violence over the Land*, by Blackhawk, 270.

17. Matthew S. Makley, *The Small Shall Be Strong*, 72–73.

18. Richard Slotkin, *Gunfighter Nation: The Myth of the Frontier in 20th Century America*, 12–13; Madley, *American Genocide*, 227, 3; Kevin Starr, *California: A History*, 99.

19. See Robert A. Caro, *The Years of Lyndon Johnson: Master of the Senate*, 15–23. Caro's characterization, which originated with the writing of commentators like Alexis de Tocqueville in the middle of the nineteenth century, referred to the Senate. For an argument that his designation may be an oversimplification, at least as it refers to its relationship with the House of Representatives, see Daniel Wirls, "The 'Golden Age' Senate and Floor Debate in the Antebellum Congress."

20. Richard Maxwell Brown, *No Duty to Retreat: Violence and Values in American History and Society*, 7–8, 34; Richard Maxwell Brown, "Western Violence: Structure, Values, Myth."

Chapter One. Encounters

1. Rohrbough in William Deverell, ed., *The Companion to the American West*, 115. There were 92,597 people in California recorded by the 1850 Census. That census did not include San Francisco, whose records had been destroyed by fire, and Contra Costa and Santa Clara Counties, whose counts were lost on the way to the census office. The state took a special census in 1852, and the count had risen to 260,949. *The Seventh Census of the United States: 1850–California*, 966, 972, https://www2.census.gov/library/publications/decennial/1850/1850a/1850a-47.pdf.

2. Stephen J. Crum, *The Road on Which We Came: A History of the Western Shoshone*, 21.

3. Angel, *History of Nevada*, 145; Zenas Leonard, *Adventures of a Mountain Man: The Narrative of Zenas Leonard*, 116–17.

4. Leonard, *Adventures of a Mountain Man*, 214–15.

5. Angel, *History of Nevada*, 146.

6. Crum, *Road on Which We Came*, 2, 13, 18–19; Scott Stine, *A Way Across the Mountain: Joseph Walker's 1833 Trans-Sierran Passage and the Myth of Yosemite's Discovery*, 63, 89; Knack and Stewart, *As Long as the River Shall Run*, 31–32.

7. Blackhawk, *Violence over the Land*, 10; James H. Simpson, *Report of Explorations Across the Great Basin of the Territory of Utah*, 109.

8. F. Dodge to Jacob Forney, Superintendent Indian Affairs, Utah Territory, January 4, 1859, "1860—Report of the Commissioner of Indian Affairs for 1859," 376, https://digicoll.library.wisc.edu/cgi-bin/History/History-idx?type=article&did=History.AnnRep59.i0013&id=History.AnnRep59&isize=M.

9. David E. Potter, ed., *Trail to California: The Overland Journal of Vincent Geiger and Wakeman Bryarly*, 189.

10. Potter, *Trail to California*, 25, 188n3.

11. Sherman L. Fleek, "The Kearny/Stockton/Frémont Feud: The Mormon Battalion's Most Significant Contribution in California," 238n15.

12. Allan Nevins, ed., *Narratives of Exploration and Adventure by John Charles Frémont*, 512–13.

13. Dale L. Morgan, *The Humboldt: Highroad of the West*, 199–202.

14. Green, *Nevada,* 68; Morgan, *Humboldt,* 198–99.

15. Simpson, *Report of Explorations,* 96. A few years after Simpson, Samuel Bowles, a famous East Coast newspaper publisher, described the area as having "forests to which the largest of New England are but pigmies." Samuel Bowles, *Across the Continent: A Summer's Journey to the Rocky Mountains, the Mormons, and the Pacific States with Speaker Colfax, 1866,* 165.

16. M. S. Makley, *Small Shall Be Strong,* 22–23.

17. M. S. Makley, *Small Shall Be Strong,* 3–4.

18. M. S. Makley, *Small Shall Be Strong,* 3; Robert W. Ellison, *First Impressions: The Trail Through Carson Valley, 1848–1852,* 20, 22–23. For a comprehensive presentation regarding the environment Euro-Americans found arriving in California, see ethnobotanist M. Kat Anderson, *Tending the Wild: Native American Knowledge and the Management of California's Natural Resources.*

19. Grace Dangberg, *Conflict on the Carson: A Study of Water Litigation in Western Nevada,* 1–3.

20. M. S. Makley, *Small Shall Be Strong,* 46. Makley points out that the fencing of the settlers' first garden "became a symbol of conquest, a tangible expression of the American colonial system that would eventually strip Washoes of all but tiny remnants of their once vast country" (49).

21. Downs, *Two Worlds of the Washo,* 73; Ellison, *First Impressions,* 23–24.

22. Downs, *Two Worlds of the Washo,* 73, 76, 78. For more regarding the Washoes and the Donner Party and sources of reporting, see M. S. Makley, *Small Shall Be Strong,* 45, 200n20.

23. J. H. Holeman, US Office of Indian Affairs, annual report of the commissioner of Indian affairs for the year 1851, Utah Superintendency, 182–84, 183–84, https://digicoll.library.wisc.edu/cgi-bin/History/History-idx?type=header&id=History.AnnRep51.

24. J. H. Holeman, US Office of Indian Affairs, annual report of the commissioner of Indian affairs for the year 1852, Utah Superintendency, 147–55, 154, https://digicoll.library.wisc.edu/cgi-bin/History/History-idx?type=header&id=History.AnnRep52.

25. J. H. Holeman, US Office of Indian Affairs, annual report of the commissioner of Indian affairs for the year 1853, Utah Superintendency, 203–7, 204, 207, https://digicoll.library.wisc.edu/cgi-bin/History/History-idx?type=header&id=History.AnnRep53.

26. Ellison, *First Impressions,* 60, 69.

27. Robert W. Ellison, *Territorial Lawmen of Nevada,* 3–4; Green, *Nevada,* 68–69; Robert Lyon, San Buenaventura, CA, November 16, 1880, in Angel, *History of Nevada,* 30.

28. Rodman W. Paul, *The Far West and the Great Plains in Transition, 1859–1900,* 175.

29. Eugene P. Moehring, *Urbanism and Empire in the Far West, 1840–1890,* 123.

30. Utah Division of Archives and Records Service, "Original Land Titles in Utah Territory," https://archives.utah.gov/research/guides/land-original-title.htm.

31. Angel, *History of Nevada,* 32–33; Ellison, *Territorial Lawmen of Nevada,* 9–25.

32. Angel, *History of Nevada*, 550; Henry Van Sickle in *Nevada Historical Society Papers, 1913–1916*, 192.

33. Grace Dangberg, *Carson Valley: Historical Sketches of Nevada's First Settlement*, 51.

34. Angel, *History of Nevada*, 32.

35. Morgan, *Humboldt*, 202.

36. M. S. Makley, *Small Shall Be Strong*, 84.

37. Lenúka, known as Captain Jim, is not to be confused with Epesuwa, a later headman who was also called "Captain Jim" by white settlers. Epesuwa traveled to Washington, DC, reportedly meeting with President Harrison in 1892. M. S. Makley, *Small Shall Be Strong*, 84.

38. Holeman, US Office of Indian Affairs, annual report of the commissioner of Indian affairs for the year 1853, Utah Superintendency, 203–7, 204, 207. The Washoes' ability to avoid contact with outsiders was well developed. Fifty years later, ethnographer J. W. Hudson wrote about difficulties searching for Washoes, who would say nothing about where they lived: "It was told me that there are over one hundred Indians in this valley, but I have searched all through this sage brush for miles yet found only seven arbors.... The only sure way to find them is to follow up a stream, necessarily afoot, and search for the water trail in a camp." M. S. Makley, *Small Shall Be Strong*, 51.

39. G. W. Ingalls in Sam Davis, ed., *The History of Nevada*, 38.

40. M. S. Makley, *Small Shall Be Strong*, 53; Ingalls in Davis, *The History of Nevada*, 38–39.

41. Morgan, *Humboldt*, 213–17, 219–21; Guy Rocha, "The Story of Jack's Valley," avepoa.com/Jacks_Valley.html.

42. Simpson, *Report of Explorations*, 98; *San Francisco Herald*, January 1, 1853.

43. *San Francisco Herald*, February 15, 1853.

44. Morgan, *Humboldt*, 203–4.

45. "1852 December 15—Eddy Annual Report, Surveyor General's Report to Governor of California" (2016), Surveyor General Reports, 3, https://digitalcommons.csumb.edu/hornbeck_usa_3_a/3. In 1859 the distance between Mormon Station, or Genoa, and Placerville was found by the army's topographical engineers to be 79.5 miles, traveling by road. Simpson, *Report of Explorations*, 98.

46. Green, *Nevada*, 69.

47. Eric R. Schlereth, "Privileges of Locomotion: Expatriation and the Politics of Southwestern Border Crossing," 997–1000, 1015–18. In 1839 one of California's expatriates, John Sutter, built a fort near Sacramento and became something of a justice of the peace for the area. He had bad relations with the Mexican government, as his settlement attracted unsavory characters, including adventurers, AWOL sailors, and rustlers and Indians who stole horses from the Mexican herds. In 1848 the discovery at his sawmill launched the gold rush. Hurtado, "Their Flag, Too," 48.

48. William Deverell, "Politics and the 20th-Century West," in *Companion to the American West*, ed. Deverell, 454; Juanita Brooks, "The Mormons in Carson County, Utah Territory," 9.

49. *Daily Alta California*, July 14, 1852.

50. Paul, *Far West and the Great Plains in Transition*, 177.

51. "Journal of Discourses," vol. 1, "A Discourse by Elder Orson Pratt, Delivered in the Tabernacle, Great Salt Lake City, August 29, 1852, Reported by G. D. Watt," 53–66, 59, 60, 61, https://jod.mrm.org/1/53.

52. *Nevada Journal*, October 6, 1854. Quote by the abolitionist is attributed to John Alexander Wills in Matthew Karp, "The People's Revolution of 1856: Antislavery Populism, National Politics, and the Emergence of the Republican Party," 524. Quote threatening to Mormonize the abolitionists is in Diane Mutti Burke, "A Contested Promised Land: Mormons, Slaveholders, and the Disputed Vision for the Settlement of Western Missouri," 30, 31–32.

Chapter Two. Lucky Bill and Other Problems

1. Archer Butler Hulbert, *Forty Niners: The Chronicle of the California Trail*, 214. Hulbert served for a number of years as archivist for the Harvard Commission on Western History.

2. Seventh Census of the United States: 1850—California, 970, https://www2.census.gov/library/publications/decennial/1850/1850a/1850a-47.pdf; Ellison, *First Impressions*, 6, 28–29; J. M. Hixon (diary) in Centennial Book Committee, *Alpine Heritage*, 19.

3. Sherman Day in Francis P. Farquhar, *History of the Sierra Nevada*, 97.

4. *San Juaquin Republican*, April 9, 1853.

5. Van Sickle in *Nevada Historical Society Papers*, 192; A. H. Hawley in *Nevada Historical Society Papers*, 176.

6. Angel, *History of Nevada*, 49.

7. Van Sickle in *Nevada Historical Society Papers*, 192. Twentieth-century histories of the Sierra played off his contemporaries' descriptions of Thorington. In 1949 George Hinkle and Bliss Hinkle wrote: "His brilliant dark eyes were lighted with quizzical humor and with what seemed, even to his victims, a profound and secret compassion. This impression of great depths of sympathy, together with a certain large urbanity of manner, was his greatest asset—a semblance which a surprisingly large number of law-abiding residents of Genoa could only describe as 'nobility'.... Lucky Bill could make a man count it a distinction to lose his shirt at a single turn of the card, and his rich baritone could make a barroom story sound like one of the Parables." George Hinkle and Bliss Hinkle, *Sierra-Nevada Lakes*, 142.

8. Quoted in David Thompson, *Nevada: A History of Changes*, 202.

9. Nancy Miluck, "How Lucky Bill's Luck Ran Out in Old Genoa," 30.

10. Austin E. Hutcheson, "A Life of Fifty Years in Nevada: The Memoirs of Penrod of the Comstock Lode (Part 1)."

11. Angel, *History of Nevada*, 36; H. Hamlin, *Knott Reminiscences, Early History of the 1850s*, 11.

12. Grace Dangberg, *Carson Valley: Historical Sketches of Nevada's First Settlement*, 127. Carson sold the sheep in California, earning $32,000. *Marysville (CA) Daily Herald*, September 15, 1853.

13. Angel, *History of Nevada*, 35–36.

14. M. S. Makley, *Small Shall Be Strong,* 2, 58–59; Knack and Stewart, *As Long as the River Shall Run,* 19, 20.

15. James W. Hulse, *The Nevada Adventure,* 78–79; Lord, *Comstock Mining and Miners,* 24, 33.

16. Morgan, *Humboldt,* 249; Gary P. BeDunnah, "A History of the Chinese in Nevada, 1855–1904," 3.

17. Jos. D. Weeks, *Report on the Statistics of Wages in Manufacturing Industries with Supplementary Reports on the Average Price of Necessaries of Life,* 31, 65, 93 or scan sequence 649, 683, 711, https://babel.hathitrust.org/cgi/pt?id=hvd.hl4p9r&view=1up&seq=5.

18. Simpson, *Report of Explorations,* 90–91.

19. Hulse, *The Nevada Adventure,* 276; Ronald M. James, *The Roar and the Silence: A History of Virginia City and the Comstock Lode,* 97–99, 153–55.

20. Lord, *Comstock Mining and Miners,* 61–63; Angel, *History of Nevada,* 413–14, 518, 522.

21. Dan DeQuille, *The Big Bonanza,* 10–11, 291–92. The more liberal of the majority focused, when attentive at all, on perceived Chinese-immigrant eccentricity. DeQuille wrote, "The Chinese are a curious people and have curious notions on all subjects. They are like Europeans in nothing. They are very superstitious and believe in ghosts and all that sort of thing, yet they sometimes act as though Satan himself could not frighten them" (292).

22. As communities developed, the prejudice against Chinese men took many forms. In Butte, Montana, labor organizations boycotted employers of Chinese immigrants because when the immigrants worked doing laundry or as cooks or as servants, they were competing with women workers. Sarah Deutch, "Landscape of Enclaves: Race Relation in the West, 1865–1990," in *Under an Open Sky: Rethinking America's Western Past,* ed. William Cronon, George Miles, and Jay Gitlin, 116.

23. Angel, *History of Nevada,* 37.

24. "Population and Industry of California: By the State Census for the Year 1852," 982, https://www2.census.gov/library/publications/decennial/1850/1850a/1850a-47.pdf.

25. Angel, *History of Nevada,* 38; Ellison, *Territorial Lawmen of Nevada,* 123; Simpson, *Report of Explorations,* 92.

26. Richard Moreno, *A Short History of Carson City,* 12.

27. Angel, *History of Nevada,* 34; *San Francisco Herald,* September 28, 1854.

28. *Records of Carson City, Utah and Nevada Territories, 1855–61* (Carson City, 1861), 76–77.

29. Angel, *History of Nevada,* 38.

30. Angel, *History of Nevada,* 50.

31. Thomas Wren, *A History of the State of Nevada,* 36.

32. Sarah Winnemucca-Hopkins, *Life Among the Piutes, Their Wrongs and Claims,* 58–59; Sally Zanjani, *Sarah Winnemucca,* 44–51.

33. For a discussion of differing stories of women in the West, see Elizabeth Jameson, "Bringing It All Back Home: Rethinking the History of Women and the Nineteenth-Century West," in *Companion to the American West*, ed. Deverell, 179–99.

34. Louise Amelia Knapp Smith Clappe, "Dame Shirley," 23, 39, 22, 54.

35. Angel, *History of Nevada,* 38. In California in the early 1850s, women made up 10 percent of the population.

36. Sally Zanjani, *Devils Will Reign: How Nevada Began,* 15.

37. Elizabeth Jameson, "Women as Workers, Women as Civilizers: True Womanhood in the American West," in *The Women's West,* ed. Elizabeth Jameson and Susan Armitage, 150–51; Page Smith quoted in Karen R. Jones and John Wills, *Women in the West: The Trailblazers and the Homesteader,* 133.

38. Zanjani, *Devils Will Reign,* 101.

39. Amelia Bass writing in the mid-1860s in Fort Collins, Colorado. Susan Armitage, "Through Women's Eyes: A New View of the West," in *The Women's West,* ed. Jameson and Armitage, 9–18, 12.

40. *San Francisco Herald,* August 27, 1857; Asa Merrill Fairfield, *A Pioneer History of Lassen County, California,* 131.

41. "Records of Carson City, Utah and Nevada Territories, 1855–61," 17, Nevada State Archives, Carson City; *Inyo County Register,* January 22, 1914.

42. Arnold R. Trimmer, unpublished manuscript, 1969, Van Sickle Collection, Douglas County Library, Minden, NV.

43. *Inyo Register,* January 22, 1914.

44. Hinkle and Hinkle, *Sierra-Nevada Lakes,* 114. Roop was good-humored as well. When he was the elected district attorney of Lassen County, he presented a document indicting a suspected horse thief. The grand-jury foreman said it was too brief and would not hold up in court. "Why not?" Roop protested. "I've got whereas in three times." Fariss and Smith, *Illustrated History of Plumas, Lassen, and Sierra Counties,* 376.

45. Knack and Stewart, *As Long as the River Shall Run,* 15–16, 2–7.

46. William Weatherlow in Fariss and Smith, *Illustrated History of Plumas, Lassen, and Sierra Counties,* 379, https://archive.org/details/illustratedhisto00sanf/mode/2up; Knack and Stewart, *As Long as the River Shall Run,* 53.

47. Fariss and Smith, *Illustrated History of Plumas, Lassen, and Sierra Counties,* 342; *Stockton Independent,* September 12, 1857; Hinkle and Hinkle, *Sierra-Nevada Lakes,* 106.

48. Seeking to govern California, Frémont engaged in a military and personal feud with Brigadier General Stephen Kearney that nearly led to open hostilities between them during the Mexican War. Frémont was court-martialed, found guilty of mutiny and disobeying orders, but was pardoned by President James Polk. See Fleek, "Kearny/Stockton/Frémont Feud."

49. Fariss and Smith, *Illustrated History of Plumas, Lassen, and Sierra Counties,* 60, 136, 333; Starr, *California: A History,* 65–70.

50. See Madley, *American Genocide.* Anthropologist Robert Heizer calculated that one hundred Indians were slain for every white man killed. In his study of the genocide, historian Lindsay concluded that this may have been an underestimation. Lindsay, *Murder State,* 184.

51. Fariss and Smith, *Illustrated History of Plumas, Lassen, and Sierra Counties,* 344–45; *Yreka Mountain Herald,* August 7, 1853, quoted in Madley, *American Genocide,* 221.

By 1855 several Northern California newspapers were reporting on, or calling for, completing the work of extermination (242–43).

52. Fairfield, *Pioneer History of Lassen County,* 30.

53. Susan Lee Johnson, *Roaring Camp: The Social World of the California Gold Rush,* 152.

54. Fariss and Smith, *Illustrated History of Plumas, Lassen, and Sierra Counties,* 343.

55. Ellison, *Territorial Lawmen of Nevada,* 155; Hinkle and Hinkle, *Sierra-Nevada Lakes,* 112–13; Fairfield, *Pioneer History of Lassen County,* 196. For a discussion of the Boundary War, see Fairfield, *Pioneer History of Lassen County,* 310–30.

56. Fairfield, *Pioneer History of Lassen County,* 268.

Chapter Three. Domesticating and Agitating

1. *Sacramento Daily Union,* July 6, 1855; Dangberg, *Carson Valley,* 51–52; *San Francisco Herald,* January 31, 1855.

2. Will Bagley, *Blood of the Prophets: Brigham Young and the Massacre at Mountain Meadows,* 4, 31.

3. *Placerville Mountain Democrat,* December 19, 1857; *San Francisco Herald,* July 17, 1855.

4. See, for example, *Daily Alta California,* December 1, 1854; *Georgetown News,* January 18, 1855; and *Shasta Courier,* November 17, 1855.

5. Brooks, "Mormons in Carson County," 17–18, 18n37; *Sacramento Daily Union,* November 7, 1856; Zanjani, *Devils Will Reign,* 62.

6. Morgan, *Humboldt,* 206.

7. Brooks, "Mormons in Carson County," 16–17; Angel, *History of Nevada,* 38.

8. Brooks, "Mormons in Carson County," 39; Ellison, *Territorial Lawmen of Nevada,* 80–81; Morgan, *Humboldt,* 249.

9. Brooks, "Mormons in Carson County," 18.

10. Ellison, *Territorial Lawmen of Nevada,* 103–4.

11. Record of Probate Court of Carson County, Utah Territory, October 2, 1855, to July 30, 1861, complaint filed May 22, 1856, 15–21, Nevada State Archives, Carson City.

12. Record of Probate Court of Carson County, complaint filed May 22, 1856, 15–21. As to the Knott and Thorington relationship, years later Knott's younger brother, Albert Adams Knott, said: "They were together in the ranch business and very friendly. Elzy liked to gamble the same as Lucky Bill." Hamlin, *Knott Reminiscences,* 15.

13. Ellison, *Territorial Lawmen of Nevada,* 107–9; Record of Probate Court of Carson County, complaint filed May 22, 1856, 21.

14. Hamlin, *Knott Reminiscences,* 15.

15. *San Francisco Herald,* April 3, 1860.

16. Angel, *History of Nevada,* 39–40.

17. Zanjani, *Devils Will Reign,* 62–63; Ellison, *Territorial Lawmen of Nevada,* 116–17.

18. Zanjani, *Devils Will Reign,* 63.

19. Abraham Hunsaker journal, August 25, 1856, quoted in Ellison, *Territorial Lawmen of Nevada,* 163.

20. *Chico Record,* November 25, 1856.

21. Dangberg, *Carson Valley,* 55; Angel, *History of Nevada,* 40.

22. *Chico Record,* November 25, 1856.

23. *Marysville (CA) Daily Herald,* January 23, 1857; *Sacramento Daily Union,* July 3, 1857.

24. Angel, *History of Nevada,* 40.

25. Angel, *History of Nevada,* 42, 64.

26. Keith J. Melville, "Theory and Practice of Church and State During the Brigham Young Era," 47–48.

27. *San Francisco Herald,* March 8, 1857.

28. Bagley, *Blood of the Prophets,* 76–77.

29. For a discussion of the Montana vigilantes' concept of social justice, see Allen, *Decent Orderly Lynching,* xviii.

Chapter Four. Major Ormsby, Mormons, and Indians

1. Hawkins to Fairfield, March 10, 1912.

2. Hamlin, *Knott Reminiscences,* 12. As an example of Ormsby's consistent publicity, in the spring of 1857, he was mentioned as carrying word of the settlers dealing with Indian threats. Then throughout the summer, newspapers reported on his activities, his pack-train and express-service businesses, and his use of his teams to test improvements to the road over the Sierra. The result was that his name appeared several times in the *Placerville Herald* and San Francisco's *Daily Alta California,* as well as in the *Sacramento Daily Union,* throughout the spring and summer, including at least three times in July.

3. Angel, *History of Nevada,* 43.

4. *Sacramento Daily Union,* July 28, 1857. The special 1852 California Census listed San Francisco's population at 34,776, and the 1860 Census listed it at 56,802. *Population and Industry of California: By the State Census for the Year 1852,* 982, https://www2.census.gov/library/publications/decennial/1850/1850a/1850a-47.pdf; *Population of the United States in 1860: State of California,* 31, https://www2.census.gov/library/publications/decennial/1860/population/1860a-06.pdf; Angel, *History of Nevada,* 42–43.

5. Hamlin, *Knott Reminiscences,* 11.

6. Fairfield, *Pioneer History of Lassen County,* 76–81. The manifesto's writers may have anticipated the actions of Atlas Fredonyer when they called those appointed "odious to the population generally." In 1862 he was convicted of "incestuous and criminal assault upon the person of his own daughter" and served a year and a half of a six-year sentence in prison. Fariss and Smith, *Illustrated History of Plumas, Lassen, and Sierra Counties,* 220–21, 228.

7. Martin Smith was Lake Valley and the Tahoe region's first Anglo settler, establishing a wilderness trading company at the foot of Johnson Pass leading to Placerville in 1851. Serving emigrants and wayfarers passing through, the hand-carved sign on his cabin read: "Groceries—Meals at All Hours—and Lodging if Required." Edward B. Scott, *The Saga of Lake Tahoe,* 191.

8. Fairfield, *Pioneer History of Lassen County,* 81–82; Hinkle and Hinkle, *Sierra-Nevada Lakes,* 132–33.

9. *Daily Alta California*, September 8, 1857.

10. Thomas Frederick Howard, *Sierra Crossing: First Roads to California*, 122–24; *Chico Record*, September 11, 18, 1857.

11. Knack and Stewart, *As Long as the River Shall Run*, 5–8; F. Dodge to Jacob Forney, Superintendent Indian Affairs, Utah Territory, January 4, 1859, "1860—Report of the Commissioner of Indian Affairs for 1859," 375–76, https://digicoll.library.wisc.edu/cgi-bin/History/History-idx?type=article&did=History.AnnRep59.i0013&id=History.AnnRep59&isize=M.

12. Knack and Stewart, *As Long as the River Shall Run*, 89–93; Michael J. Makley, *Saving Lake Tahoe: An Environmental History of a National Treasure*, 33–34.

13. M. T. Carr, 1st Lt., to W. J. Gardiner, Commander, Ft. Crook, Calif., July 2, 1858, in Knack and Stewart, *As Long as the River Shall Run*, 54.

14. William Dow and Fred Hines in Fairfield, *Pioneer History of Lassen County*, 110.

15. Madley, *American Genocide*, 175.

16. Fariss and Smith, *Illustrated History of Plumas, Lassen, and Sierra Counties*, 379.

17. See, for example, *The New York Times*, May 20, 1857; *Daily Alta California*, May 17, 20, 1857; and *Sacramento Daily Union*, June 20, 1857.

18. Bagley, *Blood of the Prophets*, 79–80.

19. *The New York Times*, July 2, 1857.

20. Bagley, *Blood of the Prophets*, 193.

21. Brooks, "Mormons in Carson County," 21–22.

22. Angel, *History of Nevada*, 42.

23. *San Francisco Herald*, October 6, 7, 1857, reprinted from the *Nevada Journal*.

24. In 1837 Samuel F. B. Morse had tried to sell his invention, the telegraph, to the federal government. It funded an experimental line that was run the thirty miles between Washington and Baltimore, but the government's administrative arm was weak in the nineteenth century, and authorities did not believe the telegraph system would be worth public ownership. So it was left to private business concerns to build segments of line they thought would be profitable. David Hochfelder, "A Comparison of the Postal Telegraph Movement in Great Britain and the United States, 1866–1900," 746–47.

25. *San Francisco Herald*, March 8, 1857; *Placerville Mountain Democrat*, May 23, 1857.

26. Downs, *Two Worlds of the Washo*, 52–53.

27. *Sacramento Daily Union*, August 17, 1857.

28. *San Francisco Herald*, August 18, 23, September 1, 1857.

29. *Sacramento Daily Union*, September 7, 1857; Ellison, *Territorial Lawmen of Nevada*, 79–85.

30. *Sacramento Daily Union*, September 10, 19, 28, 1857.

31. *Sacramento Daily Union*, October 6, 1857.

32. *Sacramento Daily Union*, October 28, November 2, 1857.

33. *Chico Record*, November 16, 1857.

34. Kimberly Johnston-Dodds, "Early California Laws and Policies Related to California Indians," California Research Bureau, 2002, 1–5, https://www.courts.ca.gov/documents/IB.pdf; Maria E. Montoya, "The Not-So-Free Labor in the American

Southwest," in *Empire and Liberty: The Civil War and the West,* ed. Virginia Scharff, 160–63. For a discussion of the Indian Act of 1850, see Andrés Reséndez, *The Other Slavery: The Uncovered Story of Indian Enslavement in America,* 2, 264–65.

35. Montoya, "Not-So-Free Labor," 163.

36. Reséndez, *Other Slavery,* 268–70.

37. In the early twentieth century, an "outing" program was established, involving Washoe Indian girls. They would be sent from Nevada to California to live with families to learn to "cook, to wash, to make and mend clothes, to sweep, to make beds—in short [girls] could be instructed in all things that are taught to white girls in homes of civilized communities." Families were able to procure a "bright young girl" by sending the superintendency $12.50 a month or $16 for one of the "better girls." (Indian boys learned agricultural or practical skills in the program.) By 1925 one hundred girls were working in California. In 1928 the Brookings Institution issued "a scathing indictment of federal Indian policy," condemning the practice of removing Indian children from their homes. M. S. Makley, *Small Shall Be Strong,* 125–28.

38. Winnemucca-Hopkins, *Life Among the Piutes,* 59–61.

39. *Sacramento Daily Union,* October 31, 1857, November 2, 1857.

40. Winnemucca-Hopkins, *Life Among the Piutes,* 61–63.

41. Katherine Gehn, *Sarah Winnemucca, Most Extraordinary Woman of the Paiute Nation,* 39.

42. Winnemucca-Hopkins, *Life Among the Piutes,* 63–64.

43. Lindsay, *Murder State,* 17–18.

44. *San Francisco Herald,* November 15, 1857.

45. Fariss and Smith, *Illustrated History of Plumas, Lassen, and Sierra Counties,* 385–386.

46. Dodge to Jacob Forney, January 4, 1859, 373–77.

47. *San Joaquin Republican,* June 19, 1859.

48. M. S. Makley, *Small Shall Be Strong,* 70.

49. Jo Ann Nevers, *Wa She Shu: A Washo Tribal History,* 52.

50. M. S. Makley, *Small Shall Be Strong,* 71–74.

51. A. B. Greenwood, *Report of the Commissioner of Indian Affairs, Accompanying the Annual Report of the Secretary of the Interior, for the Year 1859,* 22, 6–7.

52. Downs, *Two Worlds of the Washo,* 76; M. S. Makley, *Small Shall Be Strong,* 75, 86–87.

53. Greenwood, *Report of the Commissioner of Indian Affairs, 1859,* 7.

Chapter Five. Hostilities

1. Bagley, *Blood of the Prophets,* 180–82.

2. *The Deseret News,* July 15, 1857; *The New York Times,* August 26, 1857.

3. Bagley, *Blood of the Prophets,* 89.

4. Juanita Brooks, "A Place of Refuge," 15; Bagley, *Blood of the Prophets,* 184, 186.

5. *Los Angeles Star,* October 10, 1857.

6. *Placerville Mountain Democrat,* October 31, 1857.

7. See Bagley, *Blood of the Prophets;* Sally Denton, *American Massacre: The Tragedy*

at Mountain Meadows, September, 1857; and, the first of the scholarly analyses, Juanita Brooks, *The Mountain Meadows Massacre,* originally published in 1950.

8. Denton, *American Massacre,* 142.

9. Bagley, *Blood of the Prophets,* 189–90.

10. J. Forney, Superintendent Indian Affairs, Utah Territory, January 4, 1859, "1860—Report of the Commissioner of Indian Affairs for 1859," 369–71, https://digicoll.library.wisc.edu/cgi-bin/History/History-idx?type=article&did=History.AnnRep59.i0013&id=History.AnnRep59&isize=M. The Saints had survived a history of persecution. Joseph Smith, his brother Hyrum, and a beloved apostle, Parley Pratt, had all been martyred. Before surrendering to his fate, Joseph Smith had warned that his blood would "cry from the ground for vengeance." Mormon scripture stated: "Their innocent blood will cry unto the Lord of Hosts till he avenges that blood on earth." Evidence points to the fact that it was Pratt's killing in Arkansas that triggered the massacre. Bagley, *Blood of the Prophets,* 17, 268–69, 285.

11. *Los Angeles Star,* October 17, 1857; *Daily Alta California,* October 12, 1857.

12. *Placerville Mountain Democrat,* December 19, 26, 1857.

13. Bagley, *Blood of the Prophets,* 205–7.

14. Angel, *History of Nevada,* 103, 104; Howard, *Sierra Crossing,* 148; *Sacramento Daily Union,* July 9, 1857.

15. Harry Hawkins, *Douglas-Alpine History,* 29; Fairfield, *Pioneer History of Lassen County,* 130–31.

16. *Sacramento Daily Union,* June 19, 1857.

17. *San Francisco Herald,* August 27, 1857.

18. *Sacramento Daily Union,* September 8, 1857.

19. *San Francisco Herald,* August 27, 1857; Angel, *History of Nevada,* 18.

20. Karp, "People's Revolution of 1856," 524.

21. Elijah R. Kennedy, *The Contest for California in 1861: How Colonel E. D. Baker Saved the Pacific States to the Union,* 20–21; Starr, *California: A History,* 106–7. Some modern-day critics have argued that vigilantes were unpopular but swayed the public by intimidation. Frederick Allen says a more accurate analysis is that Montana vigilantes "were *popular* and acted through intimidation." He notes that leaders went on to become lawmen, legislators, governors, and judges. One specific example he cites is that in 1865, Paris Pfouts, Vigilance Committee president, was elected mayor in Virginia City, Montana. Allen, *Decent Orderly Lynching,* xvi, 314.

22. Taniguchi, *Dirty Deeds,* xvii.

23. Frederick Allen notes that the Montana vigilantes "were fully conversant with the activities of the San Francisco vigilance committee," saying they believed a core group of powerful men were best suited to run things. Allen, *Decent Orderly Lynching,* 184.

24. *Sacramento Daily Union,* September 28, 1857.

25. Van Sickle in *Nevada Historical Society Papers,* 190.

26. *Sacramento Daily Union,* November 2, 1857.

27. The Rodgers army quote was a two-line Carson Valley dispatch reprinted from an unidentified California paper. It appeared in the *Amador Ledger-Dispatch,* December 19, 1875; and *San Francisco Herald,* December 16, 1857, and February 1, 1858.

28. *San Francisco Herald,* February 8, 1858. Richard N. Allen, "Tennessee," was an outspoken critic of the anti-Mormons who would form the Carson Valley vigilantes. Of his own background he reported, "In 1856 I was on a court jury against the Vigilance Committee of San Francisco." Ellison, *Territorial Lawmen of Nevada,* 167n1.

29. *Sacramento Daily Union,* February 14, 1868; D. R. Hawkins to A. M. Fairfield, Genoa, NV, March 12, 1912, California Section, California State Library, Sacramento.

30. *Sacramento Daily Union,* June 25, 1858. (This and all quotes from the *Union* on this date come from C. N. Noteware's transcription of the Thorington trial.)

31. *Sacramento Daily Union,* June 25, 1858. The reference to "Texas boys" certainly implied their predilection for settling disputes with violence. Richard Maxwell Brown described the state in the nineteenth century as "an explosive mixture of deep-Southern and frontier-Western characteristics. In Texas, the Americanization of the common law of homicide reached its apogee." Brown, *No Duty to Retreat,* 26.

32. Effie Mona Mack, *Nevada: A History of the State from the Earliest Times Through the Civil War,* 177; Hamlin, *Knott Reminiscences,* 20.

33. Thos. J. Dimsdale, *The Vigilantes of Montana,* 13, 14. Dimsdale, born in England, slight and consumptive, had been a schoolteacher but became editor of the *Montana Post* newspaper. His book went a long way toward creating the vigilante legend. Noting how much of a cheerleader Dimsdale was for the vigilantes, Frederick Allen said that his claim that there were 102 murders in the Montana gold-rush era was unsupported by documentation. Allen's more reliable number, published in 2004, was eight. Allen, *Decent Orderly Lynching,* 9, 301.

34. *San Francisco Herald,* December 30, 1858; Hamlin, *Knott Reminiscences,* 20.

35. Allen, *Decent Orderly Lynching,* 31; Taniguchi, *Dirty Deeds,* 180, 182, 91–165 (regarding Terry).

36. *San Francisco Herald,* April 4, 18, 1858.

37. *San Francisco Herald,* April 19, 1858. The settlement of the "Utah War" involved a blanket pardon for charges of sedition and treason against Brigham Young and church officials and a promise not to interfere with their religion. In exchange, the Mormons accepted Cumming as the non-Mormon governor of the territory, missing court records and government property were produced, and, in June, the US Army peacefully entered and set up a camp in a valley fifty miles southwest of Salt Lake. Captain Jesse Gove gave a synopsis of the war: "Wounded, none; killed, none; fooled, everybody." Bagley, *Blood of the Prophets,* 202–6.

38. *San Francisco Herald,* April 25, 1858.

Chapter Six. Militias, Mobs, and Vigilantes

1. Leonard, *Adventures of a Mountain Man,* 116.
2. Nevins, *Narratives of Exploration and Adventure,* 488, 499–501.
3. Lindsay, *Murder State,* 4; Madley, *American Genocide,* 3–4.
4. Blackhawk, *Violence over the Land,* 226–27.
5. Hinkle and Hinkle, *Sierra-Nevada Lakes,* 114–15.
6. Fariss and Smith, *Illustrated History of Plumas, Lassen, and Sierra Counties,* 378.
7. Fairfield, *Pioneer History of Lassen County,* 16. For examples, see 15, 111–12, 289.

8. Lindsay, *Murder State*, 18–20.

9. Fairfield, *Pioneer History of Lassen County*, 118.

10. Fairfield, *Pioneer History of Lassen County*, 114.

11. Fairfield, *Pioneer History of Lassen County*, 289.

12. Madley, *American Genocide*, 86; Thomas D. Bonner, ed., *The Life and Adventures of James P. Beckwourth*, 99–100.

13. Fairfield, *Pioneer History of Lassen County*, 185.

14. Chauncey N. Noteware to A. M. Fairfield, Carson City, NV, n.d., California Section, California State Library, Sacramento. For an account of the San Francisco Vigilance Committee's first trial, see Taniguchi's chapter "In Secret Tribunal." The vigilantes' methods evolved until they were secretly convicting suspects before arresting them, then finding evidence, a routine that "led to increasingly arbitrary captures." Taniguchi, *Dirty Deeds*, 50–58, 85–86.

15. Taniguchi, *Dirty Deeds*, 123, 114.

16. Noteware to Fairfield, n.d.

17. Fairfield, *Pioneer History of Lassen County*, 124. In writing about "a tremendous outcry," after a murder of a young man in Montana, Frederick Allen commented, "Contrary to myth, life in the West was not cheap." Allen, *Decent Orderly Lynching*, 9. Concerning white men in Honey Lake Valley, the actions that followed sustain the observation.

18. Fairfield, *Pioneer History of Lassen County*, 125, 127.

19. Orlando Streshly to A. M. Fairfield, 1913, California Section.

20. Fairfield, *Pioneer History of Lassen County*, 123, 128.

21. Fairfield, *Pioneer History of Lassen County*, 129.

22. R. W. Young to A. M. Fairfield, August 24, 1910, California Section.

23. Noteware to Fairfield, n.d.

24. Quoted in *Sacramento Daily Union*, June 25, 1858.

25. This information and quote, and all that follows until the end of the chapter, are from the trial record printed in *Sacramento Daily Union*, June 25, 1858.

Chapter Seven. Judgment

1. Fairfield, *Pioneer History of Lassen County*, 133.

2. Fairfield, *Pioneer History of Lassen County*, 110–11, 113.

3. Fariss and Smith, *Illustrated History of Plumas, Lassen, and Sierra Counties*, 380–81.

4. Ellison, *Territorial Lawmen of Nevada*, 170n31; Chauncey N. Noteware to A. M. Fairfield, Carson City, NV, n.d., California Section, California State Library, Sacramento.

5. Ellison, *Territorial Lawmen of Nevada*, 234; Fairfield, *Pioneer History of Lassen County*, 135.

6. Dimsdale, *The Vigilantes of Montana*, 12, 13. Dimsdale's generalization was certainly colored by the case of Henry Plummer, the popular sheriff who was hanged by vigilantes. Frederick Allen describes Plummer when he arrived in Montana as "a dashing figure with a proven aura of magnetism." Plummer was elected sheriff, and, even at the time the vigilantes captured him, "the community leaders of

Bannack continued to express sharp misgivings about Plummer's complicity and plainly were not ready... to reach a guilty verdict against the sheriff." Allen, *Decent Orderly Lynching,* 68, 224.

7. R. W. Young to A. M. Fairfield, August 24, 1910, California Section.

8. D. R. Hawkins to A. M. Fairfield, Genoa, NV, March 12, 1912, California Section; Fairfield, *Pioneer History of Lassen County,* 136–37.

9. Fairfield, *Pioneer History of Lassen County,* 137.

10. *San Francisco Herald,* June 18, 1858.

11. Contemporaneous writer Thomas Dimsdale reported that a highwayman about to be hanged in Montana in January 1864 told of his gang using secret signs, such as a specific way of shaving their mustaches and goatees and using a "sailor's knot" for their neckties, to identify one another. Just as in the Carson Valley case, observers have questioned the account: Why would a small group have needed special signs to recognize one another, and why would they have advertised their common cause through their appearance? Allen, *Decent Orderly Lynching,* 215.

12. D. H. Holdridge to A. M. Fairfield, April 1, 1916, California Section; Fariss and Smith, *Illustrated History of Plumas, Lassen, and Sierra Counties,* 388.

13. Young to Fairfield, August 24, 1910.

14. Fairfield, *Pioneer History of Lassen County,* 137, 138; *Placerville Mountain Democrat,* June 26, 1858.

15. Fairfield, *Pioneer History of Lassen County,* 138; N. E. Spoon to A. M. Fairfield, January 14, 1914, box 191, Asa Merrill Fairfield Manuscript Collection, California Section; *San Francisco Herald,* June 19, 1858.

16. Fairfield, *Pioneer History of Lassen County,* 138–39.

17. Hawkins to Fairfield, March 12, 1912.

18. Taniguchi, *Dirty Deeds,* 79–80; Allen, *Decent Orderly Lynching,* 182.

19. Fairfield, *Pioneer History of Lassen County,* 140.

20. *Sacramento Daily Union,* June 14, 1858; Fairfield, *Pioneer History of Lassen County,* 140.

21. Angel, *History of Nevada,* 552.

22. Fairfield, *Pioneer History of Lassen County,* 140; Ellison, *Territorial Lawmen of Nevada,* 123n39; Hawkins to Fairfield, March 12, 1912.

23. Fariss and Smith, *Illustrated History of Plumas, Lassen, and Sierra Counties,* 388.

24. *Sacramento Daily Union,* June 18, 1858; *Sacramento Daily Bee,* June 18, 1858.

25. *Sacramento Daily Union,* June 19, 1858.

26. *Daily Alta California,* June 22, 1858.

27. Fairfield, *Pioneer History of Lassen County,* 140.

28. Angel, *History of Nevada,* 50–51.

29. *Sacramento Daily Union,* June 25, 1858.

30. *Sacramento Daily Union,* June 25, 1858.

31. Fairfield, *Pioneer History of Lassen County,* 141.

32. In *The Big Bonanza,* published in 1876, Dan DeQuille wrote that in 1859 when Peter O'Riley and Pat McLaughlin struck the great silver lode streaked with gold, H. T. P. Comstock happened by and flimflammed the men. Noting the unique quality of the find, Comstock "coolly proceeded to inform the astonished miners that they

were working ground that belonged to him." He declared that they could not work there unless they agreed to include himself and his friend Penrod in the claim. Rather than have a row about it, the discoverers agreed, and the discovery came to be named for Comstock. Like the others, Comstock and Penrod bartered their shares for relatively insubstantial sums before the big strikes, losing out on countless millions. Much of the rest of Penrod's life was spent unsuccessfully chasing another bonanza. DeQuille, *The Big Bonanza,* 24–27.

33. Ellison, *Territorial Lawmen of Nevada,* 158; Hutcheson, "Life of Fifty Years in Nevada," 62–64.

34. Emanuel Penrod to A. M. Fairfield, Genoa, NV, July 22, 1912, California Section.

35. Frederick Allen writes about a case that took place in Alder Gulch, Montana, in December 1863. A suspect named Ives, popular with a segment of the population, was charged with murdering a young man for a pouch of gold. The entirety of the evidence against Ives was the testimony of a ne'er-do-well, who was also a suspect. As in the Thorington hanging, lacking evidence in the specific case, the accusers needed to broaden the charges. Evidence was presented that Ives had committed an armed robbery, and he was accused of being a stagecoach robber by profession. There was a further imputation that he had committed other murders. The additional information bolstered the preconceived notion of his guilt, and Ives received the death sentence. Allen, *Decent Orderly Lynching,* 180.

36. Noteware to Fairfield, n.d.

Chapter Eight. Enforcement

1. Fairfield, *Pioneer History of Lassen County,* 141, 142.

2. R. W. Young to A. M. Fairfield, August 24, 1910, California Section, California State Library, Sacramento.

3. *Daily Alta California,* June 22, 1858.

4. Hamlin, *Knott Reminiscences,* 16.

5. Dangberg, *Carson Valley,* 29. Similarities between the Ives case, described in Allen's book, and the Thorington lynching end at the execution. Ives was lifted onto a box and the noose placed around his neck. Someone called out, "Men do your duty," and the box was kicked away, the noose snapping Ives's neck. Proud to have been involved, a number of men later claimed to have issued the directive, and others said they kicked out the box. The phrase "Men do your duty" became the Montana vigilante motto. Allen, *Decent Orderly Lynching,* 191–92.

6. Angel, *History of Nevada,* 51.

7. *Sacramento Daily Union,* June 22, 1858; *Placerville Mountain Democrat,* June 26, 1858.

8. Taniguchi, *Dirty Deeds,* 5.

9. *Placerville Mountain Democrat,* June 26, 1858. The Ives case in Montana again resembles the Thorington case, in that the man who served as prosecutor at the trial was convinced that had Ives survived, the prosecutor would have become a target. Allen, *Decent Orderly Lynching,* 192. As to the problem of releasing the accused, the practice caused the San Francisco Vigilance Committee massive headaches. Several

of those banished returned to file suit against them. A typical case was Charles Duane, a brawler who was head of all the city's fire-engine companies. He had been acquitted after shooting a man in the back in a barroom brawl. The vigilantes arrested him, but due to the public outcry, in which it was said he had done more to protect the city than the entire committee together, they deported him one night in a tugboat, under cover of "foggy, blackness." In 1860, after the committee had disbanded, Duane returned to the city, suing all the vigilante captains involved in his arrest and banishment. Originally winning a $7,000 award (some $230,000 today) against two of them, the case was appealed to the US Supreme Court. When the case was remanded to assess lower damages, to the great relief of vigilante leaders, Duane received $50. Taniguchi, *Dirty Deeds,* 71, 75–76, 218.

10. *Placerville Mountain Democrat,* July 3, 1858; *Sacramento Daily Union,* June 25, 1858.

11. Fairfield, *Pioneer History of Lassen County,* 142.

12. Chauncey N. Noteware to A. M. Fairfield, Carson City, NV, n.d., California Section; Van Sickle, in *Nevada Historical Society Papers,* 191. Allowing a man accused of murder to escape was not unheard of in the West. Handsome and well spoken, Henry Plummer, the Montana sheriff who was later hanged by vigilantes, had been allowed, or helped, to escape justice on at least two occasions after committing killings. In another instance, he was issued a pardon after being convicted of second-degree murder. Allen, *Decent Orderly Lynching,* 48–50, 53–54, 74–76.

13. R. W. Young to A. M. Fairfield, August 24, 1910, California Section; Fairfield, *Pioneer History of Lassen County,* 143.

14. Orlando Streshly to Fairfield, [1913],? California Section.

15. Ellison, *Territorial Lawmen of Nevada,* 164.

16. Hamlin, *Knott Reminiscences,* 16, 20, 15.

Chapter Nine. Fallout

1. Fairfield, *Pioneer History of Lassen County,* 131. Attempting to weaken Mormonism, four years later, the US Congress passed the Morrill Act that had four elements: it would ban polygamy, disincorporate the Mormon Church, prohibit churches from owning real estate worth more than $50,000, and would produce no results. Paul, *Far West and the Great Plains in Transition,* 180.

2. Fairfield, *Pioneer History of Lassen County,* 143–44.

3. Zanjani, *Devils Will Reign,* 105.

4. Nevada State Library and Archives Territorial Divorce Records, July 4, 1861.

5. *Inyo Register,* January 22, 1914; Zanjani, *Devils Will Reign,* 105–6.

6. Angel, *History of Nevada,* 18, 77, 389.

7. Bagley, *Blood of the Prophets,* 210

8. Ellison, *Territorial Lawmen of Nevada,* 179–80.

9. Russell R. Elliott, with the assistance of William D. Rowley, *History of Nevada,* 59; Angel, *History of Nevada,* 49.

10. *Daily Alta California,* November 20, 1858.

11. *Sacramento Daily Union,* December 1, 2, 1858. At the same time, telegraphic transmissions were near to uniting America and binding it to Europe, although

there were obstacles. The transatlantic cable had been completed three months earlier, in August 1858, and worked for several weeks before failing. It would not be replaced until 1866. The cable from Carson City to Omaha, Nebraska, via Salt Lake City which completed the transcontinental line, began operations on October 24, 1861.

12. Angel, *History of Nevada,* 105–6.

13. *Placerville Mountain Democrat,* November 20, 1858.

14. *Sacramento Daily Union,* November 20, 1858.

15. Zanjani, *Devils Will Reign,* 108–9.

16. *San Francisco Herald,* December 30, 1858.

17. Angel, *History of Nevada,* 51; Fairfield, *Pioneer History of Lassen County,* 144.

18. *San Francisco Herald,* December 30, 1858; Zanjani, *Devils Will Reign,* 107–9; Angel, *History of Nevada,* 42; Ellison, *Territorial Lawmen of Nevada,* 186. For information on San Francisco's Law and Order Party, see Taniguchi, *Dirty Deeds.*

19. Simpson, *Report of Explorations,* 90; Paul, *Far West and the Great Plains in Transition,* 67.

20. *Marysville (CA) Daily National Democrat,* August 13, 1859; DeQuille, *The Big Bonanza,* 7; Angel, *History of Nevada,* 59, 551; *Sacramento Daily Union,* May 30, 1859.

21. Simpson, *Report of Explorations,* 91.

22. *Daily Alta California,* September 1, 1860.

23. Simpson, *Report of Explorations,* 92, 94; Taniguchi, *Dirty Deeds,* 55–56; Allen, *Decent Orderly Lynching,* xv–xvi, 215.

24. *Sacramento Daily Union,* March 17, 1859, reprinting the Placerville account; Ellison, *Territorial Lawmen of Nevada,* 189.

25. *Sacramento Daily Union,* March 24, 1859.

26. *Sacramento Daily Union,* June 4, 1859; Simpson, *Report of Explorations,* 108n, 91, 105; Angel, *History of Nevada,* 33.

27. Simpson, *Report of Explorations,* 103, 91n.

28. Knack and Stewart, *As Long as the River Shall Run,* 66.

29. Fairfield, *Pioneer History of Lassen County,* 171–72.

30. Fairfield, *Pioneer History of Lassen County,* 172–77.

31. Fariss and Smith, *Illustrated History of Plumas, Lassen, and Sierra Counties,* 450, 380 (Weatherlow).

32. Fairfield, *Pioneer History of Lassen County,* 177.

33. *Hydraulic Press* (Nevada County, CA), June 4, 1859.

34. Fariss and Smith, *Illustrated History of Plumas, Lassen, and Sierra Counties,* 380.

35. *Daily Alta California,* May 21, 1859.

36. DeQuille, *The Big Bonanza,* 76.

37. Knack and Stewart, *As Long as the River Shall Run,* 5, 64, 89; Angel, *History of Nevada,* 148.

Chapter Ten. Disorder

1. Fairfield, *Pioneer History of Lassen County,* 84, 183–85.

2. Ellison, *Territorial Lawmen of Nevada,* 193.

3. Angel, *History of Nevada,* 552, 553.

4. Zanjani, *Devils Will Reign,* 112; *San Francisco Herald,* June 1, 1859.

5. Grant H. Smith, *The History of the Comstock Lode,* 5–11.

6. Angel, *History of Nevada,* 59.

7. Angel, *History of Nevada,* 61–62.

8. Angel, *History of Nevada,* 62–63; Mutti Burke, "Contested Promised Land," 13. For a prime example of Mormons co-opting Indian warlords, see Ned Blackhawk's description of how terrorizing Ute leader Walkara, after failing to break Mormon fortifications, attached himself and his chiefs to Brigham Young. Blackhawk, *Violence over the Land,* 242–44.

9. Angel, *History of Nevada,* 58. In April 1860 Winters became an incorporator and board of trustees member in the Ophir Company. It was organized by the first individuals to recognize that deep quartz mining was going to require large-scale enterprises. The Ophir, organized in San Francisco, began with capital of $5,040,000 and, over twenty years, earned $11 million. Smith, *Comstock Lode,* 18, 80–81, 311; Gilman M. Ostrander, *Nevada: The Great Rotten Borough, 1859–1964,* 11–12.

10. Utah Division of Archives and Records Service, "Original Land Titles in Utah Territory," https://archives.utah.gov/research/guides/land-original-title.htm.

11. Angel, *History of Nevada,* 379–80, 533–34.

12. *Daily Alta California,* September 23, 1859; Bagley, *Blood of the Prophets,* 231.

13. *Daily Alta California,* September 23, 1859.

14. Bagley, *Blood of the Prophets,* 216–18, 235; *Daily Alta California,* December 17, 1859.

15. *Sacramento Daily Union,* November 3, 1859.

16. *Sacramento Daily Union,* September 9, 14, 6, 1859.

17. *Sacramento Daily Union,* September 13, 1859.

18. *San Joaquin Republican,* September 23, 1859.

19. The name "Law and Order" does not establish the Eastern Sierra group's ideology. Not only did the antivigilante group in San Francisco use the name, but so too did a proslavery group, which frequently took vigilante-type actions in Kansas. Karp, "People's Revolution of 1856," 526.

20. Elliott with Rowley, *History of Nevada,* 59–60; Angel, *History of Nevada,* 63–64.

21. Angel, *History of Nevada,* 64.

22. Smith, *Comstock Lode,* 80. The silver block, prematurely inscribed "Nevada," was intended to be part of the monument that included blocks of stone from all the states and territories. The silver block disappeared and has never been recovered. Another block, similarly labeled "Nevada," was presented later. In the 1990s Nevada senator Harry Reid and the Nevada State Historic Preservation Office, supported by the National Park Service, failed in an attempt to discover the original block's fate, per historian Ronald M. James.

23. *Daily Alta California,* December 17, 1859; Fariss and Smith, *Illustrated History of Plumas, Lassen, and Sierra Counties,* 356.

24. Knack and Stewart, *As Long as the River Shall Run,* 44–45. For an overview of Virginia City's development and demise, see James, *Roar and the Silence.*

25. F. Dodge to Jacob Forney, Superintendent Indian Affairs, Utah Territory, January 4, 1859, "1860—Report of the Commissioner of Indian Affairs for 1859,"

375, https://digicoll.library.wisc.edu/cgi-bin/History/History-idx?type=article&did=History.AnnRep59.i0013&id=History.AnnRep59&isize=M.

26. Knack and Stewart, *As Long as the River Shall Run,* 89–90, 65–66; *Sacramento Daily Union,* May 26, 1860; Reséndez, *Other Slavery,* 265.

27. In March 1862 Indian agent Jacob Lockhart sent a report to the commissioner of Indian affairs: "The wild game is being killed by the whites, the trees from which the Indians gathered nuts are being cut down, and the grass from which they gathered seeds for winter is being taken from them." M. S. Makley, *Small Shall Be Strong,* 71.

28. *Daily Alta California,* December 17, 1859; Fairfield, *Pioneer History of Lassen County,* 186.

29. Madley, *American Genocide,* 254–55.

30. Smith, *Comstock Lode,* 20–21; Fairfield, *Pioneer History of Lassen County,* 186.

Chapter Eleven. At Pyramid Lake

1. Fairfield, *Pioneer History of Lassen County,* 197–200.

2. Fairfield, *Pioneer History of Lassen County,* 202–5.

3. Angel, *History of Nevada,* 148–49.

4. Madley, *American Genocide,* 279–81; Knack and Stewart, *As Long as the River Shall Run,* 69–70. Bret Harte, serving as a junior editor for a newspaper near Humboldt Bay, wrote a bitter denunciation of the wantonly brutal attack on the Wiyots. Because of that, he received such menacing threats against his life, he had to escape to San Francisco. Walton Bean, *California: An Interpretive History,* 189–90.

5. Much of the information about the first battle in the Pyramid Lake War that follows comes from Angel's Nevada history, published in 1880. Angel sent a writer accompanied by Warren Wasson, who for a second time was acting Indian agent, to interview Indians who had taken part in the war with white settlers in 1860. Wasson had been the agent in the early '60s and was trusted by the Indians. Through an interpreter, Wasson assured the old men that nothing they said would be used against them and so collected a large quantity of information regarding the war from the Paiutes' perspective.

6. Angel, *History of Nevada,* 150.

7. Blackhawk, *Violence over the Land,* 5; Madley, *American Genocide,* 268–69; Lindsay, *Murder State,* 335; Knack and Stewart, *As Long as the River Shall Run,* 70–71.

8. Angel, *History of Nevada,* 151.

9. *Daily Alta California,* September 1, 1860.

10. Angel, *History of Nevada,* 151. The phrase "sand in a whirlwind" was used for the title of Ferol Egan's popular history of the Pyramid Lake War, written in 1972.

11. *Sacramento Daily Union,* May 19, 1860. After the battle of Pyramid Lake, a correspondent of the *San Francisco Herald* commented, "To give you an idea of the character of these worthies, I will relate two circumstances which have occurred during the past week. There were three persons, brothers, of the name of Williams—two of whom were killed at the first massacre. The survivor made no effort to have the dead bodies of his brothers buried, and when some of the half-starved troops in

their retreat killed a few of his chickens and hogs, he charged four dollars a piece for the chickens and a proportionate price for the hogs, at the same time saying the soldiers were worse than the Indians." Quoted in *Sacramento Daily Union,* May 26, 1860.

12. Angel, *History of Nevada,* 152.

13. Knack and Stewart, *As Long as the River Shall Run,* 71; Winnemucca-Hopkins, *Life Among the Piutes,* 70–71.

14. *Daily Alta California,* May 7, 1860. Dr. Ormsby volunteered in various ways in his California communities, acting as a secretary in meetings involving public service in Sacramento and serving on the Board of Managers for Sonoma County's Agricultural Society. His one political role was in July 1857 when he served as a Democratic assembly delegate to California's state convention. *Sacramento Daily Union,* June 17, 1851; May 14, 1855; July 13, 1857.

15. *Sacramento Daily Union,* May 9, 1860.

16. For another aspect of writing as a military advantage, see Madley, *American Genocide,* 178–79. In 1850 California newspapers published a militia general's account of a strategy used to attack Indians. His narrative illustrated the capabilities of militias and the possibilities for expanded genocidal campaigns.

17. *Sacramento Daily Union,* May 15, 1860.

18. *Sacramento Daily Union,* May 15, 1860.

19. *Sacramento Daily Union,* May 15, 1860.

20. Hamlin, *Knott Reminiscences,* 14.

21. *Sacramento Daily Union,* May 21, 1860; *Daily Alta California,* May 18, 1860.

22. Hamlin, *Knott Reminiscences,* 10; *Daily Alta California,* May 18, 1860; Lord, *Comstock Mining and Miners,* 68.

23. Foreman in Ferol Egan, *Sand in a Whirlwind: The Paiute Indian War of 1860,* 120–21, 123.

24. *Sacramento Daily Union,* May 21, 24, 1860; Sessions S. Wheeler, *The Desert Lake: The Story of Nevada's Pyramid Lake,* 56–58.

25. *Sacramento Daily Union,* May 19, 1860.

26. *Sacramento Daily Union,* May 21, 1860; Foreman in Egan, *Sand in a Whirlwind,* 137–39.

27. *Sacramento Daily Union,* May 26, 1860.

28. *Sacramento Daily Union,* May 26, 1860.

29. *Sacramento Daily Union,* May 21, 1860; Angel, *History of Nevada,* 154–58.

30. *Sacramento Daily Union,* May 21, 1860; Foreman in Egan, *Sand in a Whirlwind,* 141.

31. Angel, *History of Nevada,* 157.

32. Angel, *History of Nevada,* 157.

33. Winnemucca-Hopkins, *Life Among the Piutes,* 72; Lord, *Comstock Mining and Miners,* 69.

34. *Sacramento Daily Union,* May 15, 1860. See also "Victims of the Indian Massacre," *Daily Alta California,* May 14, 1860.

35. *Sacramento Daily Union,* May 15, 1860. The following year, completed as a transcontinental device, the telegraph linked Washington, DC, with California's

federal and state authorities. The connection enabled Lincoln's government to counter any Confederate attempts to gain control of the Pacific Coast. The telegraph's military value proved itself in the Civil War, allowing the transmission of information between the Union's political centers and its field armies. Durwood Ball, "Liberty, Empire, and Civil War in the American West," in *Empire and Liberty*, ed. Scharff, 66–86, 69–71.

36. *Hydraulic Press,* May 19, 1860; *Sacramento Daily Union,* May 21, 26, 1860.

37. Wheeler, *Desert Lake,* 64–67.

38. *Daily Alta California,* September 1, 1860.

39. Wheeler, *Desert Lake,* 69–72.

40. Elliott, *History of Nevada,* 94.

41. See Office of Indian Affairs, *Annual Report of the Commissioner of Indian Affairs, 1859,* 6.

42. M. S. Makley, *Small Shall Be Strong,* 78–79.

43. M. S. Makley, *Small Shall Be Strong,* 75. Another Washoe of note, Henry Rupert, gained local fame as a Washoe shaman, or doctor, who in the early- and mid-twentieth century used his healing power across cultural and ethnic boundaries. In 2008 when the Ninth Circuit Court of Appeals ruled, for only the second time in history, that an Indian sacred site on public land be awarded federal protection, it ratified that management of Lake Tahoe's Cave Rock would reflect "prehistory through the year of Henry Rupert's death." Matthew S. Makley and Michael J. Makley, *Cave Rock: Climbers, Courts, and a Washoe Indian Sacred Place,* 29–39.

44. M. S. Makley, *Small Shall Be Strong,* 74.

45. Knack and Stewart, *As Long as the River Shall Run,* 83, 127–28.

46. Wheeler, *Desert Lake,* 76–77.

47. M. J. Makley, *Saving Lake Tahoe,* 26–27, 31; Knack and Stewart, *As Long as the River Shall Run,* 334–38; Leah J. Wilds, *Water Politics in Northern Nevada: A Century of Struggle,* 32–36.

Conclusion

1. Angel, *History of Nevada,* 41.

2. Davis, *The History of Nevada,* 232; Lord, *Comstock Mines and Miners,* 308–9.

3. Ellison, *Territorial Lawmen of Nevada,* 157–58, 160; Fairfield, *Pioneer History of Lassen County,* 143, 311–30. There was another incident illustrative of Elliott's rush to judge others. In the spring of 1861, he urged community members to peremptorily hang suspects accused of a murder. Instead, citizens decided the men needed to be sent to Carson City to stand trial. To Elliott's chagrin, the suspects were exonerated and returned to live at Honey Lake, with one remaining several years. Fairfield, *Pioneer History of Lassen County,* 250–52.

4. *Sacramento Daily Union,* July 15, 1874.

5. *Inyo Independent,* July 28, 1888; October 26, 1889; February 13, 1891; June 6, 1890.

6. Zanjani, *Sarah Winnemucca,* 45.

7. Angel, *History of Nevada,* 151.

8. *Daily Alta California,* October 12, 1857; *Placerville Mountain Democrat,* October 31, December 26, 1857.

9. *Sacramento Daily Union,* May 21, 26, 1860.

10. Blackhawk, *Violence over the Land,* 10. In discussing Ute Indians' strategies when responding to Spanish and later Mexican regimes' colonial disturbance, Blackhawk said, "Utes became feared combatants, courted allies, and eventually gracious hosts" (7). The Pyramid Lake Paiutes' strategies, when confronted by white settlers, evolved in the opposite direction. They first welcomed the settlers to homestead in Honey Lake Valley, were then courted as allies, and eventually became feared combatants. *Gold Hill Evening News,* October 21, 1872.

11. *Territorial Enterprise,* March 25, 1875.

12. Green, *Nevada,* 136.

Bibliography

Allen, Frederick. *A Decent Orderly Lynching: The Montana Vigilantes.* Norman: University of Oklahoma Press, 2004.

Anderson, M. Kat. *Tending the Wild: Native American Knowledge and the Management of California's Natural Resources.* Berkeley: University of California Press, 2005.

Angel, Myron. *History of Nevada.* 1881. Reprint, Berkeley: Howell-North, 1958.

Bagley, Will. *Blood of the Prophets: Brigham Young and the Massacre at Mountain Meadows.* Norman: University of Oklahoma Press, 2002.

Bean, Walton. *California: An Interpretive History.* New York: McGraw-Hill, 1968.

BeDunnah, Gary P. "A History of the Chinese in Nevada, 1855–1904." Master's thesis, University of Nevada, 1966.

Belew, Kathleen. *Bring the War Home: The White Power Movement and Paramilitary America.* Cambridge, MA: Harvard University Press, 2018.

Blackhawk, Ned. *Violence over the Land: Indians and Empires in the Early American West.* Cambridge, MA: Harvard University Press, 2006.

Bonner, Thomas D., ed. *The Life and Adventures of James P. Beckwourth.* 1856. Lincoln: University of Nebraska Press, 1972.

Bowles, Samuel. *Across the Continent: A Summer's Journey to the Rocky Mountains, the Mormons, and the Pacific States with Speaker Colfax, 1866.* Ann Arbor, MI: University Microfilms, 1966.

Brooks, Juanita. "The Mormons in Carson County, Utah Territory." *Nevada Historical Society Quarterly* 8, no. 1 (1965): 13–23.

———. *The Mountain Meadows Massacre.* Stanford, CA: Stanford University Press, 1950.

———. "A Place of Refuge." *Nevada Historical Society Quarterly* 14, no. 1 (1971): 13–26.

Brown, Richard Maxwell. *No Duty to Retreat: Violence and Values in American History and Society.* New York: Oxford University Press, 1991.

———. "Western Violence: Structure, Values, Myth." *Western Historical Quarterly* 24, no. 1 (1993): 4–20.

Caro, Robert A. *The Years of Lyndon Johnson: Master of the Senate.* New York: Random House, 2002.

Centennial Book Committee. *Alpine Heritage.* South Lake Tahoe, CA: Anchor, 1964.

Clappe, Louise Amelia Knapp Smith. "Dame Shirley." In *The Shirley Letters: Being Letters Written in 1851–1852 from the California Mines.* Salt Lake City: Peregrine Smith Books, 1985.

Comager, Henry Steele, ed. *Documents of American History.* 7th ed. 1934. Reprint, New York: Meredith, 1963.

Cronon, William, George Miles, and Jay Gitlin, eds. *Under an Open Sky: Rethinking America's Western Past.* New York: W. W. Norton, 1992.

Crum, Stephen J. *The Road on Which We Came: A History of the Western Shoshone.* Salt Lake City: University of Utah Press, 1994.

Dangberg, Grace. *Carson Valley: Historical Sketches of Nevada's First Settlement.* Reno: Carson Valley Historical Society, 1972.

———. *Conflict on the Carson: A Study of Water Litigation in Western Nevada.* Minden, NV: Carson Valley Historical Society, 1975.

Davis, Sam, ed. *The History of Nevada.* Vol. 1. Reno: Elms, 1913.

Denton, Sally. *American Massacre: The Tragedy at Mountain Meadows, September, 1857.* New York: Vintage Books, 2003.

DeQuille, Dan. *The Big Bonanza.* New York: Alfred A. Knopf, 1947.

Deverell, William, ed. *The Companion to the American West.* Malden, MA: Blackwell, 2004.

Dimsdale, Thos. J. *The Vigilantes of Montana.* 1866. Reprint, New York: Time-Life Books, 1981.

Downs, James F. *The Two Worlds of the Washo: An Indian Tribe of California and Nevada.* New York: Holt, Rinehart, and Winston, 1966.

Egan, Ferol. *Sand in a Whirlwind: The Paiute Indian War of 1860.* New York: Doubleday, 1972.

Elliott, Russell R., with the assistance of William D. Rowley. *History of Nevada.* Lincoln: University of Nebraska Press, 1987.

Ellison, Robert W. *First Impressions: The Trail Through Carson Valley, 1848–1852.* Minden, NV: Hot Springs Mountain Press, 2001.

———. *Territorial Lawmen of Nevada*. Vol. 1, *The Utah Territorial Period, 1851–1861.* Minden, NV: Hot Springs Mountain Press, 1999.

Fairfield, Asa Merrill. *A Pioneer History of Lassen County, California.* San Francisco: H. S. Crocker, 1916.

Fariss and Smith. *Illustrated History of Plumas, Lassen, and Sierra Counties.* San Francisco: Fariss and Smith, 1882.

Farquhar, Francis P. *History of the Sierra Nevada.* Berkeley: University of California Press, 1966.

Fleek, Sherman L. "The Kearny/Stockton/Frémont Feud: The Mormon Battalion's Most Significant Contribution in California." *Journal of Mormon History* 37, no. 3 (2011): 229–57. http://www.jstor.org/stable/23292728.

Gehn, Katherine. *Sarah Winnemucca, Most Extraordinary Woman of the Paiute Nation.* Phoenix: O'Sullivan, Woodside, 1975.

Green, Michael. *Nevada: A History of the Silver State.* Reno: University of Nevada Press, 2015.

Greenwood, A. B. *Report of the Commissioner of Indian Affairs, Accompanying the Annual Report of the Secretary of the Interior, for the Year 1859.* Washington, DC: George W. Bowman, Printer, 1860.

Hamlin, H. *Knott Reminiscences, Early History of the 1850s.* Placerville, CA: Pioneer Press, 1947.

Hawkins, Harry. *Douglas-Alpine History.* Edited by Mary Ellen Glass. Oral History Program. Reno: University of Nevada Library, 1966.

Hinkle, George, and Bliss Hinkle. *Sierra-Nevada Lakes.* 1949. Reprint, Reno: University of Nevada Press, 1987.

Hitchcock, Robert K., and Charles Flowerday. "Ishi and the California Indian Genocide as Developmental Mass Violence." *Humboldt Journal of Social Relations,* no. 42 (2020): 69–85. https://www.jstor.org/stable/26932596.

Hochfelder, David. "A Comparison of the Postal Telegraph Movement in Great Britain and the United States, 1866–1900." *Enterprise & Society* 1, no. 4 (2000): 739–61. http://www.jstor.org/stable/23699535.

Howard, Thomas Frederick. *Sierra Crossing: First Roads to California.* Berkeley: University of California Press, 1998.

Hulbert, Archer Butler. *Forty Niners: The Chronicle of the California Trail.* 1931. Reprint, Las Vegas: Nevada Publications, 1987.

Hulse, James W. *The Nevada Adventure.* 1965. Reprint, Reno: University of Nevada Press, 1990.

Hurtado, Albert. "Their Flag, Too." *Boom: A Journal of California* 1, no. 4 (2011): 45–53. https://doi.org/10.1525/boom.2011.1.4.45.

Hutcheson, Austin Ec. "A Life of Fifty Years in Nevada: The Memoirs of Penrod of the Comstock Lode (Part 1)." *Nevada Historical Society Quarterly* 1, no. 2 (1957): 59–64.

James, Ronald M. *The Roar and the Silence: A History of Virginia City and the Comstock Lode.* Reno: University of Nevada Press, 1998.

Jameson, Elizabeth, and Susan Armitage, eds. *The Women's West.* Norman: University of Oklahoma Press, 1987.

"John O'Sullivan Declares America's Manifest Destiny, 1845." https://www.americanyawp.com/reader/manifest-destiny/john-osullivan-declares-americas-manifest-destiny-1845.

Johnson, David A. "Vigilance and the Law: The Moral Authority of Popular Justice in the Far West." In "American Culture and the American Frontier." Special issue, *American Quarterly* 33, no. 5 (1981): 558–86.

Johnson, Susan Lee. *Roaring Camp: The Social World of the California Gold Rush.* New York: W. W. Norton, 2000.

Jones, Karen R., and John Wills. *Women in the West: The Trailblazers and the Homesteader.* Edinburgh: Edinburgh University Press, 2007.

Karp, Matthew. "The People's Revolution of 1856: Antislavery Populism, National Politics, and the Emergence of the Republican Party." *Journal of the Civil War Era* 9, no. 4 (2019): 524–45. https://www.jstor.org/stable/26824759.

Kennedy, Elijah R. *The Contest for California in 1861: How Colonel E. D. Baker Saved the Pacific States to the Union.* Boston: Houghton Mifflin, 1912.

Knack, Martha C., and Omer C. Stewart. *As Long as the River Shall Run: An Ethnohistory of Pyramid Lake Indian Reservation.* Reno: University of Nevada Press, 1984.

Leonard, Zenas. *Adventures of a Mountain Man: The Narrative of Zenas Leonard.* Edited by Milo Milton Quaife. 1839. Reprint, Lincoln: University of Nebraska Press, 1978.

Lindsay, Brendan C. *Murder State: California's Native American Genocide, 1846–1873.* Lincoln: University of Nebraska Press, 2012.

Lord, Eliot. *Comstock Mining and Miners.* 1883. Reprint, Berkeley, CA: Howell-North, 1959.

Mack, Effie Mona. *Nevada: A History of the State from the Earliest Times Through the Civil War.* Glendale, CA: Arthur H. Clark, 1936.

Madley, Benjamin. *An American Genocide: The United States and the California Indian Catastrophe, 1846–1873.* New Haven, CT: Yale University Press, 2016.

Makley, Matthew S. *The Small Shall Be Strong.* Amherst: University of Massachusetts Press, 2018.

Makley, Matthew S., and Michael J. Makley. *Cave Rock: Climbers, Courts, and a Washoe Indian Sacred Place.* Reno: University of Nevada Press, 2010.

Makley, Michael J. *Open Spaces, Open Rebellions: The War over America's Public Lands.* Amherst: University of Massachusetts Press, 2017.

———. *Saving Lake Tahoe: An Environmental History of a National Treasure.* Reno: University of Nevada Press, 2014.

Melville, Keith J. "Theory and Practice of Church and State During the Brigham Young Era." *BYU Studies Quarterly* 3, no. 1, article 5 (1961). https://scholarsarchive.byu.edu/byusq/vol3/iss1/5.

Miluck, Nancy. "How Lucky Bill's Luck Ran Out in Old Genoa." *Nevada Highways & Parks*, Winter 1972.

Moehring, Eugene P. *Urbanism and Empire in the Far West, 1840–1890.* Reno: University of Nevada Press, 2004.

Moreno, Richard. *A Short History of Carson City.* Reno: University of Nevada Press, 2011.

Morgan, Dale L. *The Humboldt: Highroad of the West.* Lincoln: University of Nebraska Press, 1943.

Mutti Burke, Diane. "A Contested Promised Land: Mormons, Slaveholders, and the Disputed Vision for the Settlement of Western Missouri." *John Whitmer Historical Association Journal* 36, no. 1 (2016): 13–34.

Nevada Historical Society Papers, 1913–1916. Carson City, NV: State Printing Office, 1917.

Nevers, Jo Ann. *Wa She Shu: A Washo Tribal History.* Reno: Inter-Tribal Council of Nevada, 1976.

Nevins, Allen, ed. *Narratives of Exploration and Adventure by John Charles Frémont.* New York: Longmans, Green, 1956.

Office of Indian Affairs. *Annual Report of the Commissioner of Indian Affairs, 1859.* Washington, DC: George W. Bowman, Printer, 1860.

Ostrander, Gilman M. *Nevada: The Great Rotten Borough, 1859–1964.* New York: Alfred A. Knopf, 1966.

O'Sullivan, John. "Annexation." *United States Magazine and Democratic Review* 17 (1845).

Parsons, Elaine Frantz. *Ku-Klux: The Birth of the Klan During Reconstruction.* Chapel Hill: University of North Carolina Press, 2015.

Paul, Rodman W. *The Far West and the Great Plains in Transition, 1859–1900.* New York: Harper & Row, 1988.

Potter, David E., ed. *Trail to California: The Overland Journal of Vincent Geiger and Wakeman Bryarly.* New Haven, CT: Yale University Press, 1945.

Reséndez, Andréz. *The Other Slavery: The Uncovered Story of Indian Enslavement in America.* Boston: Houghton Mifflin Harcourt, 2016.

Scharff, Virginia, ed. *Empire and Liberty: The Civil War and the West.* Oakland: University of California Press, 2015.

Schlereth, Eric R. "Privileges of Locomotion: Expatriation and the Politics of Southwestern Border Crossing." *Journal of American History* 100, no. 4 (2014): 995–1020.

Scott, Edward B. 1957. *The Saga of Lake Tahoe.* Vol. 1. Crystal Bay, NV: Sierra-Tahoe, 1964.

Simpson, James H. *Report of Explorations Across the Great Basin of the Territory of Utah.* 1859. Reno: University of Nevada Press, 1983.

Slotkin, Richard. *Gunfighter Nation: The Myth of the Frontier in 20th Century America.* New York: Atheneum, 1992.

Smith, Grant H. *The History of the Comstock Lode.* 1943. Reprint, Reno: University of Nevada Press, 1998.

Starr, Kevin. *California: A History.* New York: Random House, 2005.

Stine, Scott. *A Way Across the Mountain: Joseph Walker's 1833 Trans-Sierran Passage and the Myth of Yosemite's Discovery.* Norman: University of Oklahoma Press, 2015.

Taniguchi, Nancy J. *Dirty Deeds: Land, Violence, and the 1856 San Francisco Vigilance Committee.* Norman: University of Oklahoma Press, 2016.

Thompson, David. *Nevada: A History of Changes.* Reno: Grace Dangberg Foundation, 1986.

Weeks, Jos. D. *Report on the Statistics of Wages in Manufacturing Industries with Supplementary Reports on the Average Price of Necessaries of Life.* Washington, DC: Government Printing Office, 1886.

Wheeler, Sessions S. *The Desert Lake: The Story of Nevada's Pyramid Lake.* Caldwell, ID: Caxton Press, 2001.

Wilds, Leah J. *Water Politics in Northern Nevada: A Century of Struggle.* Reno: University of Nevada Press, 2010.

Winnemucca-Hopkins, Sarah. *Life Among the Piutes, Their Wrongs and Claims.* New York: G. P. Putnam's Sons, 1883.

Wirls, Daniel. "The 'Golden Age' Senate and Floor Debate in the Antebellum Congress." *Legislative Studies Quarterly* 32, no. 2 (2007): 193–222. http://www.jstor.org/stable/40263418.

Wren, Thomas. *A History of the State of Nevada.* New York: Lewis, 1904.

Zanjani, Sally. *Devils Will Reign: How Nevada Began.* Reno: University of Nevada Press, 2006.

———. *Sarah Winnemucca.* Lincoln: University of Nebraska Press, 2001.

Index

Page numbers in *italics* indicate illustrations.

About the Author

Michael J. Makley is the author of eight books on Western history, including *A Short History of Lake Tahoe; Saving Lake Tahoe: An Environmental History of a National Treasure;* and *Cave Rock: Climbers, Courts, and a Washoe Indian Sacred Place,* which he coauthored with his son, Matthew S. Makley.